Population Trends
in Indonesia

Population Trends in Indonesia

by Widjojo Nitisastro

Prepared under the auspices of the
Modern Indonesia Project
Southeast Asia Program
Cornell University

Cornell University Press

Ithaca and London

Standard Book Number 8014-0555-6
Library of Congress Catalog Card Number 71-106356

Printed in the United States of America
by Kingsport Press, Inc.

For my wife Darsih
and my daughter Wida

Preface

Indonesia today is the world's fifth most populous country, its approximately 120 million people ranking it below the United States and somewhat ahead of both Pakistan and Japan. Until the appearance of this book, however, no comprehensive study had been made of its population. By undertaking the first informed assessment of earlier, widely ranging population estimates and by his careful analysis of Indonesia's 1961 census, Professor Widjojo Nitisastro has made an important contribution to an understanding of Indonesia's past as well as its present problems, both political and economic.

His careful and discerning assessment of the incongruities among the several colonial surveys of Java's population and his rectification of distortions inferred from them provide a much more reliable basis for insights into the social history of nineteenth-century Java. His account of the impact of the Japanese occupation and the revolution on birth rates and population distribution is important for an appreciation of the age distribution of Indonesia's present and future population.

For those who seek to understand contemporary Indonesia and its economic and political prospects, Dr. Widjojo's masterful and painstaking analysis of the 1961 census and his projections from these data will prove of special and, indeed, indispensable importance. The remarkable accuracy of his earlier projections from the 1930 census is an indication of the soundness of his methods. The population projections which he bases on 1961 census data forecast the probable growth rate not only of Indonesia's total population but also of the different components of this population. He finds startling disparities in the sizes of age groups in the population, differences which have tremendous consequences for Indonesia's immediate future. His analysis points up the fact that, because of the low birth and high mortality rates during the Japanese occupation and the revolution, Indonesia has until now enjoyed what in effect has been a major reprieve from the necessity of rapid economic development. As a consequence, during the past two decades the annual numbers of those entering the labor market and those pressing for secondary and higher education were relatively stable. But this reprieve has ended, for as a result of the more stable economic and political conditions commencing in the early 1950's the birth rate rose markedly while mortality rates fell. Thus, the number of Indonesians in the 15–24-year age group, which began to increase gradually during the period 1967–1970, will expand much more rapidly after 1971. As Dr. Widjojo emphasizes, during the period 1966–1976 there will be "a radical rejuvenation of the working-age population," with the population component aged 15–24 years almost doubling in this one decade. As the number of those entering the labor force suddenly doubles, "each entrant will literally bring his brother along, and the brother will want a job as well."

This, of course, points up the conclusion that not only is the need for economic development in Indonesia immediate, but much of this activity should be labor-intensive. Undoubtedly the present decade (1970–1980) is the crucial period. The adverse social consequences of the rapid upsurge in the number of entrants into the labor force will be most heavily felt in Java, where the extent of the agricultural base can no longer be expanded and where two-thirds of Indonesia's population is crowded into an area smaller than the state of New York. Planned migration from Java to the outer islands and the loss of population resulting from the massacres of 1965–1966 can have only a minimal effect upon the overall picture. It is impossible to look at Professor Widjojo's data without concluding that for Java the need for birth control is desperately urgent. Birth control cannot, of course, have rapid enough results to ease the economic strains attendant upon such large numbers surging into the educational facilities and labor market in the 1970's. But from Dr. Widjojo's data one can only infer that unless the rapid and widespread practice of birth control is promptly introduced, Indonesia's population may reach approximately 227 million by 1991 (about 125 million on Java alone) and thereafter increase at an accelerating rate.

GEORGE McT. KAHIN

Ithaca, New York
January 1970

Acknowledgments

This study would never have been completed and published without the patient but effective insistence of Professor George McTurnan Kahin and Audrey Kahin. To both of them I would like to express my deepest appreciation.

Part of the present study was carried out during my graduate work at the University of California (Berkeley), part during my stay at the Modern Indonesia Project, Southeast Asia Program, Cornell University, and the rest while doing other kinds of work in Djakarta. I am particularly grateful to Professors Harvey Leibenstein, Kingsley Davis, and Henry Rosovsky for the many stimulating hours of work related to this study. I am also especially indebted to Professor Nathan Keyfitz, who aroused my interest in population studies. To my colleagues at the Faculty of Economics, University of Indonesia, I would like to acknowledge with gratitude the intellectually challenging climate they have been able to preserve during years of mounting problems and difficulties. To all others who have rendered invaluable assistance in the preparation of this book, I wish to express my heartfelt thanks.

All views expressed in this book, as well as the errors and omissions, are entirely my responsibility.

Djakarta   WIDJOJO NITISASTRO
March 1970

Contents

Appendixes

Map

Figures

Tables

Population Trends
in Indonesia

CHAPTER I

A Review of the Data and
Demographic Developments
in the Early Periods

This study of Indonesia's population covers the period between about 1775 and 1961, with projections for the years from
1961 through 1991. Although some historical data do exist from
which inferences can be drawn concerning the earlier periods,
the last quarter of the eighteenth century has been chosen as the
starting point for the present appraisal, since it is at this time that
the first known quantitative estimates originate. The significance
of the year 1961 lies in the fact that the first population census
in independent Indonesia was conducted in that year.

Because of the way in which Indonesia's history has been recorded during this period, the present study must necessarily
relate largely to Java. Colonial historiographers have been for
the most part, if not exclusively, concerned with the interests of
the colonial power rather than with those of the colonies' inhabitants. Thus, Indonesia's history after 1600 has generally been
treated from a European-centered outlook, concentrating almost
exclusively on the establishment and extension of Dutch colonial
power.[1] Because Dutch control was exercised in Java long before

[1] The shift in orientation usually found in the treatment of the
different periods in Indonesian history has been vividly described by J.
C. van Leur: "For the preceding periods, when the civilization of India
and the Islam from the worlds of the Caliphates came from overseas, the
Indocentric point of view is taken up. However, with the passage of the
West-European ships, the picture turns a hundred and eighty degrees

it was extended to the other Indonesian islands, the attention of historians has been concentrated on developments in Java.[2]

At the beginning of the seventeenth century the Dutch succeeded in establishing strongholds in Java and in the Moluccas, but at that time their position bore little resemblance to that of a dominating colonial power. Their actual domination of the whole island of Java did not begin until around 1750, and most of the other islands did not become Dutch dependencies until the nineteenth century, despite varying degrees of Dutch maritime superiority before that period.[3] In attempting to acquire the

and the Indies are from then on looked upon from the deck of the ship, from the wall of the fortress, and from the high gallery of the lodge" ("Boekbespreking: Geschiedenis van Nederlandsch Indië o.l.v. G. W. Stapel" [Book Review: *History of Netherlands Indies*, Ed. G. W. Stapel], *Tijdschrift voor Indische Taal-, Land-, en Volkenkunde*, LXXIX [1939], 590). On this subject G. W. Locher pointed out that "the history of the West is not only important for the Westerner, but is *the* history, whenever he is concerned with it," and that in such a picture of history the Indonesians "stand actually as 'natives' outside of history" ("Inleidende Beschouwingen over de Ontmoeting van Oost en West in Indonesië" [Introductory Observations on the Meeting of East and West in Indonesia], *Indonesië*, 2nd year [1949], no. 5, pp. 412–413, 419).

[2] A reflection of this one-sided emphasis on Java was the official designation of the Indonesian islands other than Java as "Buitenbezittingen" (Outer Possessions) and later on as "Buitengewesten" (Outer Provinces). Even today the term "Outer Islands" is still widely used in works in English on Indonesia. If a short collective designation is at all needed to refer to all the Indonesian islands other than Java, it seems more proper to use the term "Other Indonesian Islands" or "Other Islands."

[3] Van Leur contended that during the eighteenth century "a few European power establishments were consolidated on a very limited scale" in Asia, but that the Asian states in general "militarily, economically, and politically continued to remain as valid units, active factors in the course of events." He concluded that "the picture of Indonesia seemed rather to fit without contradiction the general picture of Asia. . . . Economically there was no [Dutch] supremacy or superiority; militarily the same could be said with respect to the land forces, [although] there was probably European supremacy in a number of seas. Politically the power of the Eastern states remained unshaken"

export crops they wanted, the Dutch concentrated initially on levying forced tributes from the Javanese people, later moving to direct management of crop production.[4] But only during the eighteenth century did the United East Indian Company succeed in gradually expanding its political control in Java by intervention in the wars of succession to the thrones of the kingdoms of Mataram and Banten.

The discovery of certain important minerals on other of the islands, and the realization that certain parts of these islands were favorable for the cultivation of rubber and tobacco, led the Dutch government during the second half of the nineteenth century to exert more control over these areas.[5] It was not until the beginning of the twentieth century, however, that they established complete domination over the whole of Indonesia.

The available data on population growth in Indonesia thus relate almost exclusively to Java. Data for the other islands were primarily limited to guesses and were concerned largely with the areas of Dutch exploitation. Even in the 1930 census, which, though primitive in some respects, represents the best effort at collecting population data in Indonesia during the colonial era, the information concerning many of the islands other than Java

---

("Eenige Aantekeningen Betreffende de Mogelijkheid der 18e Eeuw als Categorie in de Indische Geschiedschrijving" [Some Notes on the Possibility of the 18th Century as a Category in the Historiography of the Indies], *Tijdschrift voor Indische Taal-, Land- en Volkenkunde,* LXXX [1940], 551, 560, 561).

[4] For a summary of the succeeding economic policies of the Dutch East Indian Company and, later on, of the Dutch colonial government, see G. Gonggrijp, *Schets ener Economische Geschiedenis van Neder-lands-Indië* (Sketch of an Economic History of the Netherlands Indies), 3rd ed. (Haarlem, 1949).

[5] The extent to which many areas outside Java were still free from Dutch domination even at the end of the past century has been pointed out by, among others, G. J. Resink, "Veronachtzaamde Uitspraken" (Neglected Utterances), *Indonesië,* 8th year (1955), no. 1, pp. 1–26. For an overall view of this aspect of Indonesian history, see W. F. Wertheim's work, *Indonesian Society in Transition* (The Hague, 1959), pp. 63–66.

was drawn mainly from reports by local leaders rather than from actual population counts.

A series of population figures exist for Java from the late eighteenth century, and official yearly figures for the different regions of the island after 1849 are available (see Table 1). Between 1880 and 1905, so-called "quinquennial censuses" were held on the island. These population figures were often quoted in official and unofficial publications, sometimes accompanied by warnings regarding their limited reliability. More often than not, however, in the studies based on these data the warnings have been ignored, and the figures have provided the basis for speculations about an inferred high rate of annual population increase and its causes. Traditional explanations have referred to the high fertility of the soil, the attainment of a *pax neerlandica* resulting in fewer famines due to wars, and the introduction of smallpox vaccination.[6]

Recently, more sophisticated arguments have been added. Some writers have searched for psychological explanations. One contention has been that the allegedly rapid population increase in Java was probably due to a disruption of the island's culture by the Dutch, which made its inhabitants strive for emotional security through greater sexual activity. Others have asserted that the introduction of the system of forced cultivation of export crops, known as the "cultivation system," provided a positive incentive for increasing the size of the family.

All these speculations are of interest. But they are rendered largely irrelevant by the almost complete failure to scrutinize properly the basic data from which they are drawn. Especially where such speculations form part of some sweeping generalization, an appraisal of the available data appears to be in order. Whether or not the appraisal confirms the impression of a very rapid rate of increase of Java's population over the past century, its conclusions should lead to more reliable use of the data.

[6] See, for example, Departement van Economische Zaken, *Volkstelling, 1930* (Population Census, 1930), VIII (Batavia, 1936), 10.

Table 1. Total population by region, Java, 1815–1930 *

Region	1815	1845	1850	1855	1860	1865	1870	1875
Banten	231,604	389,556	470,381	498,419	550,254	610,726	685,202	729,288
Djakarta	439,952	676,893	755,333	866,156	978,443	1,084,684	1,175,929	1,225,041
Priangan	194,048	728,061	737,466	806,672	830,755	895,937	1,034,814	1,217,318
Tjirebon	233,956	616,858	574,730	704,219	904,588	933,803	1,037,678	1,200,367
Pekalongan	293,857	535,902	479,788	552,127	778,848	913,344	1,246,143	1,378,657
Semarang	448,521	1,179,866	966,495	1,228,602	1,514,577	1,651,410	1,931,996	2,113,100
Rembang	207,421	478,708	536,478	585,160	691,438	746,776	853,561	960,816
Banjumas	‡	401,840	336,724	419,268	537,482	698,912	855,981	951,356
Kedu	‡	972,293	928,785	1,066,258	1,194,456	1,405,878	1,736,807	1,880,008
Madiun	236,135	404,767	395,307	440,352	517,713	587,454	713,018	885,208
Kediri	269,954	235,243	240,766	315,154	356,668	454,450	571,980	659,307
Surabaja	218,659	938,989	939,087	1,064,618	1,187,037	1,297,151	1,435,707	1,571,980
Madura	156,913	298,403	345,171	352,226	508,868	573,210	662,720	757,953
Pasuruan	65,131	570,404 ⎫	895,708	694,019 ⎱	779,525	849,175	952,289	1,059,824
Besuki		260,243 ⎭		304,820 ⎰	339,997	367,670	425,010	456,114
Total, region under direct Dutch control	2,996,151	8,607,238	8,602,219	9,808,070	11,670,649	13,070,580	15,318,835	17,046,346
Jogjakarta	1,620,109 ‡	349,166 ⎱	364,045	331,662	352,800	369,597	397,120	437,760
Surakarta		505,193 ⎰	603,759	686,426	695,268	728,239	736,213	851,672
Total, region of the Principalities	1,620,109	854,359	967,804	1,018,088	1,048,068	1,097,836	1,133,333	1,289,432
Total, Java	4,615,270	9,461,597	9,570,023	10,916,158	12,718,717	14,168,416	16,452,168	18,335,778

Table 1 (continued)

Region	1880	1885	1890	1895	1900	1905	1917 †	1920	1930
Banten	594,141	530,171	666,362	699,185	812,170	895,390	878,009	897,391	1,028,628
Djakarta	1,246,315	1,291,065	1,450,268	1,601,550	1,938,006	2,109,352	2,444,642	2,787,345	3,059,359
Priangan	1,597,666	1,622,045	1,977,849	2,195,109	2,435,582	2,666,767	3,358,022	3,810,632	4,639,469
Tjirebon	1,295,476	1,346,267	1,484,924	1,556,285	1,660,679	1,709,005	1,671,111	1,711,778	2,069,690
Pekalongan	1,459,833	1,518,107	1,627,323	1,746,261	1,893,176	1,990,286	2,264,007	2,268,571	2,640,124
Semarang	2,113,281	2,220,128	2,337,633	2,449,458	2,685,015	2,614,923	2,792,335	2,737,416	3,166,416
Rembang	1,052,348	1,176,580	1,277,592	1,328,895	1,470,525	1,496,798	1,640,702	1,663,814	1,829,324
Banjumas	1,016,367	1,096,039	1,208,289	1,251,963	1,368,298	1,486,129	1,627,690	1,767,529	2,067,490
Kedu	1,965,562	2,005,406	2,094,585	2,198,286	2,358,545	2,338,683	2,713,517	2,456,591	2,536,932
Madiun	996,183	996,002	1,085,199	1,111,490	1,233,653	1,349,472	1,602,242	1,594,655	1,668,547
Kediri	771,103	943,082	1,120,524	1,267,704	1,512,921	1,774,545	2,151,660	2,011,993	2,411,209
Surabaja	1,714,477	1,856,635	2,054,203	2,181,332	2,360,909	2,436,963	2,529,844	2,460,180	2,790,506
Madura	810,135	1,373,948	1,592,679	1,630,510	1,758,511	1,493,289	1,778,243	1,743,818	1,962,462
Pasuruan	1,221,482	1,351,809	1,468,007	1,620,622	1,824,407	2,022,170	2,054,345	2,241,231	2,741,105
Besuki	509,266	585,043	673,337	743,352	837,081	972,475	1,215,976	1,498,865	2,083,399
Total, region under direct Dutch control	18,363,635	19,912,417	21,968,774	23,672,002	26,149,538	27,386,247	30,722,345	31,651,809	37,594,489
Jogjakarta	463,433	501,043	785,473	814,959	1,084,327	1,118,705	1,374,168	1,282,815	1,559,027
Surakarta	967,437	1,053,985	1,160,317	1,210,740	1,512,773	1,593,056	2,060,870	2,049,547	2,564,848
Total, region of the Principalities	1,430,870	1,555,028	1,945,790	2,025,699	2,597,100	2,711,761	3,435,038	3,332,362	4,123,875
Total, Java	19,794,505	21,467,445	23,914,564	25,697,701	28,746,638	30,098,008	34,157,383	34,984,171	41,718,364

* The administrative divisions of 1920 are used in this table. Changes in boundaries and designations of the various regions have been taken into account as far as possible.
† The figures for 1917 were compilations from local officials, as were the figures for previous years. Unlike the data for 1880–1895, however, they were not based on actual counts.
‡ Banjumas and Kedu are included in Jogjakarta and Surakarta.

Source: Thomas Stamford Raffles, *The History of Java*, 2nd ed. (London, 1830), I, 70, and II, 265–332; P. Bleeker, "Bijdragen tot de Statistiek der Bevolking van Java" (Contributions to the Statistics of Population of Java), *Tijdschrift voor Neêrland's Indië*, 9th year (1847), I, 39–41, and IV, 1–25; *Koloniaal Verslag* (The Hague) for 1845–1922; Departement van Economische Zaken, *Volkstelling, 1930* (Population Census, 1930), 8 vols. (Batavia, 1930–1936).

The present author's attempt to appraise part of the available information on Indonesia's population makes no pretension at providing an exhaustive treatment. In examining the available demographic data, attention will be given primarily to the procedures of arriving at official population figures, the implied or explicit assumptions used by "authorities" in estimating vital rates, the internal consistency of the different data, the consistency of the data as compared with general tendencies found in many other populations, the extent to which the data agree with other nondemographic information, and the degree of agreement between the data and analytically probable configurations. The purpose, however, is not solely to point out the shortcomings of defective data. Rather, by not taking any data for granted, it is hoped that the data can be brought into more plausible proportions, thus achieving a somewhat better understanding of the implied problems and permitting a more reliable use of the data in the future.

For purposes of convenience, the presentation will be made by periods, using the following somewhat arbitrary dates: 1775–1815, 1815–1880, 1880–1905, 1905–1940, 1940–1950, 1950–1960. A separate treatment of the 1961 population census will follow, to be concluded by population projections for the period 1961–1991.

Between the years 1775 and 1815 several estimates were made by Radermacher, Nederburgh, and Raffles, among others. Between 1815 and 1880, estimates exist for the years 1825–1831 and for 1845 (supplied by Bleeker) and yearly figures for 1849–1879. Quinquennial counts were conducted between 1880 and 1905. These data all pertain almost exclusively to Java. During the period 1905–1940, however, two censuses, conducted in 1920 and 1930, supplied information on the population of the other Indonesian islands as well. In addition, some data on vital statistics are available for parts of this period. The decade between 1940 and 1950 witnessed the Japanese occupation, from the beginning of 1942 to the middle of 1945, and the war of independence, from 1945 to the end of 1949. It is to be expected that the events of the forties had an important bearing on demographic features, which in turn had an effect on the composition of the present and future population. The decade of the fifties also encompassed important demographic events that have definite implications for the present and future growth and composition of the Indonesian population.

Much emphasis will be given, especially for the early periods, to the actual procedures used in arriving at the estimates, since these estimates provide little information on the composition of the population. With regard to age distribution even the more recent data of the colonial era contain very little information. The 1930 census, for example, used only three age classifications: children who cannot yet walk, other nonadults, adults. Some effort will be made to draw some inferences from this type of information.

A cursory survey of some demographic developments in the early periods may provide a historical perspective against which the data may be better viewed. Archeological findings and comparative studies in languages and agricultural methods suggest that the earliest migration to Indonesia occurred in prehistoric times from what is now southern China via the Indo-China and Malay peninsulas. But no estimates of the magnitude of this migration are available. This is also the case with speculations concerning migrations from the Indian subcontinent, which have been inferred from the impact of the Hindu culture on many parts of Indonesia. There are a number of conflicting opinions as to the nature of these movements. The existence of large-scale Indian migrations has recently been refuted, and it has been contended that, on the contrary, the few Indians who had an actual impact on religion and the arts were priests and artists giving "technical assistance" to the Indonesian kingdoms.[7]

[7] The conflicting opinions are discussed in F. D. K. Bosch, *Het Vraagstuk van de Hindu-Kolonisatie van den Archipel* (The Problem of the Hindu Colonization of the Archipelago) (Leiden, 1946). J. C.

The present discrepancy between the population density of Java and that of the other Indonesian islands is undoubtedly not a recent phenomenon. This can be inferred from the existence of huge temples, which in Indonesia are almost exclusively found in Java. The intensive method of land cultivation, made possible by the high fertility of the recent volcanic soil and the availability of the right amount of rainfall, enabled certain areas in Java to support a relatively large population with a commensurate seasonal labor input. Thus, the Javanese villages were able to support large kingdoms and armies and to mobilize manpower for the building of temples.[8] As the population increased, new areas came under cultivation. For example, it has been deduced that only about two centuries ago several parts of West Java started to be populated by people growing rice on irrigated fields.[9]

Unlike Java, in many parts of the other Indonesian islands, where the absence of recent volcanoes has resulted in less fertile soil, shifting cultivation has been (and in many regions still is) commonly practiced, with a small area of jungle being cleared and cropped for two or three years and then abandoned. It was

---

van Leur dismissed the possibility of a political invasion from India, or a large settlement by Indians, or any "decisive Indian cultural influence on the courts of rulers and nobles [which] originated from the trading quarters" of Indian merchants. Instead, he contended that "the course of events amounted essentially to a summoning of Indian *condottieri* and Indian court artificers," a process which also took place in southern India, Ceylon, and southern Indo-China ("On Early Asian Trade" [a translation of van Leur's dissertation "Eenige Beschouwingen Betreffende den Ouden Aziatischen Handel" (Some Observations on the Old Asian Trade), Middelburg, 1934], *Indonesian Trade and Society* [The Hague, 1955], pp. 102–104).

[8] B. Schrieke, *Indonesian Sociological Studies*, Pt. II: *Ruler and Realm in Early Java* (The Hague, 1957), pp. 299–301. Schrieke also speculated that the heavy pressures exerted on the population for building these grand temples resulted in migration and settlement in uninhabited areas of Java, and that through the resulting depopulation the "central Javanese royal culture was destroyed by its own temples" (p. 301).

[9] G. J. A. Terra, "Some Sociological Aspects of Agriculture in South-East-Asia," *Indonesië*, 6th year (1953), no. 5, p. 449.

impossible to support a concentrated population by such methods. Thus, from the turn of the sixteenth century, while most of the kingdoms on Java were densely populated inland states primarily based on irrigated agriculture, on the other islands they were mainly harbor principalities oriented toward overseas trade, with sparsely settled but highly mobile populations.[10]

Prior to colonial rule, migration within and between the different Indonesian islands was reportedly extensive. Settlements of several population groups were established in distant regions and islands within and outside the boundaries of present-day Indonesia. Centuries ago foreign traders—Chinese, Arabs, and Indians—were also already settling in separate quarters of the coastal centers.[11]

Although all these probable developments during the early periods of Indonesia's history raise different and challenging hypotheses, no adequate information has been available to gauge the magnitude of the population movements nor to assess the accuracy of speculations concerning them.

[10] Following in the steps of Max Weber, van Leur described the inland states of Java as being based on a patrimonial, bureaucratic hierarchy, while a closed aristocratic community formed the backbone of the harbor states in the other Indonesian islands ("On Early Asian Trade," pp. 104–105).

[11] For a survey of the different types of migration, see *ibid.*, pp. 100–103, mainly based on C. van Vollenhoven's findings in *Het Adatrecht van Nederlandsch Indië* (The Adat Law in the Netherlands Indies) (Leiden, 1918–1933).

CHAPTER 2

Early Estimates and Raffles' Data on the Population of Java, 1775–1815

During the eighteenth century, the Dutch East India Company gradually extended its control over Java by intervening militarily in the internal disputes of the kingdoms of Mataram and Banten. A growing demand for Asian products on the European market led the company to seek to increase coffee production in Java by a system known as "contingents and compulsory deliveries." These were forced tributes exacted from the population, contingents being overt tributes in kind and compulsory deliveries being tributes under the guise of trade. The system was started in western Java and later extended to other areas of the island. Despite its huge profits from coffee production, however, the corruption of company officials and the growing debts, which took large proportions of the profits, resulted in the progressive weakening of the company until in 1799 the Dutch government took over its assets and debts. As an asset of the company, Java then came under the direct rule of the Dutch government. From 1811 to 1816, Dutch rule was interrupted by the British occupation. It was during the British interregnum that Lieutenant Governor Raffles introduced the "land-rent" system, for which population data were collected.

For the period between 1775 and 1815, several estimates of the population of Java are available.[1] J. C. M. Radermacher and W.

---

[1] Estimates pertaining to the years before this period include Valentijn's estimate of 31,161,250 persons (!) for Java in the early part of the

van Hogendorp published estimates in 1779, which were revised in 1781. Although the components of their estimates of the total population did not refer to one single year, their figures will be considered as referring to the year 1775. Nederburgh reported certain estimates for the year 1795, and in 1863 an estimate appeared for the year 1802 without any indication as to its original sources. Governor General Daendels reportedly made estimates for the year 1807, and Raffles compiled a comparatively detailed estimate of Java's population for 1815. A summary of these estimates would run as follows:

Year	Population of Java [2]	Compiler
c.1775	2,029,915	Radermacher and van Hogendorp
1795	3,500,000	Nederburgh
1802	3,647,167	Bleeker (1863)
c.1807	3,770,000	Daendels
1815	4,615,270	Raffles

Only the estimates for the years 1775, 1795, and 1815 will be discussed here, not only because they (especially the one for 1815) are the figures most frequently quoted, but also because they contain comparatively more information than the other two.

Radermacher's and van Hogendorp's Data for 1775

In their report published in 1779, Radermacher and van Hogendorp drew attention to the then customary practice in Java of calculating the population in terms of tjatjahs,[3] or families,

---

eighteenth century (François Valentijn, *Oud en Nieuw Oost-Indiën* [Old and New East-Indies], IV [Dordrecht, 1726], 53) and Bleeker's report of a total Javanese population of 2 million between 1750–1755 and of "more than 2 millions" for 1770–1776 (P. Bleeker, "Statistisch-Ekonomische Onderzoekingen en Beschouwingen op Koloniaal Gebied: De Bevolkingstoename op Java" [Statistical Economic Enquiries and Observations in the Colonial Field: The Population Increase in Java], *Tijdschrift voor Nederlandsch Indië*, n.s., 1st year [1863], I, 192–193).

[2] The term "Java" includes the adjoining island, Madura.

[3] Pronounced "chachas."

reportedly consisting of "two weapon-carrying men, two women, and two children." At that time they estimated Java's population at 143,200 *tjatjah*s, or 915,588 persons.[4]

A supplement published two years later contained corrections to these estimates. In revising their figures, they contended that the *tjatjah*s included only the *bumi*s (the descendents of the original founders of a village), and the *numpang*s (who were people from neighboring areas), but not the *budjang*s (who were said to be unmarried and strangers).[5]

More importantly, on the basis of what they described as "new reports," they now estimated that the population of Java amounted to 2,029,915 persons, distributed geographically as follows: [6] Banten, 90,000; Djakarta, 340,915; Tjirebon, 90,000; and Java's east coast,[7] 1,509,000.

Various methods were used in arriving at these new estimates. With regard to Banten, it was stated that "Banten . . . is inhabited by around 30,000 men, and thus it can be expressed as 90,000 inhabitants." [8] The calculation of one adult male for

---

[4] J. C. M. Radermacher and W. van Hogendorp, "Korte Schets van de Bezittingen der Nederlandsche Oost-Indische Maatschappye Benevens eene Beschrijving van het Koningrijk Jaccatra en de Stad Batavia" (Short Sketch of the Possessions of the Netherlands East-Indian Company, Along with a Description of the Kingdom of Jaccatra and the City of Batavia), *Verhandelingen van het Bataviaasch Genootschap van Kunsten en Wetenschappen*, 3rd ed. (Batavia, 1825; 1st printing, 1779), I, 8. The figure "94,200 *tjatjah*s or 565,200 souls" referred to in the article as being the population of Java is a mistake. This figure refers to Java's northeast coast.

[5] J. C. M. Radermacher and W. van Hogendorp, "Bijvoegsels tot de Beschrijving der Sundasche Eilanden: Java, Borneo en Sumatra" (Supplements to the Description of the Sunda islands: Java, Borneo, and Sumatra), *Verhandelingen van het Bataviaasch Genootschap van Kunsten en Wetenschappen*, 2nd ed. (Batavia, 1824; 1st printing, 1781), III, 271.

[6] *Ibid.*, p. 274.

[7] This term refers to the whole region east of Tjirebon, comprising both the territories of the Principalities of Surakarta and Jogjakarta (which previously made up the kingdom of Mataram) as well as the areas under direct Dutch control.

[8] Radermacher and van Hogendorp, "Bijvoegsels," pp. 271–272.

every three persons was apparently based on their understanding that one *tjatjah* included two adult males. The estimate of 30,000 men derived from information that 15,000 men in the coastal areas were able to work and the assumption of an equal number of men in the interior.[9]

The area designated as Djakarta (including Priangan) consisted of the city of Djakarta, the area surrounding the city, the Djakarta regencies, and the Priangan lands. In accordance with "a better survey" it was estimated that in 1779 the populations of the city of Djakarta and of the surrounding area were respectively 12,121 and 160,986 persons. The number of persons in the Djakarta regencies, including 1,324 *budjangs*, amounted to 68,351 persons. In the Priangan regencies there were 15,724 houses and 5,103 *budjangs*, a total of 99,447 persons.[10] The implied assumption in these figures is that the average number of persons in a house is six, or equal to the average number of persons in a *tjatjah*.

For Tjirebon, the original estimates of 15,000 *tjatjahs*, or 90,000 persons, were not changed, since there were "no new reports." [11]

Concerning Java's east coast, Radermacher and van Hogendorp observed that in the year 1738, when the whole area was under control of the Susuhunan (the title of the king of Mataram), the population amounted to 309,700 *tjatjahs*, or 1,858,200 inhabitants. They pointed out:

Although it cannot be presumed that the region is much less inhabited, it was not possible in 1774 to count more than:

69,000 *tjatjahs* under the Company,
85,450 *tjatjahs* under the Susuhunan [of Surakarta],
87,050 *tjatjahs* under the Sultan [of Jogjakarta],
10,000 *tjatjahs* on Madura
———
251,500 *tjatjahs* or 1,509,000 inhabitants.[12]

[9] *Ibid.*, p. 272 n.   [10] *Ibid.*, pp. 272–273.   [11] *Ibid.*, p. 273.
[12] *Ibid.*, p. 274.

The impression is given that some kind of count or enumeration was conducted in 1774 revealing the existence of 251,500 *tjatjahs*. Another source, however, reported that the number of *tjatjahs* in the regions under control of the Susuhunan and the Sultan (respectively 85,450 and 87,050) were not for the year 1774, but rather referred to the year 1755, when the kingdom of Mataram was partitioned into Surakarta and Jogjakarta.[13]

It can thus be concluded that the various components of this estimate of Java's total population did not refer to the same year; that even the years governing each of the components were not definite; that in almost all cases the number of persons were inferred from the alleged number of *tjatjahs* or of houses or of men, and assumed a fixed relation in each of these three cases; and that the actual methods of estimating the number of *tjatjahs*, houses, or men were either guesses or not known.

Nederburgh's Data for 1795

For the year 1795, Nederburgh reported the population of Java to be over 3.5 million.[14] The territorial distribution was as follows:

The Principalities [15]	1,500,000 persons
Java's northeast coast [16]	1,495,908 persons
The regencies of Djakarta and Priangan	206,494 persons

[13] See the discussion on Nederburgh's estimates for 1795, which follows.

[14] Quoted in "Bevolking van Java en Madura" (Population of Java and Madura), *Tijdschrift voor Neêrland's Indië*, 2nd year (1839), I, 160. The article was reproduced from *De Statistiek van 1832* (The Statistics of 1832).

[15] "The Principalities" (De Vorstenlanden) was the term used by the Dutch for designating jointly the Principalities of Surakarta and Jogjakarta.

[16] This term referred to the region east of Tjirebon under direct control of the Dutch (thus excluding the territories of the Principalities).

The city of Djakarta and

surrounding areas   144,026 persons

Tjirebon   90,000 persons

Banten   90,000 persons

The reliability of these figures can be partly assessed from the methods Nederburgh employed in arriving at his estimates. He first pointed out that when the kingdom of Mataram was partitioned in 1755, Susuhunan Pakubuwono III of Surakarta reigned over 85,450 *tjatjah*s and Sultan Hamengkubuwono of Jogjakarta over 87,050 *tjatjah*s. He then referred to the fact that in 1774 Governor van den Burgh reportedly succeeded "not without much difficulty" in setting up new registers, showing that the numbers of *tjatjah*s in each of these two principalities had increased to over 100,000. From these figures, and assuming each *tjatjah* to consist of six persons, Nederburgh inferred that "because after that time Java has been in peace and order, it can be posed with certainty that [the population of these two principalities] since then has still increased considerably, and at present it can be estimated to be 1,500,000 souls." [17]

The figures for Java's northeast coast together with those for the regencies of Djakarta and Priangan were reported to be the result of *een opname* (a survey) conducted by Governor van Overstraten in 1795. Nederburgh presented the data on the population of the city of Djakarta and surroundings separately from the estimate of the population of the regencies of Djakarta and Priangan. For the city of Djakarta and surroundings and also for Tjirebon and Banten he used the preliminary estimates of Radermacher and van Hogendorp.[18]

The objective of the *opname*, as stated in the instructions issued by van Overstraten, was "to make possible a calculation on firm grounds, to what extent the cultivation of desired crops

[17] *Op. cit.*, pp. 158–159.

[18] *Ibid.*, p. 159. The figure for the city of Djakarta and surroundings was actually erroneous and was corrected by Radermacher and van Hogendorp in 1781 ("Bijvoegsels," p. 272).

could be extended."[19] For this reason estimates included the number of buffaloes and the extent of the ricefields. No instructions have been found regarding the methods of conducting the survey or their actual implementation. The terms *opname* or *opneming* are not self-explanatory. As will be seen in the discussions on later decades, they were frequently used to describe different types of activities vaguely connected with the collection of population data. Sometimes they were used interchangeably with the terms *telling* (count or enumeration) or even *volkstelling* (population census).

Some idea of the accuracy of what was reported to be an *opname* can be obtained from the data for the Djakarta and Priangan regencies. Together, these consisted of eleven regencies, and the average number of districts per regency was reported to be between three and eighteen. From the data it is inferred that the average number of villages per district in these regencies ranged between 11 and 330, and that the average number of persons per village in these eleven regencies ranged between 23 and 218.[20] The large discrepancies found in the average number of villages per district and in the average number of persons per village indicate the very conjectural nature of the data.[21]

[19] Quoted in J. J. Verwijk, "Het Verzamelen van Gegevens voor de Bevolkingsstatistiek op Java en Madura" (The Gathering of Data for the Population Statistics on Java and Madura), *Tijdschrift voor het Binnenlandsch Bestuur*, II (1889), p. 8.

[20] Engelhard, "Overzigt der Bevolking en Plantagiën van de Batavia'sche en Preanger-Regentschappen 1795" (Summary of the Population and Plantations of the Batavia and Preanger Regencies, 1795), reproduced in *De Opkomst van het Nederlandsch Gezag over Java: Verzameling van Onuitgegeven Stukken uit het Oud-Koloniaal Archief* (The Rise of the Dutch Authority over Java: Compilation of Unpublished Documents from the Old Colonial Archives), ed. J. K. J. de Jonge and M. L. van Deventer (The Hague, 1884), p. 390.

[21] Another estimate of the population of Java's northeast coast in 1802 was 1,850,571 persons (see P. Bleeker, "Statistiek der Bevolking van het Goevernement van Java's Noordoostkust" [Statistics of Population of the Government of Java's Northeast Coast], *Tijdschrift voor Neder-*

Raffles' Data for 1815

Most often used as a starting point in discussions on the growth of Java's population is the 1815 figure associated with Thomas Stamford Raffles, lieutenant governor of Java during the British occupation from 1811 to 1816. Raffles' *The History of Java* contains a "Table exhibiting the Population of Java and Madura, according to a Census taken by the British Government, in the year 1815" (see Table 2), which classifies the population by sex and ethnic group (that is, Indonesians and Chinese) for the different regions of Java and also shows the population density of each of these regions.[22] His "Account of the Several Principal Divisions of Java and Madura" is even more detailed.[23] Here there are tables showing, for every district within each residency,[24] the total population by sex and whether they were "Attached to the Cultivation of the Soil" or "Employed in other Avocations;" these categories are subdivided into "Javans" and "Chinese and other Foreigners." The tables also enumerate the number of buffaloes, horses, and ploughs, and for some regions classify the population into men, women, boys, and girls. For all the districts of each residency the data also include the number of villages, the different types of land—cul-

---

landsch Indië, n.s., 4th year [1866], II, 325–338). Another source reported that the figure was 1,879,559 (see P. J. Veth, *Java: Geographisch, Ethnologisch, Historisch* [Java: Geographically, Ethnologically, Historically], 2nd ed., ed. Joh. F. Snelleman and J. F. Niermeyer [Haarlem, 1907], p. 8). There was also an estimate of Java's population of 3,647,167 for the same year (see Bleeker, "Statistisch-Ekonomische Onderzoekingen," p. 193). None of these references indicate the sources of the estimates.

[22] Thomas Stamford Raffles, *The History of Java*, 1st ed. (London, 1817), I, 63.

[23] *Ibid.*, II, 241–291.

[24] During the British interregnum, the territory under direct British control was divided into residencies, each headed by a resident. Each residency, in turn, was divided into districts, each headed by a *bupati* (regent). A district consisted of several divisions, headed by officers of divisions, and each division consisted of several villages.

Table 2. Population by sex and region, Java, 1815, as given by T. S. Raffles

Division	Total population	Male	Female	Natives: Total	Natives: Male	Natives: Female	Chinese: Total	Chinese: Male	Chinese: Female	Square statute miles	Estimated population per sq. mi.
Java											
European Provinces											
Bantam	231,604	106,100	125,504	230,976	111,988	118,988	628	352	276	3,428	67½
Batavia and environs *	332,015	180,768	151,247	279,621	151,064	128,557	52,394	29,704	22,690	2,411 (Batavia and Buitenzorg together)	169⅓ (Batavia and Buitenzorg together)
Buitenzorg	76,312	38,926	37,386	73,679	37,334	36,345	2,633	1,591	1,042		
Priangen Regencies	243,628	120,649	122,979	243,268	120,289	122,979	180	86	94	10,002	24⅓
Cheribon	216,001	105,451	110,550	213,658	99,837	113,821	2,343	1,193	1,150	1,334	162
Tegal	178,415	81,539	96,876	175,446	80,208	95,238	2,004	915	1,089	1,297	137⅓
Pakalung'an	155,442	53,187	62,255	113,396	52,007	61,389	2,046	1,180	866	607	190⅙
Semarang *	327,610	165,009	162,601	305,910	154,161	151,749	1,700	848	852	1,166	281
Kedu	197,310	97,744	99,566	196,171	97,167	99,004	1,139	577	562	826	238¾
Grobogan and Jipang	66,522	31,693	34,829	66,109	31,423	34,686	403	223	180	1,219	54⅓
Japara and Jawana	103,290	55,124	48,166	101,000	54,000	47,000	2,290	1,124	1,166	1,025	100⅔
Rembang	158,530	75,204	83,326	154,639	73,373	81,266	3,891	1,831	2,060	1,400	113
Gresik	115,442	58,981	56,461	115,078	58,807	56,271	364	174	190	778	148
Surabaya *	154,512	77,260	77,252	152,025	76,038	75,987	2,047	1,010	1,037	1,218	126¾
Pasuruam	108,812	54,177	54,635	107,752	53,665	54,087	1,070	522	548	1,952	58⅛
Proboling'go	104,359	50,503	53,856	102,927	49,797	53,130	1,430	706	724	2,854	36½
Banyuwangi	8,873	4,463	4,410	8,554	4,297	4,257	319	166	153	1,274	7
Native Provinces †											
Sura-kerta	972,727	471,505	501,222	970,292	470,220	500,072	2,435	1,285	1,150	11,313 (Sura-kerta and Yugya-kerta together)	147½ (Sura-kerta and Yugya-kerta together)
Yugya-kerta	685,207	332,241	352,966	683,005	331,141	351,864	2,202	1,201	1,001		
Madura											
Bankalang and Pamakasan	95,235	47,466	47,769	90,848	45,194	45,654	4,395	2,280	2,115	892	106¾
Sumenap	123,424	60,190	63,234	114,896	55,826	59,070	8,528	4,364	4,164	728 ‡	146
Total, Java and Madura	4,615,270	2,268,180	2,347,090	4,499,250	2,207,836	2,291,414	94,441	51,332	43,109	45,724	100+

* The figure includes the population of the capital city. Raffles estimates the populations of the cities as follows: Batavia and its immediate suburbs, 60,000; Semarang, 20,000; Surabaja, 25,000.

† The figure for the Principality of Jogjakarta includes the population of the European-controlled city of Pachitan, which Raffles estimates as about 22,000. He estimates he population of the city of Surakarta as 105,000 and of Jogjakarta as "somewhat less."

‡ According to Raffles, this figure "does not include the dependent islands, on which a considerable portion of the population is scattered."

Source: Thomas Stamford Raffles, ***The History of Java*** (London, 1817), I, 63.

tivated land, irrigated land (*sawah*), nonirrigated land (*tegal*), coffee ground, teak forest, land capable of being cultivated, unfit land, jungle land, and so on—the outputs of rice and corn, and the estimated values of these products. According to Raffles, the description may "be considered as faithful a view of the population of the country as could be expected, and as such, notwithstanding the inaccuracies to which all such accounts are liable, it is presented with some confidence to the public."

The collection of these data originated because of the introduction of the "land-revenue" system, one of Raffles' many innovations and one that had important bearings on future developments throughout the colonial period. Briefly the system was as follows: Since proprietary right to the soil was originally vested only in the sovereign, the actual cultivators had to dispose of part of their produce to the government. The government's share, preferably paid in cash, depended on the type of land and was to range from one-fourth to one-half of the total output, "as the actual quantity of produce left from each for the use of the renter is wished to be nearly the same." [25] The introduction of this "land rent" was supposed to be in lieu of all other types of taxes, forced deliveries, and forced services rendered to the government or to the local heads. [26] As the government intended to deal directly with each cultivator, it needed to collect information concerning every cultivator and his possessions. In addition, "to equalize in some measure the payments from all ranks of people, a tenement tax (or more properly a small rent for the ground on which their houses stand) should be levied from those who contribute nothing to the land rents." [27] Therefore, a distinction was made between cultivators and persons "Employed in other Avocations."

[25] "Revenue Instructions," reproduced as App. L, no. II (*ibid.*, II, cclv).
[26] After the return of Java to the Dutch, the land-rent system was continued, not in lieu of, but rather in addition to, other obligations imposed on the population.
[27] "Revenue Instructions," Raffles, *op. cit.*, II, ccxlix.

Government officials, called collectors, assisted by division officers and village heads, were charged with implementing the system. Raffles gave the following account of the collection of the data:

A detailed account of the peasantry of each village was first taken, containing the name of each male inhabitant, with other particulars, and from the aggregate of these village lists a general statement was constructed of the inhabitants of each subdivision and district.[28]

Some idea of the degree of reliability of the data collected can be gained by glancing through the instructions issued by Raffles himself for gathering the information. After emphasizing that the government must be "furnished with the fullest and completest view of the actual resources of the country," he remarked:

The best mode to be adopted will be as follows: The collector, attended by his native assistant, and such servants as are necessary, must himself proceed to the chief station in each division, where he will cause to be assembled the head inhabitants of the several villages contained in it. To these he must clearly explain the nature of the information desired; and through their means it is expected that it will be obtained without difficulty.

Whenever it may be necessary, the collector will visit the village itself, and on the spot cause such inquiries to be made as are requisite.[29]

From this account it can be concluded that even if Raffles' instructions were strictly carried out, there was to be no actual enumeration. Raffles' data for the different regions were merely a compilation of figures provided by the village heads. While the latter might well know all heads of household in their village who were cultivators or noncultivators, it seems unlikely that

[28] Raffles, *op. cit.*, I, 61.
[29] *Ibid.*, p. ccxlviii. The term "head inhabitant" referred to the village head: "The head inhabitant therefore (whether recognized under the name of *Petingi, Bukul, Lura, Kuwu, Mandor,* or otherwise)" (p. ccxlvi).

they had population records or were well informed about the size and composition of every household.

Even if these village heads possessed all this information, it is questionable whether they would supply the correct statistics to the British colonial government. In his accounts Raffles tried to create the impression that the British, in contrast to the Dutch, had won the confidence of the inhabitants.[30] This picture appears unacceptable in terms of collecting population data, however, since that activity was directly related to some form of taxation. The village heads performed a double function: on the one hand, they were agents of the government, responsible, among other things, for the collection of revenues from the household-ers; on the other hand, they were the traditional elected repre-sentatives of the villagers, their salary consisting of a certain portion of the village land. It seems probable, therefore, that these village heads would prefer to minimize the amount of revenue assessed to the inhabitants of their villages by reporting a lower output of the land, or a smaller area of land cultivated by the villagers, or a smaller number of cultivators. Since in the "Revenue Instructions" forms only the names of the household-ers (cultivators or noncultivators) were registered,[31] together with the numbers of men and women in their households, the exclusion of several heads of households automatically elimi-nated a corresponding number of entire households.

Another point relates to the coverage of Raffles' data. By Raffles' own account with regard to Banten, it appears that information could only be collected for the population of the northern part of the region, while the figures for the rest of the area were outright guesses. This was also the case with parts of

[30] E.g., *ibid.*, I, 61.

[31] A point emphasized by Raffles was the need to give every head of household a number, for, as he correctly pointed out, "in registering names alone, very great confusion may arise, not only by the same being possessed by numerous individuals, but by the singular practice which frequently occurs among the Javans, of persons, from the most capricious motives, assuming new appellations" (*ibid.*, II, ccxlix).

Tjirebon.[32] As to the data for the Principalities, Raffles himself asserted that "as the information they convey rests principally upon native authority, the same reliance cannot be placed upon them as upon the tables for the provinces under the immediate direction of the European government." [33] The data for Madura were presented in an entirely different form from that for the other regions,[34] probably indicating that Raffles' instructions were not followed there.

Another test of the accuracy of the data is to compare the figures for the different regions with some known characteristics of the regions. Raffles' data show a plausible geographical distribution of the population. From later accounts it is known that Central Java was more densely populated than the eastern part of the island. Raffles' figures indicate that the residency of Semarang in Central Java was the most densely populated region (281 persons per square mile) and Banjuwangi, on the eastern tip of the island, was the least populated (7 persons per square mile).[35]

A comparison of the average number of persons per village in the different regions, as calculated from Raffles' data, gives the following results: the arithmetical mean of the number of persons per village in each region ranges between 46 (for Surabaja) and 300 (for Banten). Within the regions there are even larger differences between average numbers for the different divisions. For example, in Banten the range is between less than 90 and more than 1,300; for Surabaja it is between less than 20 and more

[32] *Ibid.*, pp. 243, 253.
[33] *Ibid.*, p. 288. To this assertion Raffles added an afterthought: "There is no reason, however, to believe they are essentially wrong, as they were framed with great care and every attention to accuracy, on the part of the native officers employed."
[34] *Ibid.*, pp. 284–286. The population was classified into chiefs, priests, males above fifty years, females above fifty years, males middle-aged, females middle-aged, young men, young women, boys, girls. There was no division into cultivators and noncultivators.
[35] *Ibid.*, I, 63.

than 100. The likelihood that these differences were the result of underreporting or limited coverage of the data is strengthened by the large discrepancies between the average village population figures of adjoining regions. For example, the mean for Semarang is 203 persons per village,[36] while for the adjoining region of Kedu it is 50.

In another set of directives Raffles spelled out the duties of local authorities in compiling population statistics. The village heads were "directed to keep a register of all persons under their authority, describing the name, age, country, occupation, size, and appearance of each individual, with any other remarks that may be deemed necessary. They will also, with the assistance of the village priest, form a register of the births, marriages, and deaths, which occur within their jurisdiction. These will be drawn up every six months, according to forms to be furnished to them by the Resident. A copy of each will be retained in the village, and another will be forwarded to the police officer of the station." The police officers were instructed to forward to the *bupatis* "every six months abstract accounts of births, marriages, and deaths, which have occurred in their division, and of the general state of cultivation and population, with such remarks accompanying them as may seem requisite." In turn, the *bupatis* "shall, every six months, furnish to the Resident abstract accounts of the state of cultivation and population within their districts, according to forms which will be given to them, and accompanied with such remarks as may suggest themselves." [37]

The "Regulation . . . for the more effectual administration of justice" also contained directives to be observed by the village heads "whenever a stranger arrives for the purpose of settling in a village, or any one of its former inhabitants absconds." [38] It also

[36] These calculations are based on figures in *ibid.*, II, 241–289.

[37] "Regulation, A.D. 1814, Passed by the Honourable the Lieutenant Governor in Council, On the 11th of February 1814, for the more effectual administration of justice in the Provincial Courts of Java," reproduced as part of Appendix D in *ibid.*, pp. lii–liii, liv, lviii.

[38] *Ibid.*, p. liii.

prescribed the steps to be taken whenever some members of a village started to build new settlements in new villages.[39]

Few of these directives were put into force during the short British occupation. With the exception of minor details, however, such as the description of the "appearance of each individual," the directives were adopted by the Dutch colonial government when they returned to Java, and for decades to come they were the sole source of population data. And even in the years prior to the first population census in independent Indonesia in 1961, official population statistics, such as those published by the Central Bureau of Statistics, were based on these village registers as reported to the civil service.

Raffles' directives probably cannot be considered as the first introduction of population registers into the villages since, as has been pointed out, the Indonesian kings and princes had based the earlier administrative divisions of their territory on the number of inhabitants reported by the local and village heads. Moreover, Dutch administrators, such as Daendels, had also asked the local heads to supply data on population. Nevertheless, Raffles' directives were not only the most specific, but, more importantly, were the model for future directives on this subject. Although his directives concerning the registers on village inhabitants are indicative of a police state eager to keep full control of its population, they became the main source of population data for years to come.

[39] The village heads were to take certain steps "when, from caprice or other cause, any of its members are allowed to leave the main part, or *désa*, to go and reside in lonely and remote spots, forming thereby small settlements of two or three cottages only together, termed *dukus*," since, on the one hand, these settlements "which being necessarily from their distance without the guard of night watches, &c. must frequently become liable to be attacked and plundered, or more often, perhaps, from the absence of all controul, will themselves form the resort and shelter of robbers and other abandoned characters;" while at the same time, "on the other hand, it not being wished to repress too much this outsettling, as by the creation of new villages (which must owe their formation to such small beginnings), a great part of the land, at present waste, may be brought into cultivation" (*ibid.*, p. liv).

From this account of Raffles' data several conclusions can be drawn. The figures for the different regions were compiled, not from a census, but from the information supplied to local officers by the village heads. The impression given by Raffles that there was "a settlement . . . made with each individual cultivator," [40] thus implying a high degree of accuracy, is not borne out by his own instructions on the methods for collecting the data. In spite of Raffles' confidence, the degree of unintentional and deliberate underreporting was probably high, especially because of the direct relation between the collection of population data and the levying of taxes. Although the data referred to every region of Java, the coverage of a number of regions was very likely far from adequate. As compared to Radermacher's and Neder-burgh's data and all other information available up to that time, Raffles' figures were definitely more accurate, but the shortcomings we have discussed indicate that the resulting total population figures for Java were a gross underestimate.

[40] *Ibid.*, p. 243. See also *ibid.*, I, 61.

CHAPTER 3

Lack of Evidence of Rapid
Population Growth, 1815–1880

Large-scale and ruthless exploitation of Java's human and natural resources characterized Dutch rule in the nineteenth century. Throughout the century the colonial exploitation took different forms, but its objective remained the same, as did the heavy burdens it imposed on the population.

The century's last major revolt against Dutch colonial rule in Java was led by Prince Diponegoro and lasted from 1825 to 1830. It resulted in the complete devastation of large areas of the island and must have had a considerable impact on Java's population growth. In order to rehabilitate its finances, which had suffered immeasurably because of the revolt, the colonial government introduced in 1830 the infamous "cultivation system." [1] The system called for the cultivation of certain crops in high demand in the European market, forced delivery of the produce, and forced labor services for government projects such as building roads to transport the produce. [2] In order to achieve a high

[1] For a description of the cultivation system, see G. Gonggrijp, *Schets ener Economische Geschiedenis van Nederlands-Indië* (Sketch of an Economic History of the Netherlands Indies), 3rd ed. (Haarlem, 1949), pp. 101–145.
[2] The Dutch colonial government insisted on tribute in kind for their main source of revenue, while the British, in contrast, stimulated the use of money by discouraging revenue payments in kind and by introducing the land-rent system. This difference was probably related to the different states of development of the two countries. The interest of the Netherlands was in acquiring a supply of goods from its colonies

degree of efficiency in implementing the forced cultivation of crops and delivery of produce, the colonial power strengthened the authority of those members of the traditional aristocracy who were willing to cooperate by granting them hereditary status and ownership of land, and they functioned as agents of the colonial government in exploiting the population. The Dutch economic historian Gonggrijp referred to this period as "the most humiliating pages of our colonial history." [3]

After the end of British rule in 1816, little of importance occurred in the field of collecting population data until the beginning of the third quarter of the nineteenth century. A government regulation in 1819 stipulated that the village heads keep a register of the inhabitants of their villages. This regulation resembled that issued by Raffles, with the improvement that only the occupation and the age of the inhabitants were to be entered in the registers.[4] Several governors general ordered the collection of statistical data, but very little is known about the success of their efforts or intentions. It was not until 1839 that a series of population statistics were published for the years 1826–1831. Although these were said to be the result of a "general census" (*algemeene volkstelling*), a superficial examination reveals that their quality was very questionable.

During this period, interest in population statistics seems to have declined, and even when data were collected in the differ-

---

by exacting overt and disguised tributes to be traded in Europe. Britain, on the other hand, had already reached the stage of being capable of producing large amounts of textiles and other industrial commodities, and thus also needed markets for the output of its manufacturing industries.

[3] *Op. cit.*, p. 10.

[4] Article 14 of Reglement op de Administratie der Policie en de Criminele en Civile Regtsvordering onder den Inlander in Nederlandsch Indië, Besluit van Commissarissen Generaal over Nederlandsch Indië van 10 Januari 1819, no. 6 (Regulation on the Administration of Police and Criminal and Civil Legal Action among the Natives in Netherlands Indies, Decision of the Commissioners General of Netherlands Indies of January 10, 1819, no. 6), *Indisch Staatsblad*, no. 20.

ent regions, they were apparently not forwarded to the central government. P. Bleeker, an industrious student of Java's population, was unable to find population data in the government agencies in Djakarta, but on his trips throughout Java in the middle of the forties he succeeded in collecting data from the local officials. Summing up the figures for all regions, Bleeker estimated that in 1845 Java's population numbered 9.5 million.

Probably in part as a reaction to Bleeker's efforts, the Dutch government began in 1849 to publish annual data on the population of Java in *Koloniaal Verslag* (Colonial Report), the yearly report of the Dutch minister of colonies to the Dutch parliament. These data were the sum totals of the reports of local officials, as were those of Bleeker, but were less detailed.

The degree of reliability of these official figures will be shown later by comparing them with the results of an *opneming* (survey) conducted in the residency of Tjirebon in West Java and finished in 1858. This survey was intended to provide data for the implementation of the land-revenue system as well as the cultivation system and the imposition of forced-labor services. A similar survey was later conducted in the residency of Banjumas, followed by surveys, known as cadastral and statistical *opnemingen*, in the residencies of Kedu, Tegal, Pekalongan, Semarang, and Bagelen, all in Central Java.

Data for 1826–1831

In 1839 an article appeared entitled "Bevolking van Java en Madura." This contained a table (reproduced here as Table 3) for the years 1826–1831 on the population of Java, excluding the Principalities of Jogjakarta and Surakarta, distributed by residencies. The general contention of the article was that there had been an increase in population, and this was attributed to several main causes. In earlier periods, it argued, there were constant wars between the different kingdoms and the population was continuously subject to "the torments and slavery oppressions of their kings." In contrast, with the "increased settlements of

Table 3. Population by region, Java, 1826–1831 (a reproduction of the 1832 data)

Residency	1826	1827	1828	1829	1830	1831
Bantam	230,431	245,751	270,876	298,860	337,169	337,169
Batavia	185,716	194,876	203,870	212,460	223,596	223,596
Buitenzorg	127,423	154,380	181,790	216,840	240,812	240,812
Krawang	62,573	67,430	71,520	65,480	79,445	79,445
Preanger Regent-						
schappen	341,473	370,882	406,281	433,862	471,928	471,928
Cheribon	310,780	339,898	363,785	396,852	429,576	429,576
Tagal	122,641	135,420	147,692	153,780	168,644	168,644
Pekalongang	170,863	183,767	205,998	225,756	249,897	249,897
Samarang	280,840	301,617	324,791	352,680	385,366	385,366
Kadoe	242,590	251,431	268,370	282,460	307,339	308,978
Bagaleen	280,860	302,677	329,270	348,461	379,382	441,653
Banjoemaas	280,671	310,842	342,790	380,640	421,554	421,554
Madion	197,827	212,504	231,472	248,361	268,130	268,130
Kedirie	111,718	126,803	138,971	150,216	167,183	167,183
Japara en Joanna	211,580	238,671	267,840	294,768	324,777	324,777
Rembang	301,670	321,580	356,471	381,670	413,334	413,334
Soerabaija, waaronder						
Madura & Grissee	438,168	470,201	503,840	528,961	560,792	560,792
Passaroeang	157,868	170,681	186,521	208,460	229,543	229,543
Bezoekie en Banjoe-						
wangie	245,860	261,685	272,540	206,470	296,386	296,386
Total, Java						6,018,763

Source: "Bevolking van Java en Madura" (Population of Java and Madura), *Tijdschrift voor Neêrland's Indië*, 2nd year, (1839), I, 158; reproduced from *De Statistiek van 1832* (The Statistics of 1832).

Europeans, naturally many sources of industry and welfare came into being for the aborigines." The article then went on to point out that there was peace and order under colonial rule, and many people stayed alive due to vaccination, which was introduced "already before the year 1780." [5] The subject matter of this part of the article, the allegedly sharp contrast between the general conditions before and after the settlement of the Dutch rule and their consequent impact on population increase, will be discussed more fully later.

The article then went on to criticize Raffles, pointing out that his figures were "imaginary" and that his conclusion "ought not

[5] "Bevolking van Java en Madura" (Population of Java and Madura), *Tijdschrift voor Neêrland's Indië*, 2nd year (1839), I, 155–156; reproduced from *De Statistiek van 1832* (The Statistics of 1832).

to occur to someone who is looking for the truth and is thinking logically."[6] This criticism of Raffles, presented without any supporting evidence, is quite understandable in the light of Raffles' own sharp criticism of Dutch colonial rule and his many innovations.

The article presented its own table on the population of Java between 1826 and 1831, contending that "we can rely more on the results of the general population census that has taken place in our days."[7] The table shows, for the year 1831, a population of 6,018,763 for Java exclusive of the Principalities of Jogjakarta and Surakarta. The population of the two Principalities, according to the article, numbered about one million. Thus, the total population of Java was accordingly estimated as somewhat more than seven million. One quick glance at the original table, however, reveals that for seventeen out of the nineteen residencies the 1831 population figures were identical to those of 1830. The table also shows improbable annual rates of increase for the total population. (By adding together the populations of the different regions for each of the years, a basis can be found for calculating the annual rates of increase.) As shown in Table 4, the annual growth rates implied were 80.3, 85.0, 59.7, 100.2, and 10.7 per

Table 4. Total population and annual rate
of increase, Java, 1826–1831

Year	Total population	Annual rate of increase (per 1,000)
1826	4,301,552	
1827	4,661,096	80.3
1828	5,074,688	85.0
1829	5,387,037	59.7
1830	5,954,853	100.2
1831	6,018,763	10.7

Source: Computed from Table 3. Figures are for all Java excluding the Principalities of Jogjakarta and Surakarta.

[6] Ibid., p. 157.   [7] Ibid.

1,000 persons. This simple calculation is probably enough to indicate the general unreliability of these data.[8]

For a large part of Java the existence of any kind of enumeration during the reported period was definitely out of the question. From 1825 to 1830, the revolt against the Dutch colonial government, known as the Java war, raged over vast areas of Central and East Java, so that many of the regions were under alternate control of the contesting forces. It therefore seems fair to conclude that the figures presented for the period 1826–1831, allegedly derived from a census or enumeration, are at least of a very questionable character.

Bleeker's Data for 1845

When Bleeker traveled through Java during the middle of the forties, he collected from local officials the population data that he had been unable to find in the government offices in Djakarta. He summed up the figures and published them as data for the year 1845, with the exception of two regions [9] (see Table 5).

[8] In an article in 1863, Bleeker gave data for the years 1824, 1826–1830, 1832, 1834, 1837, and 1838. According to this information, the population decreased from 6,368,090 in 1824 to 5,295,542 in 1826, and from then on there was an annual rate of increase of between 60 and 100 per 1,000 persons until 1830 (total population 7,064,936). Bleeker's speculation was that this erratic behavior was a consequence of the Java war which took place between 1825 and 1830. He points out that if only the figures for 1824 and 1830 were taken into account, an annual growth rate of 18.2 would result. Bleeker did not supply a source for any of these figures, however, nor did he indicate how the figures were arrived at (P. Bleeker, "Statistisch-Ekonomische Onderzoekingen en Beschouwingen op Koloniaal Gebied: De Bevolkingstoename op Java" [Statistical and Economic Enquiries and Observations in the Colonial Field: The Population Increase in Java], *Tijdschrift voor Nederlandsch Indië*, n.s., 1st year [1863], I, 193–194).

[9] P. Bleeker, "Nieuwe Bijdragen tot de Kennis der Bevolkingsstatistiek van Java" (New Contributions to the Knowledge of the Population Statistics of Java), *Bijdragen tot de Taal-, Land-, en Volkenkunde van Nederlandsch Indië*, IV (1869), 447–448. See also P. Bleeker, "Bijdragen tot de Statistiek der Bevolking van Java" (Contributions to the Statistics of the Population of Java), *Tijdschrift voor*

Table 5. Total population by
residency of Java, 1845

Residency	Total population
Besuki	503,175
Pasuruan	336,472
Surabaja	1,237,392
Kediri	235,243
Rembang	478,708
Madiun	314,979
Patjitan	89,788
Djepara	422,035
Semarang	757,831
Kedu	357,188
Pekalongan	236,620
Surakarta	505,193
Jogjakarta	349,166
Bagelen	615,105
Banjumas	401,840
Tegal	299,282
Tjirebon	616,858
Priangan	728,061
Krawang	133,065
Bogor	260,311
Djakarta	283,517
Banten	389,556
Total, Java	9,551,385

Source: P. Bleeker, "Bijdragen tot
de Statistiek der Bevolking van Java"
(Contributions to the Statistics of the
Population of Java), *Tijdschrift voor
Neêrland's Indië,* 9th year (1847), IV,
15.

With regard to the reliability of his collection, Bleeker reported:
"The value of the figures for the different residencies are judged
differently by the local authorities. In general, however, it can
be accepted that for no residency are the reported figures too
high. For many residencies they are definitely too low." He

Neêrland's Indië, 9th year (1847), I, 39–41, and IV, 1–25. The figure for
the residency of Bagelen was for 1843. Bleeker reported that there were
no records for the Indonesian inhabitants of Surakarta and that the
figure shown in the table was an estimate by the local officials ("Bijdragen tot de Statistiek," 9th year [1847], I, 40). He calculated that the
population of Bagelen was 700,000 while that of Surakarta was over
800,000.

concluded: "It can be safely assumed, that at present the true number of population already exceeds 10,000,000." [10] It has to be emphasized, however, that Bleeker's figures were collections of those reported to him by the local authorities. Bleeker's reference to his figures as population records containing "the figures of the population census [or population enumeration, *volkstelling*] of 1845," the heading of his main table as "General population record of Java, for the greater part according to the enumeration [*telling*] of 1845," [11] and the references by later writers to these figures as constituting the results of an enumeration have been quite misleading. Nothing is known as to how the local authorities arrived at their figures. Very probably they were at best additions and subtractions of population changes that had been orally reported by the village heads.[12] There is nothing in the accounts of Bleeker's journeys to indicate that any enumeration was conducted or that Bleeker had any opportunity to check the reliability of the data he received.[13] In short, what Bleeker did was to act as a substitute for the negligent central government by collecting and adding up the information received from local officials.

Annual Data for 1849–1879

Beginning in 1849, the colonial reports submitted to the Dutch parliament each year by the ministers of colonies contained official population figures for Java.[14] Warnings appeared in

[10] "Bijdragen tot de Statistiek," 9th year (1847), I, 40.

[11] *Ibid.*, pp. 40, 39.

[12] This is how W. B. Bergsma described the collection of earlier data in "Hoe de Bevolkingscijfers van de Inlanders op Java en Madoera Worden Verzameld" (How the Population Figures of the Natives in Java and Madura Are Collected), *Tijdschrift voor het Binnenlandsch Bestuur*, VII (1892), 310.

[13] Bleeker's accounts of his travels were published in "Fragmenten eener Reis over Java" (Fragments of a Journey through Java), *Tijdschrift voor Nederlandsch Indië*, 11th year (1849), II, 17–55, 117–145, 177–190, 266–270.

[14] *Koloniaal Verslag* (The Hague), for 1849–1880.

practically every issue that the figures were of limited reliability. Actually they were compilations of figures from local officials, who were supposed to collect the data from lower officials, who in turn were to get the information from village heads. With a few exceptions, the data for both the total population and for the different regions generally indicate very high rates of increase. As is shown in Table 6, the annual rates of increase during the

Table 6. Total population and annual rate of increase, Java, 1850–1880 (computed from official data)

Year	Total population	Annual rate of increase (per 1,000)
1850	9,570,023	
		22.3
1855	10,916,158	
		30.5
1860	12,718,717	
		21.6
1865	14,168,416	
		29.5
1870	16,452,168	
		21.7
1875	18,335,778	
		15.5
1880	19,794,505	

Source: based on population figures in Koloniaal Verslag (The Hague) for 1850–1882.

six five-year periods between 1850 and 1880 are 22.3, 30.5, 21.6, 29.5, 21.7, and 15.5 per 1,000 persons. The data for the different regions show even higher rates, reaching in some cases 60 or 70 (see Table 7). For many regions the rates also appear to be very erratic. For example, for these five-year periods the annual growth rates for the residency Tjirebon are 40.6, 50.1, 6.3, 21.1, 29.1, 15.2; for Pekalongan, 28.0, 68.8, 14.0, 62.1, 20.2, 11.4; for Madura, 4.0, 73.6, 23.8, 29.0, 26.8, 13.3. These data also show a great discrepancy between the rates of increase in the territory under direct Dutch rule and those in the Principalities during the period 1850 to 1870. For those four five-year periods, the annual

Table 7. Annual rate of increase per 1,000 persons, by region, Java, 1850–1880

Region	1850–1855	1855–1860	1860–1865	1865–1870	1870–1875	1875–1880
Banten	11.6	19.8	20.8	23.0	12.5	−41.0
Djakarta	27.4	24.5	20.6	16.1	8.2	3.4
Priangan	17.9	5.9	15.1	28.8	32.5	54.4
Tjirebon	40.6	50.1	6.3	21.1	29.1	15.2
Pekalongan	28.0	68.8	14.0	62.1	20.2	11.4
Semarang	48.0	41.8	17.3	17.9	17.9	0.0
Rembang	17.4	33.4	15.4	26.7	23.7	18.2
Banjumas	43.8	49.7	52.5	40.5	21.1	13.2
Kedu	27.6	22.7	32.6	42.3	15.8	8.9
Madiun	21.6	32.3	25.3	38.7	43.2	23.6
Kediri	53.2	24.7	48.4	46.0	28.4	31.3
Surabaja	25.1	21.7	17.7	20.3	18.1	34.9
Madura	4.0	73.6	23.8	29.0	26.8	13.3
Pasuruan	21.8	23.2	17.5	22.9	21.4	28.4
Besuki		21.8	15.6	28.9	14.1	22.0
Average, region under direct Dutch control	28.0	32.9	22.6	31.7	21.4	14.9
Jogjakarta	−18.6	12.3	9.3	14.3	19.5	11.4
Surakarta	25.6	2.1	9.2	2.2	29.1	25.5
Average, region of the Principalities	10.1	5.8	9.3	6.3	25.8	20.8
Average, Java	22.3	30.5	21.6	29.5	21.7	15.5

Source: Based on population figures in Koloniaal Verslag (The Hague) for 1850–1882. The administrative divisions of 1920 are used in this table.

growth rates in the former are 28.0, 32.9, 22.6, and 31.7, while for the latter they are 10.1, 5.8, 9.3, and 6.3.

These differences might all have been due to interregional migrations, which appear to have occurred on an extensive scale. As has been pointed out by others, during earlier periods the population of the island had reacted to pressures by moving to uninhabited areas and setting up new settlements.[15] The years

[15] For example, in reference to the services performed by the population in earlier periods in building temples, Schrieke pointed out that "we are aware that the Javanese are able to endure great pressure: history provides any number of examples of it. But there is a limit. If that limit is transgressed—soccage service is particularly burdensome —the people move to other regions where the pressure is less heavy, and lay out sawahs [irrigated fields] once more" (B. Schrieke, Indonesian

presently under consideration cover part of the period when the "cultivation system" was being implemented. This system exerted tremendous economic pressure on the peasant population,[16] but since it was not enforced in all regions (in the territories of the Principalities, for example), and since the resulting pressures were not equally heavy in the different regions, it is quite plausible that it led to large population movements between the regions.[17]

If these movements were indeed the consequence of the differential pressures of the economic system, however, their directions, as can be inferred from the differential growth rates, are not plausible. For example, one of the residencies that suffered most was Tjirebon, but the data show a very high rate of population increase there during several five-year periods. On the other hand, the territories of the Principalities, which were not directly subject to the pressures of the system, reportedly experienced the smallest growth rates for the whole island during most of the period. Aside from "noneconomic" factors, a

---

Sociological Studies, Pt. II: *Ruler and Realm in Early Java* [The Hague, 1957], p. 300). Raffles also pointed out that "it has been ascertained, that, on the first establishment of the Dutch in the eastern part of the island, the inhabitants of whole districts at once migrated into the Native Provinces. Every new act of rigour, every unexpected exaction, occasioned a further migration, and cultivation was transferred to tracts which had previously scarcely a family on them." He also asserted that "the inhabitants of the province of *Demak*, one of the richest in the eastern districts, fled into the Native Provinces; and when an order was given for the rigid enforcement of the coffee monopoly, every district suffered in its population, in proportion to the extent of service levied upon it" (Thomas Stamford Raffles, *The History of Java*, 1st ed. [London, 1817], I, 65).

[16] Gonggrijp, *op. cit.*, p. 101.

[17] In 1866 a large-scale exodus was reported from the Djepara region to escape the burdensome forced labor services, which compelled peasants to neglect their own fields ("Bijdragen tot de Kennis van het Landelijk Stelsel op Java" [Contributions to the Knowledge of the Land-Rent System in Java], *Tijdschrift voor Nederlandsch Indië*, n.s., 4th year [1866], II, 274–302).

large-scale population movement from the Principalities to the regions under direct Dutch control would have been plausible only if, despite the strains imposed by the compulsory cultivation and delivery of crops and a multitude of compulsory labor services, the level of income in the Dutch-controlled areas was higher than anywhere else. From historical accounts of the actual working of the cultivation system, this assumption seems improbable.

It seems more plausible to infer, therefore, that the differential growth rates, with respect both to the different regions and the different years, were primarily the consequence of the quality of the data rather than of the impact of actual population movements. For Java as a whole, there are no reports or indications of any large-scale migration from other Indonesian islands or from other countries.[18] In the absence of significant migration, a growth rate of 30 for the whole island, assuming a crude birth rate of 45, would imply a crude death rate of 15 per 1,000 persons, something rather unlikely during that period.

The colonial reports, in explaining the high rates of increase, repeatedly argued that the earlier data (those of the previous year) were defective and that the later data were of superior quality. Thus, each year, the figures collected were considered more reliable than all previous figures; but by the next year these in turn were said to have underreported the actual population

[18] For example, according to the colonial reports, the number of non-Indonesians in Java during the years 1855, 1865, and 1875 was 178,612, 214,504, and 246,479, compared to a total population of, respectively, 10,916,158, 14,168,416, and 18,335,778 persons. The majority of these non-Indonesians were Chinese. Several settlements are known to have been established in the other islands, including Kalimantan, by persons who originally came from Java. It is also known that there was migration from Banten (the westernmost region of Java) to Lampung, on the southern tip of Sumatra. But the settlement in Java of persons originating from the other Indonesian islands was very small compared to the total population of Java, and took place mainly around Djakarta. Only during very recent years are there indications of a large population influx from these islands to Java.

numbers. If this official explanation is accepted, it implies that there was a cumulative degree of underreporting for the earlier years and that consequently the average annual growth rate was actually smaller than the figures indicate.[19]

Whenever the rate of increase was comparatively small or the later figures were less than those for previous years, this was usually attributed to the effect of some epidemic. The plausibility of this explanation can be estimated by comparing the population figures with the reports on health conditions, which were also contained in these colonial reports, but were apparently prepared by different officials. These reports show that epidemics also occurred in regions that were reported to have experienced a rapid population increase. In a number of cases the epidemics in the regions with supposedly decreasing (or very slowly increasing) populations were reported to have been more limited than in the other regions.

The reports further ascribed any small increases or decreases in the population of certain regions to the return of inhabitants of other regions to their original places of residence. It was stated that in many cases these persons had left their home areas because of some action of local officials that had resulted in heavier burdens being laid on the population; the repeal of such regulations after several years resulted in the return of the population. In the colonial reports for the years in which this out-migration reportedly occurred, however, none of these movements was estimated to have had an effect on the population either of

[19] This reasoning contains an implicit assumption that can be seen more clearly in the following way: Denote the estimated population of year i based on the reports in year j by $_jP_i$. Thus, the estimated population of the year 1865, based on the reports of the same year, was $_{1865}P_{1865}$, and based on the reports of the year 1866, it was $_{1866}P_{1865}$. A continuous improvement in reporting implies that $_{j+n}P_i > _jP_i$, but the implication that the average annual growth rate is actually smaller contains the implicit assumption that

$$\frac{_{j+n}P_{i+n}}{_jP_{i+n}} \leqq \frac{_{j+n}P_i}{_jP_i} \, .$$

the regions of departure or of the regions of arrival. Similarly the return of these persons did not have any reported effect on the population of the original places of residence. Only the effect of their departure from the regions where they had temporarily stayed was reported. This is understandable, since local officials were unlikely to take pride in population decreases and were more likely to submit reports which transferred the blame from their own shoulders.[20]

In some cases the decrease or lower rate of increase of population was supposedly a consequence of too high estimates for the earlier years. At any rate, in the case of any unlikely discrepancy between figures of different years the earlier ones were blamed. This attitude characterizes almost all the later reports. Such an explanation may or may not have been correct, but it is something that can be expected from official reports.

Since the official data for the period under consideration have been frequently used as evidence of a very rapid population increase, attributed primarily to improved health conditions, it may be of some use to supply some data relating to the activities of the Dutch government in this field. Much emphasis has been given to the effects of smallpox vaccination, even to the extent of implying that at the beginning of the nineteenth century a full-fledged campaign against smallpox was undertaken. Although vaccination was begun in the early decades of the nineteenth century, the extent of its use has been grossly overemphasized. The colonial reports supply the following data: in 1855

[20] "Nothing is less agreeable to a resident [head of a residency] than to find out that in his monthly registers or in his yearly reports he has to record that the population in some districts has decreased" (V. L., "De Afschaffing van het Passenstelsel" [The Repeal of the System of Passports], *Tijdschrift voor Nederlandsch Indië*, n.s., 1st year [1863], II, 237). The article also mentioned "that hundreds of natives often move from one region to the other without possessing passports and without being sent back, because it is in the interests of the native heads not to have them reported (increase of population)" (p. 237).

around 110,000 persons were reportedly vaccinated; in 1865 about 500,000; in 1880, 520,000. On the basis of the official population figures, which were likely to be underestimates, these vaccinations affected respectively 1, 3, and 2.5 per cent of the population. For earlier periods, D. Schoute, a medical historian, asserted that "the vaccination was only applied to those natives who came in daily contact with Europeans." [21] In 1870 the number of medical doctors in Java was fifty-three, of whom half were military doctors. [22] The existing hospitals were almost exclusively military. Even at the turn of the present century, efforts in the field of health were primarily confined to the army. [23] It is interesting to note that nowhere has there even been mention of the possibility that the spread of diseases might have resulted from closer contact between the population and the foreigners, although a glance at the colonial reports shows that a very high proportion of the members of the Dutch army were carriers of contagious diseases. It seems reasonable to accept Schoute's statement that during the last century practically nothing was done in the field of public health, with the exception of smallpox vaccination. [24] Even this latter was carried out on a far more limited scale during that century than is often thought.

To sum up, the colonial reports were indeed correct in their warnings that the official data for the period were of limited reliability. The very high growth rate for Java as a whole, which the data indicate, appears most unlikely, while the differential growth rates between regions and years are actually indications of the deficiencies of the data. When the colonial reports cite a

[21] "De Geneeskunde in Nederlandsch Indië gedurende de Negentiende Eeuw" (Medicine in the Netherlands Indies during the Nineteenth Century), *Geneeskundig Tijdschrift voor Nederlandsch-Indië*, LXXIV (1934), 950.

[22] *Koloniaal Verslag, 1871*, p. 350. The official estimate of the total population was 16.5 million.

[23] Schoute, *op. cit.*, LXXV (1935), 1476.   [24] *Ibid.*, p. 1560.

high degree of underreporting at each point in time, this implies that there must have been a much smaller actual rate of increase throughout the whole period. Thus, the view that these years witnessed a very rapid population growth, primarily due to improved health conditions, is not supported by evidence. It seems more likely that actually little was done in the field of public health during the past century.

Data Based on Regional Surveys

The extent of underenumeration in the official figures discussed in the preceding section can be demonstrated by comparing them with the results of a number of regional surveys (*opnemingen*). The first of these, completed in 1858, was carried out in the residency of Tjirebon in West Java. This survey was intended to provide improved data for implementing the land-revenue system, as well as the cultivation system and the imposition of forced-labor services. The land-revenue system, as originally conceived, was to consist of payments from individual peasants directly to the government. For this purpose the individual holdings of every peasant had to be known. Since the government did not want to increase its expenditures by measuring the holdings of every individual, however, it circumvented this procedure by making assessments of a whole village as one unit rather than of each individual villager. Nevertheless, even for this more simple form of taxation the total arable land of every village had still to be measured. As early as 1818 the desirability of such measurements was recognized, but not until almost forty years later did they begin in Tjirebon. These land surveys were conducted simultaneously with military topographical surveys, and an estimate of the number of inhabitants of these regions was attached.

This interest in surveys was also related to the cultivation system. To rehabilitate its finances, which were in a chaotic condition after the Java war, the Dutch government ordered the execution of this system, which was, briefly, based on the compulsory production of export products and government monopoly on the trade of these products.[25] The villagers were to produce certain crops, which were to be delivered freely to the government, supposedly in lieu of paying land revenue in cash. The villagers were also to provide "cultivation services" (*cultuurdiensten*), which were compulsory labor services in government enterprises. These were in addition to the already existing *heerendiensten* (literally, "gentlemen services")—forced-labor services for such government projects as roads and fortifications —and other traditional unpaid services performed for the interest of individual government officials.[26]

Since from the outset the cultivation system dealt with a whole village as a single unit rather than with individual peasants, there was no need to collect data on individual holdings. A proper implementation of the system as originally envisaged would have necessitated knowledge both of the available arable land and of the labor force available to perform the compulsory services. Nevertheless, no serious efforts to collect information were made, and a decision in 1844 to conduct some kind of survey was never implemented.[27] The Dutch government reportedly shrank from financing such efforts. Some supporters of the idea contended that government expenditures in collecting the data would soon be more than compensated for by the increased revenue that would result from improved information on the available land and labor, since they had some suspicion that the information presented by the village heads was inten-

[25] Gonggrijp, *op. cit.*, pp. 101–146; J. S. Furnivall, *Netherlands India: A Study of Plural Economy* (Cambridge, Eng., 1944), pp. 115–147.

[26] This last type of service was known as *pantjendiensten*. There were also unpaid services to be performed for the village as a whole, such as serving as night watchman and maintaining the irrigation works.

[27] Decision of Governor General Markus of June 20, 1844, no. 5. See *Encyclopaedie van Nederlandsch Indië*, 2nd ed. (The Hague, 1921), IV, 105.

tionally too low.[28] The Dutch government, however, had a much more effective, and at the same time much less cumbersome and costly, device to maximize the stream of desired export crops, by an ingenious combination of low salaries and harsh punishments for government officials, on the one hand, and attractive "cultivation premiums" (*cultuurprocenten*) and certain hereditary functions, on the other.[29]

The Dutch government's interest in acquiring population data was illustrated by a letter from a minister of colonies, Cornets de Groot van Kraayenburg, to the Royal Commission for Statistics, which had been set up to study the possibility of conducting population censuses in the colonies. The letter stated:

The population censuses to be held should appear as little as possible as something extraordinary, and in the new regulations concerning that matter, where they are unavoidable, less what is desirable [but] rather what is useful should be aimed at. Also all increase of writing [or deskwork, *schrijfwerk*], where it is not absolutely necessary, ought to be avoided.[30]

The surveys conducted in Tjirebon were later repeated in the Banjumas residency in Central Java. In 1864 it was decided that similar surveys, known as cadastral and statistical surveys, should be conducted in the residencies of Kedu, Tegal, Pekalongan, Semarang, and Bagelen.[31] In the reports of these surveys emphasis seems always to have been given to the measurement of land,[32]

[28] T. J. Willer, "Maandelijksch Overzigt der Indische Letterkunde: Volkstelling in Nederlandsch Indië" (Monthly Survey of the Indies Literature: Population Census in Netherlands Indies), *Tijdschrift voor Nederlandsch Indië*, 24th year (1862), I, 388.

[29] *Ibid.*, p. 391; Gonggrijp, *op. cit.*, pp. 109–110, 123–124.

[30] Quoted in *Encyclopaedie van Nederlandsch Indië*, 1st ed. (1905), IV, 585.

[31] Decision of the Governor General of the Netherlands Indies of Nov. 2, 1864, no. 31, *Indisch Staatsblad, 1864*, no. 166.

[32] Although these surveys were called cadastral surveys, they were not to determine the area of individual landholdings, but rather to measure the total land belonging to each of the villages (see "Uittreksel der

while little was reported on the procedure of collecting population data. The data on population were called the result either of
the statistical survey (*statistieke opneming*) or of the population
census (*volkstelling*), without further explanation or description.[33] The cadastral offices set up in each of the five residencies
were to supervise the population registration, a task formerly
performed by the civil service. In the villages the registers were
kept up to date by the village secretary, who was a member of
the village government. The statistics compiled by the cadastral
bureaus were then sent to the central government. The steps
involved in compiling the data at least allowed less possibility of
arithmetical errors than had been the case with the data compiled
by local officials.

A comparison of the reports of the local officials and the
results of the survey yields the following results: For the residency of Tjirebon the local officials reported a population
of 598,131 persons in 1852; the survey showed a population of
775,430 persons in 1858, giving an annual average increase
of around 5 per cent. For the residency of Banjumas the 1857
population according to the civil service reports was 436,174
persons, while the survey gave the 1862 population as 688,906,
an average annual increase of around 14 per cent.

For the other residencies the comparisons referred either to
the same years or to years which were not too far apart.[34] The
results of the comparisons for the combined population of the

---

Verschillende Halfjaarlijksche Verslagen over de Statistieke Opneming
van Java, Samengesteld door Rost van Tonningen, 24 November 1867"
[Summary of the Different Biannual Reports on the Statistical Surveys
of Java, Written by Rost van Tonningen, November 24, 1867], reproduced in "Stukken betrekkelijk de Statistieke en Kadastrale Opneming
van het Eiland Java" [Documents concerning the Statistical and Cadastral Survey of the Island of Java], ed. Rost van Tonningen, *Tijdschrift
voor Nederlandsch Indië*, 3rd ser., 2nd year [1868], II, 70).

[33] *Ibid.*, p. 59.

[34] For Kedu, see *ibid.*, pp. 59–60; for Bagelen, *ibid.*, p. 61; for Pekalongan, *ibid.*, p. 63; for Tegal, *ibid.*, p. 64; for Semarang, *ibid.*, p. 62.

regencies of Magelang and Temanggung in the residency of Magelang are given in Table 8.

For the regencies of Karanganjar, Kebumen, Ambal, and Kutoardjo in the residency of Bagelen, the civil service reported a total population of 455,560 in 1864, while the result of the survey in 1866 was 541,460, an increase of 18.8 per cent in two years. For the five districts in the residency of Pekalongan the

Table 8. Population of Magelang and Temanggung, 1866

Age group	Report of the civil service	Result of the survey	Increase (%)
Men	121,292	174,840	44
Women	144,029	192,685	34
Girls of nonmarriageable age	141,466	119,816	−15
Boys under 14 years	114,960	126,667	10
Total population	521,747	614,008	18

Source: "Uittreksel der Verschillende Halfjaarlijksche Verslagen over de Statistieke Opneming van Java, Samengesteld door Rost van Tonningen, 24 November 1867" (Summary of the Different Biannual Reports on the Statistical Surveys of Java, Written by Rost van Tonningen, November 24, 1867), reproduced in "Stukken betrekkelijk de Statistieke en Kadastrale Opneming van het Eiland Java" (Documents concerning the Statistical and Cadastral Survey of the Island of Java), ed. Rost van Tonningen, *Tijdschrift voor Nederlandsch Indië*, 3rd ser., 2nd year (1868), II, 60.

difference between the population figures given in the civil service report of 1865 and those in the 1866 survey is 35 per cent. For the total of five districts in the residency of Tegal the difference is 9.3 per cent. For the total of five districts in the residency of Semarang it is 9 per cent.

Even though it is not known how accurate the survey was, these comparisons do give some idea of the underreporting of the population figures in official records. Part of the discrepancy might be due to natural increase or in-migration from other regions, but the main difference was probably due to more accurate reporting in the surveys. One interesting aspect of the figures is that the degree of underreporting of men and boys is higher than that of women and girls. This can readily be understood given the then existing economic system. As a Dutch minister of colonies explained, the main cause of the discrepancy lay in the inaccuracies of the civil service reports, based as they were on the information from the village heads, "who had an interest in reporting the [labor] force of the village as small as possible." [35]

The areas of arable land were also underreported. For example, according to the survey, the area of irrigated fields (*sawah*) in Tjirebon in 1858 was about 16 per cent larger than was indicated in the reports of the local officials for the same year.[36] The discrepancies for some of the other residencies are even larger.

The cadastral offices, which were set up in seven residencies and were in charge of recording the changes in arable land and keeping the population records up to date, were never expanded to other residencies and were finally abolished in 1879. The collection of population data became once more part of the activities of the civil service.[37] The statistical division at the General Secretariat, which was the central government agency to which statistical data from the residencies were sent and which was in fact the beginning of a central statistical agency, was abolished in 1884.

[35] "Inlichtingen betreffende de Statistieke en Kadastrale Opmetingen van de Residentiën Cheribon en Banjoemas, Nota van de Minister van Koloniën, I. D. Fransen van de Putte, van 12 Mei 1863" (Information concerning the Statistical and Cadastral Surveys of the Residencies Tjirebon and Banjumas, Statement of the Minister of Colonies, I. D. Fransen van de Putte, of May 12, 1863), reproduced in van Tonningen, "Stukken betrekkelijk de Statistieke en Kadastrale Opneming van het Eiland Java," p. 41.

[36] "Nota betreffende de Statistieke Opneming in de Residentie Cheribon, Samengesteld door de Inspecteur Belast met de Leiding der Statistieke Opneming op Java, Rost van Tonningen, 7 Maart 1866" (Statement concerning the Statistical Survey in the Residency of Tjirebon, Written by the Inspector in Charge of the Statistical Survey in Java, Rost van Tonningen, March 7, 1866), reproduced in *ibid.*, pp. 51–52.

[37] Decision of the Governor General of the Netherlands Indies of May 10, 1879, no. 4, *Indisch Staatsblad*, no. 164.

CHAPTER 4

Population Enumerations
and Compulsory Labor
Services, 1880-1905

During the last quarter of the nineteenth century, the cultivation system—the huge government enterprise of state capitalism that had enjoyed a monopoly for decades—was gradually replaced by private capital from Dutch and other sources.[1] With the opening of the Suez Canal and the resultant stimulation of trade between Asia and Europe, Indonesia became one of the major world areas of investment in such primary products as rubber, palm oil, tin, petroleum, and other raw materials for industry, as well as in such agricultural consumption goods as coffee, sugar, tea, and tobacco. But the ending of the government monopoly in exports did not mean the end of forced cultivation and forced labor. The forced cultivation of coffee continued until around 1920, while compulsory labor was not abolished in Java until 1916 and was never abolished in the other islands.

Although the form of colonial exploitation changed, the living conditions of the peasants did not, and at the turn of the century, according to some reports, there was even a decline in their welfare.[2] The sugar industry later played an important role in

[1] See G. Gonggrijp, *Schets ener Economische Geschiedenis van Nederlands-Indië* (Sketch of an Economic History of the Netherlands Indies), 3rd ed. (Haarlem, 1949), pp. 147–169.

[2] See, for example, C. Th. van Deventer, *Overzicht van den Economischen Toestand der Inlandsche Bevolking van Java en Madoera* (Review of the Economic Situation of the Native Population of Java and Madura) (The Hague, 1904).

Java, renting from the peasants irrigated land to grow sugar cane on a rotation basis, alternating with foodcrops planted by the peasants themselves. The industry made use of advanced technology for planting and processing, but its presence served to strengthen the traditional characteristics of the society, for in order to ensure use of the best lands it was necessary to deal with the local officials rather than with the individual peasants. As a result, the peasants became paid workers on their own land at subsistance wages.[3]

The year 1880 saw the beginning in Java of what were sometimes called quinquennial population censuses, which were directly related to the system of compulsory labor services. The regulations concerning the collection of population statistics printed in the *Indisch Staatsblad, 1880*, no. 80, stipulated that before the end of those years in which the compulsory labor services were revised, a survey (or enumeration, *opneming*) was to be made of the population, of those persons who were subject to compulsory services, and of livestock. Since the compulsory services were revised every five years, beginning in 1880, the population surveys were also held every five years.

This period also marked the increasing use in Dutch official reports of statistics on the population of the other Indonesian islands. Data on a number of regions other than Java were already available before 1880, but they pertained mainly to the population of coastal areas and as a rule were no more than outright guesses. In this respect, the reported figures for 1880–1905 were actually not much better.

The Quinquennial Population Enumerations

The procedure for the quinquennial population enumerations was described as follows: In each village every yard was to be numbered, and a number plate given to the head of the household that occupied the yard. On a specified day the heads of the

[3] J. van Gelderen, *Voorlezingen over Tropisch-Koloniale Staathuishoudkunde* (Lectures on Tropical-Coloinal Economics) (Haarlem, 1927), p. 116.

households were to assemble, each of them carrying the number plate of his yard. A commission consisting of one or more government officials, the village head, and two village elders was to register the inhabitants of each yard. Only the names of the owner of the yard or of the head of the household were to be entered in the forms. Behind the name of the household head they were to record the numbers of men, women, boys, and girls occupying the yard, the names of persons subject to compulsory labor, their degree of liability for compulsory services, and the number of livestock (horses, cows, buffaloes).

This procedure recalls the one stipulated by Raffles, with some added improvements, such as numbering the yards, which were the units of enumeration. While in Raffles' directives the division officers were to proceed to the villages only if necessary, the 1880 regulations stipulated that a survey was to be held in every village, although they did not in fact rule out the possibility of assembling the household heads of several villages in one place. According to these directives the Dutch district officer (*controleur*) was to be a member of the commission, but full use seems to have been made of a proviso that if he was unable to be present, the commission was to consist of local officials and local heads recommended by him. W. B. Bergsma, who had an important role in the compilation of population statistics in Java, pointed out that "the *controleur* attends the enumeration whenever he *can*, since he necessarily has to make a choice out of hundreds of villages, even though it takes several months before all [villages] are surveyed." [4] Actually, the officials had one whole year to cover their territory, a fact that posed serious problems whenever there were intensive population movements. Regarding this, H. E. Steinmetz, a civil service officer, complained of the lack of directives concerning those who were

[4] "Hoe de Bevolkingscijfers van de Inlanders op Java en Madoera Worden Verzameld" (How the Population Figures of the Natives in Java and Madura Are Collected), *Tijdschrift voor het Binnenlandsch Bestuur*, VII (1892), 319.

absent, "as is for that matter also the case for other particulars," and about the passive role of the population, who were "indifferent and phlegmatic, and, without saying anything, let themselves with pleasure be counted more than once." Citing, in addition to these difficulties, the lack of personnel and funds, he contended that as a result the job was carried out "as conveniently as possible." [5]

J. J. Verwijk, another civil servant, had already pointed out that the method of registering the name of only the head of household probably led to a considerable degree of underenumeration. "The experience has taught us that this method of entering [in the forms] results in love of ease and is the cause of many miscounts." He indicated that apart from the widespread negligence of those in charge of the enumeration, the respondents frequently forgot to include infants. "Does the state also have to know the babies?" was an exclamation he often heard. [6]

The main reason for doubting the reliability of these enumerations, however, lies in their direct relation to the system of compulsory labor. It seems that the registration of persons liable for compulsory services was an important, if not the main, part of the whole activity. Underreporting could be expected to result from attempts to evade this type of draft. Bergsma pointed to "the alarming phenomenon of established farmers disappearing from their villages [minggat, secretly making off] to resume the struggle for life somewhere else." He noted that this occurred not only in barren regions, but also in those areas with the

[5] "Volkstellingen op Java en Madoera" (Population Census in Java and Madura), Tijdschrift voor het Binnenlandsch Bestuur, XVIII (1900), 90–91.

[6] "Het Verzamelen van Gegevens voor de Bevolkingsstatistiek op Java en Madura" (The Gathering of Data for the Population Statistics on Java and Madura), Tijdschrift voor het Binnenlandsch Bestuur, II (1889), 20. Other difficulties that Bergsma indicated were problems related to the absence of family names and the widespread custom in large parts of the island for a person to call himself after his first child rather than after his father (op. cit., p. 311).

best-irrigated fields.[7] Evading different types of taxation by disappearing without notice was reported to be fairly common among the people, as was their preference in new places of settlement "not to know" where they came from.[8]

Another consequence of the direct connection between enumeration and compulsory labor services was probably a tendency to class young men in the category of boys for as long as possible. The widespread low sex ratio (the number of males per female) among adults, and the corresponding high sex ratio among children, were therefore, partly at least, falsified. In addition, girls were probably considered adults at a younger age than were boys.

During the period between consecutive enumerations, any changes in the population were to be reported by the village heads to the district or subdistrict heads either orally or, wherever possible, in writing. A form was provided for this purpose listing the number of the yard and the name of the household head, with the following additional columns: born, added, left (went away), died. The first of these columns was divided into boys and girls, the others into men, women, boys, and girls. Thus, here again the unit was the yard, and changes were recorded only by number, without registering the name of each of the persons involved. These additions and subtractions were to become the official population figures for the years between enumerations.

Initially the colonial reports published the population figures for each year. After 1895, however, only the results of the quinquennial enumerations were published, because "the value of the data derived from the village registers [recording the changes in population] cannot in the long run justify the efforts of the civil service officers in compiling them for publication in the colonial reports." [9] That the annual figures were indeed of even less value than the results of the enumerations is apparent.

[7] *Op. cit.*, p. 320.   [8] *Ibid.*, p. 311.
[9] *Koloniaal Verslag, 1897*, p. 1.

Some idea of their reliability can be inferred from Table 9, where the rates of annual increase jump after every five-year enumeration. The annual growth rates for the five-year periods between 1880 and 1905 calculated from these data are shown in Table 10. It appears that these rates are relatively less than for the preceding period. Between 1850 and 1880 the annual rates of increase for the five-year periods range from 15.5 to 30.5 per 1,000 persons, while during the period 1880–1905 the range is between 9.2 and 22.4. The latter data, however, show the same erratic

Table 9. Annual rates of increase, Java, 1879–1895

Period	Rate of increase (per 1,000)	Period	Rate of increase (per 1,000)
1879–1880	26	1887–1888	17
1880–1881	15	1888–1889	9
1881–1882	8	1889–1890	39
1882–1883	18	1890–1891	9
1883–1884	14	1891–1892	6
1884–1885	26	1892–1893	13
1885–1886	25	1893–1894	19
1886–1887	24	1894–1895	25

Source: Based on population figures in *Koloniaal Verslag* (The Hague) for 1881–1897.

course as for the earlier period. The comparatively low growth rate during the years from 1900 to 1905 was reportedly in part the consequence of crop failures and a cholera epidemic. But for a number of regions the growth rates go up and down in a very unlikely fashion. For example, the growth rates for Jogjakarta in each of the five-year periods are consecutively 15.6, 89.9, 7.4, 57.1, and 6.2 per 1,000 persons; for Madura, 105.6, 17.9, 18.3, 15.1, and −32.7; for Surakarta, 17.1, 19.2, 8.5, 44.5, and 10.3; for Djakarta, 7.0, 23.2, 30.8, 27.2, and 16.9. Within each five-year period there are also large discrepancies between regions, and during the periods 1880–1885 and 1900–1905 there are even negative growth rates for a number of residencies. Very few

Table 10. Annual rates of increase per 1,000 persons, by region, Java, 1880–1905

Region	1880–1885	1885–1890	1890–1895	1895–1900	1900–1905
Banten	−22.8	26.8	28.5	29.9	19.5
Djakarta	7.0	23.2	30.8	27.2	16.9
Priangan	3.0	37.6	20.8	20.8	20.4
Tjirebon	7.7	2.6	9.4	13.0	5.7
Pekalongan	7.6	13.9	14.1	16.1	10.0
Semarang	9.8	10.3	9.3	18.3	−5.3
Rembang	22.3	16.5	7.8	3.2	2.5
Banjumas	15.1	19.5	7.1	17.8	16.5
Kedu	5.0	8.7	9.6	14.0	−1.7
Madiun	−0.2	17.1	4.8	20.8	17.9
Kediri	40.3	34.5	6.2	35.3	31.9
Surabaja	15.9	20.2	15.0	15.8	26.5
Madura	105.6	17.9	18.3	15.1	−32.7
Pasuruan	20.3	16.5	19.8	23.7	20.6
Besuki	27.3	28.1	19.8	23.7	30.0
Average, region under direct Dutch control	16.2	19.6	14.9	19.9	9.2
Jogjakarta	15.6	89.9	7.4	57.1	6.2
Surakarta	17.1	19.2	8.5	44.5	10.3
Average, region of the Principalities	16.1	44.8	8.0	49.9	8.6
Average, Java	16.2	21.6	14.4	22.4	9.2

Source: Based on population figures in *Koloniaal Verslag* (The Hague) for 1882–1907. The administrative divisions of 1920 are used in this table.

regions, however, exhibit such constantly low or high rates of increase that they can be designated areas of in- or out-migration. If the data can be trusted, Tjirebon and Kedu were areas of out-migration, while Pasuruan and Besuki were areas of in-migration. It is well known that the two last-mentioned regions received a large number of settlers from Madura. In general, however, it is hard to draw inferences concerning the extent and direction of migration from these data. For example, Kediri had growth rates which were constantly higher than 30 per 1,000 persons during four five-year periods, but in 1890–1895 its rate of increase was reported as only 6.2. This seems unlikely, but during that same period growth rates lower than 10 per 1,000 persons were reported in nine out of seventeen regions. The

sudden increase in the rate of growth of the residency of Priangan from 3.0 in 1880–1885 to 37.6 in 1885–1890 looks improbable, but similar events occured concurrently in Banten and
Djakarta.

The regulations concerning the collection of population statistics did not apply to the regions outside direct control by the
colonial government—that is, the territories of the Principalities
and, initially, the island of Madura. The population figures recorded for these regions were said to reflect a higher degree of
underreporting than was the case for the areas under direct
control. During the first half of the eighties, Madura came under
direct government control, and the population increase of 88 per
cent recorded in that island within the next ten years was said to
be the result of improved reporting.[10] Veth also reported that an
exhortation by the resident of Jogjakarta in 1885 to the regent
(rijksbestuurder) resulted in the population figure's jumping by
28.5 per cent within one year.[11] There is no reason to believe,
however, that the later reports were consequently more accurate
than the earlier figures, especially when they were not subject to
close examination.

Another point is that according to the colonial reports, the
figures for many regions did not include the inhabitants of what
were called "private estates" (Particuliere Landerijen). These
large tracts of land, totaling around 1.5 million hectares, had
been sold by the government to private persons, at first mainly
Dutch, but later also Chinese, British, and French. On these
lands the landlords largely replaced the government as sovereign.
They were entitled to one-fifth of the produce of the land tilled
by the peasants, they levied rents, and they were supposed to
assume the duties normally carried out by the civil service. As
could be expected, they were far more interested in the first two

[10] P. J. Veth, Java: Geographisch, Ethnologisch, Historisch (Java:
Geographically, Ethnologically, Historically), 2nd ed., ed. Joh. F.
Snelleman and J. F. Niermeyer (Haarlem, 1907), p. 138.

[11] Ibid., p. 18.

of these activities and completely neglected the last.[12] As a rule they did not know the number of people on their estates, and it was not known how the population figures for these areas had been arrived at and to what extent they approximated the actual numbers. Although in terms of the total population of Java the number of inhabitants of these estates was relatively small, their exclusion from the reported figures indicates a limited coverage of the data for a number of regions. It seems quite probable that the erratic population figures for such regions as Tjirebon were partly the result of the inclusion or exclusion of some of the population of these estates in the different reports.

Whatever the shortcomings of the enumerations, one clear advantage of them to the government was that they did not cost anything. All the work entailed in the enumeration and in keeping the registers was merely part of the normal duties of the local government and not a separate operation. The disadvantages of such an arrangement, however, were obvious and many did press for improved methods. For example, Controleur van Aalst pointed out that the majority of the persons collecting or processing the statistics were not qualified to perform the work satisfactorily. Many of the officials at the local level did not have the time to exercise proper control over the implementation. "It can be safely posited that, as long as the processing remains in the hands of those assigned to this work [the district and subdistrict heads, who made their clerks do the greater part of the job], the end results will remain unreliable, despite the best enumeration." [13] Van Aalst proposed the establishment of a separate statistical bureau.

Another critic, attacking the government policy of no cost, asked rhetorically: "But is this [policy of] no expense really a virtue, if as a result we have to manage with defective means and

[12] J. S. Furnivall, *Netherlands India: A Study of Plural Economy* (Cambridge, Eng., 1944), p. 313.
[13] J. van Aalst, "Bevolkingsstatistiek" (Population Statistics), *Tijdschrift voor Binnenlandsch Bestuur*, XXXII (1907), 13–14.

as a matter of course be content with very mediocre results." [14]

It is rather interesting to note the government's justifications for persisting in this kind of enumeration, which was specifically designed for purposes of compulsory labor services. They are well summed up in the following:

In justification of the method used it is maintained [by the government] that it is in harmony with the state of civilization of the Javanese people; that it does not rouse the suspicion which the native harbors with respect to any individual enumeration [hoofdelijke opneming], which from experience he gets to know as the forerunner of new or more severely collected tax or personal services; while it finally has the merit of costing the colonial exchequer nothing.[15]

From the preceding account it can be inferred that the population counts were directly coupled to the system of herendiensten, that comparatively little attention was given to enumerating those people who were not subject to compulsory services, and that the counting was concerned with the inhabitants of yards rather than with all individuals. Moreover, the counts were conducted by civil service officers who were not properly trained for the assigned tasks, as is shown by the absence of directives. One must also take into account the probable attitude of villagers and village officials, the extended period of enumeration, and, consequently, the differing times of conducting the actual counting in the various regions. All this, when coupled with the fact of uncentralized processing by untrained personnel without proper guidance from their superiors, renders the reliability of the results quite inadequate. While some of these factors could make results that were too high or too low equally probable, such factors as the attitudes of the villagers

[14] Steinmetz, op. cit., p. 95.
[15] "Uitkomsten der Volkstellingen op Java en Madoera" (Results of the Population Censuses in Java and Madura), editorial in Nieuwe Rotterdamsche Courant, Dec. 14, 1902; reprinted in Tijdschrift voor Binnenlandsch Bestuur, XXIV (1903), 109.

and the village elders would be likely to bias the figures in a downward direction.

For a number of years the colonial reports also contained data on the number of births and deaths among Indonesians. These figures were compiled from local data obtained from village heads. There are several indications of their limited reliability, such as the very erratic character of the data for different regions in consecutive years—particularly for the Principalities, but for many other regions as well. For example, the number of births in Banten during the years 1889, 1890, and 1891 were, respectively, 16,500, 25,300, and 14,700. The number of deaths during the same years in the residency of Tegal were reported to be 20,500, 31,400, and 28,800; in the residency of Kedu there were 21,600, 29,200, and 20,600.

Despite those shortcomings the data may throw some additional light on the reliability of the reported total population numbers. By using the average annual number of births of 1879, 1880, and 1881, the crude birth rate for Java in 1880 may be computed as 29 per 1,000 persons.[16] These figures would imply an annual rate of increase of 4, 11, and 6 per 1,000 persons, a much lower growth rate than would appear from the official population figures for these years (see Tables 9 and 10). The crude death rate computed from these data of about 25 per 1,000 persons does not seem improbable. The number of registered deaths was probably far from complete, however, and if a large number of deaths were indeed unreported, this would imply a larger total population. Thus, these data on deaths can be considered additional evidence of the underreporting of the total population.

Nearly all contemporary critics of the colonial government's methods of collecting population statistics in Indonesia understandably cited the fact that the British colonial government in India had been conducting censuses there since 1871. N. P. van

[16] For 1875, the crude birth and death rates computed from these data were respectively 30 and 25 per 1,000 persons.

den Berg, for example, after describing the censuses in British India, urged that there be no further delay "with the implementation of a task, from which we, as a first-rate colonial power, can no longer withdraw." [17] Another critic argued against the contention that there were insurmountable obstacles to holding a census in Java. "When it comes to the point, then we will after all be able to do what the English did ten years ago on a scale ten times larger, while the difficulties to be overcome were at least ten times as big. . . . Everything argues this time to show that we occupy an honorable place among the great colonial powers." [18] In 1909 the government decided to conduct decennial censuses, starting in 1915, but the decision was not implemented until 1920.

Some Data on the Population of the Indonesian Islands Other than Java

The colonial report of 1849 supplied some figures purporting to show the population of some of the Indonesian islands other than Java. These figures were reportedly based on information supplied by heads of local governments and from "other sources." Subsequent colonial reports contained similar data, although they always warned the reader not to place reliance on the reported figures for the "Outer Possessions." To emphasize their doubts the compilers of the official Netherlands East Indies yearbooks (*Koloniaal Verslag*) did not sum up the figures, even for the separate islands,[19] explaining in a note that "due to the incompleteness of the reports no totals are shown." Table 11, which shows the totals of the reported figures for the different regions and islands, sufficiently demonstrates the questionable quality of the data. The total figures decreased from 10.5 million

[17] "Volkstelling in Indie" (Population Census in the Indies), *De Economist*, I (1902), 354.

[18] H. C. Kerkkamp, "Hoe Java's Bevolking Toeneemt" (How Java's Population Increases), *De Economist*, II (1908), 622.

[19] With the exception of the colonial reports of 1849 and 1905.

Table 11. Total population of the
Indonesian islands other than Java,
1849–1905 (official estimates)

Year	Total population
1849	10,473,500
1855	5,036,801
1860	2,965,450
1865	2,895,115
1870	4,285,353
1875	4,557,413
1880	6,284,357
1885	6,413,578
1890	6,767,700
1895	7,834,696
1900	6,575,878
1905	7,304,552

Source: Koloniaal Verslag (The
Hague) for 1849–1907.

in 1849 to 3.0 million in 1860 and 2.9 million in 1865 and then
increased to 4.3 million in 1870. No information was provided as
to how the local officers arrived at these estimates.

Starting in 1876, the reported figures were classified into three
groups: "(1) figures which can be considered as rather accurate,
(2) figures which were obtained by approximation, (3) figures
based on sheer guesses." There is absolutely no indication, however, as to the criteria for these classifications. Only the data on
the residency of Sumatra's west coast, grouped into the "rather

Table 12. Population of the Indonesian islands other than Java by island or island group,
1849–1905

Island or group	1849	1855	1860	1865	1870
Sumatra	3,550,000	1,718,809	1,552,179	1,619,900	2,436,096
Kalimantan	1,200,000	700,386	873,305	697,685	1,185,733
Sulawesi	3,175,000	392,040	336,338	466,573	459,108
Maluku *	543,500	378,681	134,312	110,957	196,254
Nusa Tenggara	2,005,000	1,846,885	39,316		8,162
Total, islands	10,473,500	5,036,801	2,965,450	2,895,115	4,285,353

* Includes West Irian.

accurate" category, are known to have originated from an *op-nemïng*, conducted every five years from 1880. This effort was apparently carried out on the initiative of the local officers, but unfortunately there is no account of how it was implemented. The colonial reports sometimes referred to this effort as "so-called enumeration." [20] The report for the year 1900 observed that the quinquennial enumerations had been expanded, "as far as feasible, to other regions." [21] In the same reports, however, the footnotes to the tables are full of indications that the coverage was limited for Sumatra, Kalimantan, Sulawesi, and the other islands and that the data for many other regions referred only to areas under direct Dutch control.[22] The data for 1900, by eliminating the group of "sheer guesses," implied that the quality of the data had improved. For 1905 all classification of the data was dropped and, in contrast with the preceding reports, the sum total of the figures was included. Nevertheless, the report for 1905 indicated that there was no question of an accurate *opnemïng* in the "Outer Possessions." [23]

To give some impression of the data, the totals for the different islands are shown in Table 12. The figures for the earlier years are obviously unreliable. But even those for 1900 and 1905 are questionable. The increase in the total population of all these islands from 6.6 million to 7.3 million within this five-year period

Table 12 (continued)

1875	1880	1885	1890	1895	1900	1905
1,890,077	2,719,896	2,882,869	3,003,700	3,277,483	3,183,880	4,067,141
1,227,654	981,601	1,011,819	1,112,100	1,133,772	1,076,910	1,172,864
561,725	886,111	818,097	964,200	1,986,635	870,525	835,825
208,756	378,549	360,093	352,100	394,206	405,254	401,491
69,201	1,318,200	1,340,700	1,335,600	1,042,600	1,039,309	827,231
4,557,413	6,284,357	6,413,578	6,767,700	7,834,696	6,575,878	7,304,552

Source: Koloniaal Verslag (The Hague) for 1849–1905.

[20] *Koloniaal Verslag, 1897.*   [21] *Koloniaal Verslag, 1902*, pp. 1–2.
[22] *Ibid.*, Appendix A, pp. 6–7.   [23] *Koloniaal Verslag, 1907*, p. 2 n.

was attributed primarily to a population increase in Sumatra of about 30 per cent in five years; in most other islands there was allegedly a population decrease.

Based on these considerations, it seems fair to conclude that the available data on the population of the Indonesian islands other than Java until 1905 are insufficiently reliable to be of any use.[24]

[24] It has to be pointed out, however, that the data for some smaller regions, such as Sumatra's west coast, are definitely more reliable than the other figures.

CHAPTER 5

Population Censuses, Migration, and Resettlement, 1905–1930

The early decades of the twentieth century witnessed the development of a sector of the economy concentrating on plantation agriculture and mining and producing primary products for export to foreign markets. The highly capital-intensive character of the production process in these enterprises, geared as it was exclusively to the demand of foreign markets, produced a dichotomy in the economy wherein peasant small holders producing mainly food and using traditional labor-intensive methods existed alongside large-scale plantations using modern technology and producing almost exclusively for export.

The development of the plantation sector was not designed to absorb the existing excess labor supply from the traditional sector, and between the two sectors virtually no links existed that might become channels for introducing new and more efficient methods of production to the tradition-bound peasants. Nor was the introduction of the modern sector with its high capital-labor ratio designed to increase the level of income of the population. Indeed, there are no firm indications that any improvement in the general level of living occurred during this period. On the contrary, a number of sources point to a possible deterioration in living conditions in the period subsequent to the beginning of World War I.[1]

[1] See, for example, J. W. Meijer Ranneft and W. Huender, *Onderzoek naar de Belastingdruk op de Inlandsche Bevolking* (Investigation into the Pressure of Taxation on the Native Population) (Weltevreden, 1926).

After the turn of the century, foreign private capital continued to concentrate on investments in the Indonesian islands outside of Java, particularly in Sumatra. This emphasis was related to the rapidly increasing demand in the world market for industrial raw materials rather than nonindustrial agricultural products. Thus, rubber plantations and petroleum and tin-mining enterprises developed rapidly in Sumatra. The colonial government assisted these enterprises in many ways, including helping them solve the problem of labor scarcity by promoting the migration of workers from Java to the plantations and mines in Sumatra. In addition, it also started a resettlement program with the object of transferring part of Java's rural population to the more sparsely populated regions of the other islands, particularly South Sumatra.

During these years a number of programs were started in the fields of public health, education, agricultural extension service, village banking, irrigation, and other public works. These programs were modest in scale compared with the size of the population and the area of the territory. Moreover, these efforts were closely linked to the development of Dutch and other foreign investments in plantation agriculture, mining, and related activities. Thus, educational programs were designed to meet the need for elementary clerical and technical skills; the development of roads, ports, and railways complemented the growth of the business firms; irrigation works were best developed in those areas where cane was produced for the sugar factories.

In 1909 the government decided that in 1915 and every ten years thereafter "a general enumeration [*algemeene telling*] of the population and of their horses, livestock, vehicles, ships, and other vessels" was to be conducted.[2] However, probably because of the war in Europe, this ordinance was repealed.[3]

Another ordinance in 1920 stipulated that a census be conducted that year, but no reference was made to periodic cen-

[2] *Indisch Staatsblad, 1909,* no. 575.
[3] *Indisch Staatsblad, 1915,* no. 669.

suses. The 1905 enumeration, which was the last of the series of quinquennial enumerations, had already included such topics as marital status and occupation. The 1920 census was a further improvement, not only in terms of the topics included, but also in terms of organization. The processing, however, was still carried out locally.

In this respect the 1930 census showed further improvement. Although the actual enumeration was still carried out by local officers, the processing was done centrally. There is no doubt that this census was superior to all preceding enumerations, despite the primitive treatment of such topics as age classification.

The Population Census of 1920

The 1920 census was a *de jure* count and the topics included name, sex, marital status, whether children or adults, ethnic group, daily language used, literacy, ability to read and write in Dutch, physical disabilities (blindness and deaf-mutism), and housing. For the country as a whole a "leader of the census" was appointed, but the heads of the residencies were in charge of the census in their respective territories, each assisted by a "residential leader of the census." The enumerators, called "population enumerators," were appointed by the regional heads and selected from government employees. The census legislation stipulated that village heads, village secretaries, and other members of the village government were to be given preference in these selections and that as a rule they were not to receive any remuneration.[4] Every enumerator was assigned to an enumeration district, which in principle was one village provided that the inhabitants numbered around one thousand persons. The whole enumeration lasted for one month. In the case of Europeans, the householder method was employed, while for Indonesians the enumerators filled in the questionnaires, "except where the per-

[4] Volkstellingsordonantie, 1920 (Census Ordinance, 1920), *Indisch Staatsblad, 1920,* no. 117.

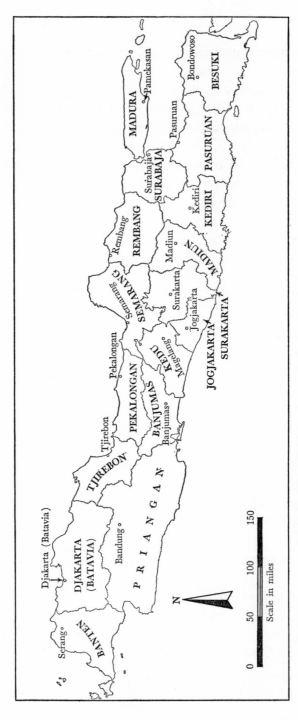

Administrative divisions (regencies), Java, 1920

son to be enumerated expresses the desire to fill in [the question-naire] himself." [5]

Since the actual enumeration started on November 1 and the regional leaders of the census were instructed to assume their responsibilities not earlier than September 1 of the same year, it is unlikely that intensive preparations were made. A numbering of houses preceded the enumeration, and some use was made of skeleton maps, but these were restricted to certain urban centers. The processing was carried out locally, first by the enumerators themselves and afterwards at the subdistrict office, the district office, the subdivision office, the division office, and the residency office. The colonial report of 1922 stated that much of the processing was actually conducted in subdistrict offices rather than by the enumerators in the villages, but that even so the totals reported for the different regions were not always correct.

According to the 1920 census, the population of Java was 35.0 million, which implies an annual rate of increase of 10 per 1,000 persons during the period 1905–1920. Computed on this basis, the growth rates for the different regions show sharp contrasts. While Banten and Tjirebon had rates of increase of 0.1, Besuki's growth rate was 62.2 per 1,000 persons. Two-thirds of the administrative regions in Java had rates of increase of less than 10 per 1,000 persons.[6] The population of the different regions is shown in Table 1.

Compared with the official population estimates of growth rates during the previous century, the computed rate of increase between 1905 and 1920 was relatively small. It is quite probable that the influenza epidemic that raged through large areas of the world at the end of the First World War had a great impact on

[5] Uitvoeringsvoorschriften (Instructions Concerning the Execution of the Census), *Indisch Staatsblad, 1920,* no. 162.
[6] It is known that since the earlier enumerations there had been population movements out of Banten, which is the most western region in Java, to Lampung in South Sumatra, but this was mostly the tempo-rary migration of workers to harvest pepper there. Besuki was known to be an in-migration region, especially after the turn of the century.

Indonesia's population. It was reported that the number of deaths during the second half of 1918 increased suddenly as a consequence of this epidemic. The registered number of deaths during November 1918 was 416,000 more than that for the same month the previous year.[7] From the official death rates, it is difficult to gain an accurate idea of the course of mortality during those two years. For a number of years the colonial

Table 13. Annual number of
reported deaths, Java,
1916–1926

Year	Deaths
1916	586,757
1917	673,830
1918	1,227,121
1919	930,095
1920	764,316
1921	815,268
1922	689,613
1923	634,058
1924	655,827
1925	706,554
1926	753,688

Source: Based on popula-
tion figures and crude death
rates in Koloniaal Verslag
(The Hague) for 1917–
1927.

reports contained population figures (Indonesians only) based on local records, and the computed crude death rate was derived from these data and the reported number of deaths. Since the reliability of both the numerator and denominator of these crude death rates is unknown, it would appear more desirable to compare the number of reported deaths for the different years than to compare the estimated death rates. As is shown in Table 13, from 1917 to 1918 the number of reported deaths increased by about 80 per cent, and the figure for 1919 was higher than for the subsequent years. Without excluding the possibility of dif-

[7] Koloniaal Verslag, 1919, pp. 173–175.

ferent degrees of accuracy in reporting, it can be assumed that the sudden increase in the number of deaths was a real one.

Between 1905 and 1920 no enumeration was conducted, but population figures for 1917 based on the reports of local civil service officers have been published. Using these data, the annual growth rate of Java's population for the period 1905–1917 was

Table 14. Annual rates of increase per 1,000 persons, by region, Java, 1905–1920, 1905–1917, 1917–1920

Region	1905–1920	1905–1917	1917–1920
Banten	0.1	−1.6	7.3
Djakarta	15.2	12.3	43.7
Priangan	23.0	18.3	42.1
Tjirebon	0.1	−1.9	8.0
Pekalongan	8.7	10.7	0.7
Semarang	3.0	5.5	−6.6
Rembang	7.0	7.6	4.7
Banjumas	12.2	7.6	27.5
Kedu	3.3	12.4	−33.2
Madiun	11.1	14.3	−1.6
Kediri	8.4	16.1	−22.4
Surabaja	0.6	3.1	−9.3
Madura	10.3	14.5	−6.5
Pasuruan	6.9	1.3	29.0
Besuki	62.2	18.6	69.7
Average, region under direct Dutch control	9.6	9.6	9.9
Jogjakarta	9.1	17.1	−22.9
Surakarta	16.8	21.5	−1.8
Average, region of the Principalities	13.7	19.7	−10.1
Average, Java	10.0	10.5	8.0

Source: Based on population figures in Koloniaal Verslag (The Hague), 1907, 1918, 1923.

10.5 per 1,000 persons, and for 1917–1920 it was 8.0. The annual rates of growth for the different regions are shown in Table 14. For 1905–1917 the rates ranged between −1.9 and 21.5, while for 1917–1920 the range extended from −33.2 to 69.7 per 1,000 persons. Eight of the fifteen regions showed a population decrease between 1917 and 1920. Almost all these regions were reported to have very high crude death rates in 1918. Other regions with reportedly high crude death rates, however, also showed high growth rates between 1917 and 1920. It seems probable that an underreporting of the total population in 1917 led to the official crude death rates and rates of increase being greater than was actually the case.[8]

Thus, it seems plausible that the actual growth rate during most of the period up to 1918 was higher than the reported 10.0 per 1,000 persons and that between 1918 and 1920 the rate of growth was very small or, probably, negative. In addition, if account is taken of the firmly held opinion in the 1930 census report that a high degree of underreporting occurred in the 1920 census,[9] then the annual growth rate for the whole period between 1905 and 1920 was probably higher than 10.0 per 1,000 persons.

The other Indonesian islands were accorded only limited coverage in the 1920 population census. For extensive areas of these islands the population data were not, as in Java, the result of a census, but were based on information supplied by the local heads of the administration. The 1930 census report repeatedly pointed out that the results of the 1920 census for the islands other than Java were much less reliable than the 1930 census figures, and that the published 1920 population figures for these islands were too small.[10] The unreliability of the returns for 1920 and 1905 is further indicated by the implausibly high annual rates of increase, as shown in Table 15. For these islands as a whole the annual growth rate from 1905 to 1920 was reportedly

[8] For example, Banjumas, Pasuruan, and Besuki were reported to have crude death rates of, respectively, 36.0, 57.8, and 51.0 per 1,000 persons in 1918, but their annual rates of increase during 1917–1920 were 27.5, 29.0, and 69.7 per 1,000 persons. The sharp contrast between these figures and the growth rates for the earlier period, 1905–1917, in these three regions, which were respectively 7.6, 1.3, and 18.6 per 1,000 persons, also points to the conclusion that there was an underreporting of the total population in 1917.

[9] Departement van Economische Zaken, *Volkstelling, 1930* (Population Census, 1930), VIII (Batavia, 1936), 9.

[10] *Ibid.*, IV (1935), 4, V (1936), 3, 11.

Table 15. Reported annual rates of population increase in
Indonesian islands other than Java by island and island
group (per 1,000 persons), 1905–1930

Island or group	1905–1920 (Indonesians only)	1920–1930 Indonesians only	1920–1930 Total population
Sumatra	25.3	26.3	26.6
Kalimantan	17.9	27.4	28.8
Sulawesi	86.8	30.5	30.9
Maluku	28.2	35.9	36.1
Nusa Tenggara	78.7	24.2	24.4
Average, islands	42.8	27.4	28.0

Source: Based on population figures in Koloniaal Verslag (The
Hague) for 1907 and 1922 and Departement van Economische
Zaken, Volkstelling, 1930 (Population Census, 1930), Vols. IV
(Batavia, 1935) and V (Batavia, 1936).

42.8 per 1,000 persons, and for some islands it was even higher,
Sulawesi being reported to have an annual rate of increase of
86.8 and the group of islands of Nusa Tenggara (including Bali)
78.7 per 1,000 persons.

The Population Census of 1930

The 1930 population census incorporated a number of improvements over that of 1920. The census was conducted
throughout the entire country, although simpler methods of
enumeration were applied in extensive areas outside Java. In
contrast to the 1920 census, the organization, or more precisely
the processing of the data, was centralized. The actual enumeration still relied largely, however, on the civil service officers,
whom van Gelderen, the director of the census, called "the
backbone of the whole system." [11] The preparations were superior to those for the preceding census, and the length of time of
the actual enumeration was shorter. Also, use was made of me-
chanical processing. It seems that a number of the essential

[11] J. van Gelderen, "The Census of 1930 in the Netherlands East
Indies," Bulletin de l'Institut International de Statistique, XXV, no. 3
(La Haye, 1931), 136.

features of a modern census were incorporated in the 1930 census,[12] but in some respects, such as the primitive treatment of ages, the census was quite deficient.

The head of the Central Office of Statistics was appointed head of the temporary census office. It is obvious from the census legislation that great reliance was placed on the local government apparatus. As in 1920, the legislation stipulated that the heads of the regional administration were to be responsible for carrying out the census in their respective territories.[13] They were assisted by regional census leaders, nearly all of whom were recruited from among civil service officers. The enumerators, appointed by the regency heads, consisted mainly of village heads, village officials, schoolteachers, and other persons in government employment.[14]

The census legislation stipulated that population censuses were to be held every ten years from 1930, and that the *de facto* population was to be enumerated, although in the islands outside of Java there was to be a *de jure* count. The implemental legislation also listed the topics to be covered. For Indonesians these consisted of: name; sex; whether head of family or not; marital status; number of wives; age group classification of "children who could not yet walk," other nonadults, and adults (there was a provision to record "for those, for whom such can be stated with certainty, the age in years"); principal means of livelihood (*middel van bestaan*) as well as main additional means of livelihood (with status in each); literacy; ability to write in Dutch; level of education; ethnic group (*landaard*); district of residence; district of birth; physical disabilities (blindness and deaf-mutism); and religion (for the Batak, Menadonese, and Ambonese ethnic groups only).

In addition to a provision concerning the duty of every person

---

[12] Compare United Nations, *Handbook of Population Census Methods*, I (New York, 1958), 4–5.

[13] Volkstellingsordonantie, 1930 (Census Ordinance, 1930), *Indisch Staatsblad, 1930*, no. 128.

[14] Van Gelderen, "Census of 1930," p. 143.

to furnish information for the census, and the stipulation of punishment with imprisonment for anyone "who willfully hinders, prevents, or frustrates an act" of the census officers, the basic census legislation also determined that "he who in any way rouses popular feeling against the census or the methods of its execution is to be punished with detention." [15] There was no legal guarantee whatsoever as to the confidential nature of the information furnished to census officers.

In Java the actual enumeration was conducted in two stages. During the first stage, which officially lasted two weeks, the required information was entered. The second stage (officially the evening of October 7, 1930) was used for checking the available information and bringing it up to date. These stages were officially designated as "periodical" and "instantaneous" enumerations (*periode en moment telling*). Accordingly, there were periodical and instantaneous enumeration districts, and periodical and instantaneous enumerators. Each periodical enumeration district covered about 1,000 to 1,200 persons and consisted of three to four instantaneous enumeration districts.

Four methods were used in the other Indonesian islands to arrive at population figures: [16] a periodical enumeration followed by an instantaneous enumeration as in Java; a periodical enumeration only; a count by village heads as in earlier times; and guesses made by local officers. The first method was carried out in only a few areas, primarily in the cities. The second was the principal method used in most of Sumatra and the other islands. The third was applied to large parts of Kalimantan and parts of some other islands, while guesses were made when none of the three first methods was possible.

Local officers of the civil service were responsible for the actual management of the enumeration at the regional and local

[15] In article 6 of the census ordinance of 1930. In 1920 the penalties consisted of fines only. The more severe punishments in the 1930 census legislation were probably related to the armed uprising in a number of regions of Java and Sumatra in 1926–1927.

[16] *Volkstelling, 1930*, IV, 3–4, V, 2–3.

levels, as well as for the preparatory activities, such as determining the enumeration districts and giving instructions to the enumerators. The operational unit of identification was the housing unit, and for that purpose a house-numbering preceded the enumeration, as in 1920. The fact that no special geographic and cartographic work formed part of the preparatory activities, however, must have influenced the subdivision into enumeration districts, and therefore the number of omissions and duplications in the actual enumeration. Only in some urban areas were the enumerators provided with maps of their respective districts.[17] Nor does it appear that any intensive and careful training was given to the enumerators. Although manuals were distributed to civil service officers, instructions to enumerators were very probably by word of mouth. "They [the Dutch civil service officers] are especially entrusted with the *oral* instruction of Native Service officials and Native heads of population, who in their turn have to instruct the enumerators." [18]

The writers of the census report were convinced that the results from the census returns were of a high degree of reliability. They asserted that few individuals were counted more than once and that the questions were answered properly because they were simple and because there was no reason not to answer or to give untrue answers.[19] These contentions have to be taken on trust, since there is no indication in the census report that any reliability tests were made on the returns. Taking into consideration the extent of the preparations and the care taken in the publication of the results, however, there is no doubt that this census was far superior to all preceding enumerations.

The Population of Indonesia in 1930

According to the census, the total population of Indonesia in 1930 was 60.7 million, of which 41.7 million lived in Java and 19.0 million in the rest of the country. The geographical distri-

---

[17] Van Gelderen, "Census of 1930," p. 144.   [18] *Ibid.,* p. 143.
[19] *Volkstelling, 1930,* VIII, 1.

bution of the population is shown in Table 1 and Table 16. The census figure implies an annual rate of increase of 17.6 per 1,000 persons in Java during the period 1920–1930. The census report contended, however, that such a high rate of growth was "no doubt due to the too low figures for 1920"[20] and asserted that the actual growth rate was probably 15 per 1,000.

Table 16. Population (by sex), area, and density, by region, Indonesia, 1930

| Region | Population | | | Area | Density |
	Male	Female	Both sexes	(sq. kms.)	(per sq. km.)
West Java *	5,587,000	5,810,146	11,397,146	46,877	243.0
Central Java †	7,478,854	7,786,650	15,265,504	37,375	408.2
East Java	7,358,371	7,697,343	15,055,714	47,922	492.0
Total, Java	20,424,225	21,294,139	41,718,364	132,174	316.1
Sumatra	4,271,456	3,983,387	8,254,843	473,606	17.5
Kalimantan	1,102,886	1,065,775	2,168,661	539,460	4.0
Sulawesi	2,095,895	2,136,011	4,231,906	189,035	22.4
Maluku and West Irian	390,555	367,495	893,400	496,456	1.8
Nusa Tenggara ‡	1,719,533	1,740,526	3,460,059	73,614	47.0
Total, Indonesia	30,004,550	30,587,333	60,727,233	1,904,345	31.9

* Including Djakarta.
† Including Jogjakarta and Surakarta.
‡ Including Bali.
    Source: Based on Departement van Economische Zaken, *Volkstelling, 1930* (Population Census, 1930), 8 vols. (Batavia, 1930–1936).

The resulting population figures give a population density of 31.9 persons per square kilometer for Indonesia as a whole, 316.1 for Java, and 10.7 for the rest of the country. These figures clearly show the very unequal distribution of Indonesia's population. But in Java itself there were many areas with even higher population densities. Among the extensive areas with very large populations were south-central Java (with a population density of 679.3 persons per square kilometer), the Bandung plateau (671.1), and the Tjirebon plain (656.9). Many smaller areas had yet higher population densities: Adiwerna (1,637.9), Pekalon-

[20] *Ibid.*, p. 9.

gan (1,485.6), and Plumbon (1,074.8). Although a few regions of the other islands had high population densities, they were still far below the average density of Java as a whole. Thus, on Bali and Lombok there were 175.2 persons per square kilometer and on the Agam plateau in Central Sumatra 117.1. The contrast can also be illustrated by the fact that more than 77 per cent of the total area of the Indonesian islands outside of Java had population densities of less than 10 persons per square kilometer, while 84 per cent of the total area of Java had 150 inhabitants per square kilometer.[21]

A comparison of the figures of the 1920 and 1930 population censuses shows that during the twenties Java's population increased at an annual rate of 17.6 per 1,000 persons and that of the other islands at an annual rate of 28.0 per 1,000 persons. As mentioned previously, the census report considered these rates to be exaggerated, due to the underenumeration of the 1920 census. The annual rates of increase for the different regions in Java during 1920–1930 are shown in Table 17. The differential growth rates shown here appear to be less divergent than in any earlier statistics, which may indicate a higher degree of reliability. The residency of Besuki at the eastern tip of Java had the highest rate of increase (32.9), a consequence of the continuous migration into that area. The high rate of growth of the residency of Djakarta, which included the city of Djakarta, was probably related to the expansion of the urban center. On the other hand, the residencies of Kedu and Rembang, both in Central Java, experienced the slowest growth rate with respectively 3.2 and 9.5 per 1,000 persons; these were very probably regions of out-migration. The census report asserted that the computed rates of growth for the other Indonesian islands were exaggerated and that no inference could be drawn from them concern-

[21] Of course, there were smaller areas with high population densities in some of the other islands. Thus, Gianjar in southern Bali had 453 inhabitants per square kilometer and in the district of Old Agam there were 237 persons per square kilometer.

Table 17. Annual rates of population increase by region, Java, 1920–1930

Region	Annual rate of increase (per 1,000)
Banten	13.7
Djakarta	27.2
Priangan	19.7
Tjirebon	19.0
Pekalongan	15.2
Semarang	14.6
Rembang	9.5
Banjumas	15.7
Kedu	3.2
Madiun	21.1
Kediri	18.1
Surabaja	12.6
Madura	11.8
Pasuruan	20.1
Besuki	32.9
Average, region under direct Dutch control	17.2
Jogjakarta	19.5
Surakarta	22.4
Average, region of the Principalities	21.3
Average, Java	17.6

Source: Based on population figures in *Koloniaal Verslag, 1922* (The Hague) and Departement van Economische Zaken, *Volkstelling, 1930* (Population Census, 1930), 8 vols. (Batavia, 1930–1936). The administrative divisions of 1920 are used in this table.

ing the course of population growth there between 1920 and 1930.[22] From the census data these islands as a whole registered a rate of population increase of around 28.0 per 1,000 persons. As shown in Table 15, Maluku had the highest growth rate with 36.1 and Nusa Tenggara the lowest with 24.4 per 1,000 persons.

With respect to rural-urban distribution it was reported that about 7.5 per cent of the total population for Indonesia as a whole lived in what the census report called "areas with more or less urban appearance." In Java the percentage was 8.5, in Suma-

[22] *Volkstelling, 1930*, VIII, 39.

tra, 6.4, and in the other regions 4.3. One city (Djakarta) had a population of more than half a million (533,015); only six other cities had more than 100,000 inhabitants each—Bandung, Semarang, Jogjakarta, Surakarta, and Surabaja (all in Java) and Palembang in Sumatra.

In the census the whole population was divided into the following groups: Indonesians (called "natives"), Europeans (including Americans, Japanese, Egyptians, Armenians, Turks, and others, who were all legally treated as Europeans);[23] Chinese; and other Asians (called "other nonindigenous Orientals," mostly Arabs). Their respective numbers were 59.1 million (97.4 per cent), 240,000 (0.4 per cent), 1.2 million (2 per cent), and 115,000 (0.2 per cent). About 20 per cent of the Europeans were in Java, while more than 50 per cent of the Chinese lived in the other islands, particularly in East Sumatra, Riau, Bangka, and West Kalimantan. In the residency of Bangka almost 45 per cent of the population were Chinese, most of whom worked in the tin mines.

The census also contained information on the different Indonesian ethnic groups. According to the census report, these groupings were mainly based on "social criteria, such as the language spoken, customs and habits."[24] Among the sixty-one ethnic groups classified in the census reports, the Javanese constituted more than 47 per cent of the total population (27.8 million), followed by the Sundanese (8.6 million), the Madurese (4.3 million), the Minangkabaus (2.0 million), the Buginese (1.5 million), the Bataks (1.2 million), and the Balinese (1.1 million). The data on ethnic groups, combined with data on place of residence and place of birth, give some information about migration and population distribution.

[23] Indonesians who legally had equal rights as Europeans (*gelijkgestelden*) were grouped as Europeans, but the Chinese who had acquired these equal rights were classified as Chinese. Moreover, all women who married those classified as Europeans were grouped as Europeans. See *ibid.*, VI, 144.

[24] *Ibid.*, VIII, 44.

Apart from the contrast in terms of population densities between Java and the rest of Indonesia, attention has also been
drawn to the difference in the sex composition. The earlier
enumerations in Java consistently show a low sex ratio. In 1930
the sex ratio was found to be 95.5 males per 100 females. In
contrast, the average sex ratio for the other Indonesian islands as
a whole was found to be 100.7, although only in Sumatra,
Kalimantan, and Maluku did the sex ratio actually exceed one
hundred (they were respectively 102.8, 101.1, and 105.9). For
Sulawesi and Nusa Tenggara the ratio was closer to that in Java:
97.7 for Sulawesi and 98.6 for Nusa Tenggara. Commenting on
the high sex ratios in many of the other islands, the census report
correctly pointed out that only in certain regions, such as the
residency of Sumatra's east coast, could this phenomenon be
explained by net in-migration. The report's further speculation
that these high sex ratios were probably "symptoms of unfavorable expectation of life amongst the women, possibly connected
with the reduced strength of certain of the races living in those
districts," [25] seems to be a somewhat strained argument. Interest-
ingly enough, the census report did not consider the possibility
that an underenumeration of females had resulted in a high sex
ratio.

The report itself showed that in some areas sex selectivity in
migration might have had an important effect on the sex composition. Using the concept of "persons born in a certain district"
(*geboortebevolking*) [26]—the number of persons born in a district (both those who are still resident there and those who have
left the district) not including those resident in that district who
were born elsewhere—it was found that the sex ratio for each of
the islands or groups of islands in Indonesia, excepting Maluku,
was less than one hundred, with the sex ratio of Java remaining
the smallest.

As mentioned earlier, three very crude age group classifica-

[25] *Ibid.*, p. 38.   [26] *Ibid.*, p. 5.

tions were used in the census: (i) "children who could not yet walk," (ii) other children, and (iii) adults (see Table 18). Throughout the census report it was assumed that the first group consisted of persons aged up to fifteen or eighteen months.[27] The report contended that in contrast with categories ii and iii the distinction between i and ii presented no problems.[28] It is true that a physical feature, such as the ability to walk, appears to be a clear-cut distinction. Since such a physical feature also has a social value, however, and since it is probable that the enumerators accepted the word of the parents rather than in each case attempting to find out for themselves, the report's sanguine attitude toward the reliability of this distinction seems to be unwarranted. As to the distinction between "other children" and adults, the report pointed out that probably females were considered adults at an earlier age than the males (fourteen to fifteen years for females versus sixteen to seventeen for males), since the former marry when they are younger. The report added, however, that in regions where younger boys were subject to forced labor, they were considered adults at the age of fourteen or fifteen.[29] In any case, the proportion of adult females appeared to be consistently higher than adult males. In certain regions known from other characteristics to be in-migration areas, the proportion of adults was relatively high.

The proportion of "children who could not yet walk" was smaller in urban centers than anywhere else. The report stated that this phenomenon had drawn much attention, but that it had not been established whether it was the result of a low birth rate or of a high infant mortality rate.[30] This differential proportion, however, does not necessarily indicate either of the two. As a result of net in-migration, the proportion of adults in the urban centers was higher than elsewhere, while the ratio of "children

[27] For example, *ibid.*, I (1933), 94, III (1934), 39–40. This assumption was reportedly "according to experts."

[28] *Ibid.*, I, 94, II (1934), 102, III, 98.

[29] *Ibid.*, VIII, 48.   [30] *Ibid.*

Table 18. Population by sex, age group, and region, Indonesia, 1930 (Indonesians only, in thousands)

Age group	Java			Other islands			Indonesia		
	Male	Female	Both sexes	Male	Female	Both sexes	Male	Female	Both sexes
I*	1,116	1,128	2,244	501	501	1,002	1,617	1,629	3,246
II†	7,686	6,793	14,479	3,184	2,769	5,953	10,870	9,562	20,432
III‡	11,142	12,956	24,098	4,976	5,335	10,311	16,118	18,291	34,409
Total §	19,976	20,915	40,891	8,688	8,635	17,323	28,664	29,550	58,214

* Children who could not yet walk.
† Other nonadults.
‡ Adults.
§ Includes those with unknown ages.
Source: Departement van Economische Zaken, *Volkstelling, 1930* (Population Census, 1930), VIII (Batavia, 1936), 98–99.

who could not yet walk" to "other children" was similar to that of the rest of the country. This necessarily implies that the proportion of "children who could not yet walk" was smaller in the urban centers than elsewhere.

The same three age categories were also used for most of the Indonesians in the islands other than Java. For certain ethnic groups, however, the ages in years were recorded and published. The age composition of one group originating from Minahasa is shown in Table 19.[31] Some tests of the reliability of this data have been carried out by computing sex ratios (the number of males per 100 females) and age ratios (the ratio of an age group to the mean of the two adjacent age groups computed separately for each sex). From these tests it was found that the degree of reliability of these data is quite low.[32]

The census figures showing the number of persons employed in different economic activities reflect the existence of two sectors in the economy (see page 63). As can be seen from Table 20, 20.9 million persons were engaged in some type of economic activity, of which 67.7 per cent were employed in agriculture, including small-scale farming, large-scale plantation farming, forestry, fishing, and animal husbandry. Around 57.7 per cent of the total number of workers were in small-scale agriculture, while only 6.7 per cent were employed on the plantations. In Java there were about one million plantation workers, and in the rest of the country around 400,000. This small proportion of plantation workers clearly indicates that the development of these plantations was in no way designed to absorb the increasing labor supply of the country. (The same was true with regard to the mining industry, which employed

[31] The data on ages for two other ethnic groups, those originating from Sangir and Talaud, covered only a small number of persons, and the data on persons originating from Ambon covered less than 50 per cent of the total numbers of this ethnic group.

[32] The age-ratio score for each of the sexes was 5.7, the sex-ratio score was 5.8, and the joint score, allowing for the smallness of the population, was 24.8.

Table 19. Population of Sulawesi originating from Minahasa,
by age, 1930

Age group	No. Male	No. Female	% of population from Minahasa Male	% of population from Minahasa Female
0– 4	21,273	20,538	17.12	16.42
5– 9	17,603	16,861	14.17	13.48
10–14	15,869	15,120	12.77	12.09
15–19	13,957	13,807	11.23	11.04
20–24	10,002	11,095		
			14.94	16.30
25–29	8,560	9,291		
30–34	7,204	7,909		
			10.42	11.67
35–39	5,749	6,689		
40–44	5,179	5,547		
			7.97	8.19
45–49	4,724	4,692		
50–54	4,814	4,310		
			6.56	5.93
55–59	3,537	3,102		
60–64	2,325	2,377		
			3.12	3.09
65–69	1,548	1,482		
70–74	1,046	1,044		
			1.25	1.25
75–79	512	519		
80–84	309	350		
			0.36	0.41
85–89	141	161		
90+	118	161	0.09	0.13
Total, known ages	124,270	125,055	100.00	100.00
Unknown ages	3,324	4,121		
Total, all ages	127,594	129,176		

Source: Departement van Economische Zaken, Volkstelling, 1930
(Population Census, 1930), V (Batavia, 1936), 62, 77–79.

less than one per cent of the total working population.) The
great emphasis given by Dutch and other foreign private capital
to investment in Sumatra can be seen from the fact that 45.2 per
cent of the working population in East Sumatra were plantation
workers. The colonial government's successful program to help
these plantations solve their problem of labor scarcity was also
borne out by the census data: out of 370,000 plantation workers

Table 20. Employed persons by economic activity, Indonesia, 1930

Economic activity	Indonesians only (in thous.)			Total population	
	Male	Female	Both sexes	No. (in thous.)	%
Agriculture *	10,518	3,502	14,020	14,118	67.7
Mining	55	41	96	147	0.7
Manufacturing	1,477	628	2,105	2,209	10.6
Trade	801	290	1,091	1,293	6.2
Transportation	225	66	291	317	1.5
Services	661	317	978	1,025	4.9
Others and unknown	1,070	628	1,698	1,761	8.4
Total, all activities	14,807	5,472	20,279	20,870	100.0

* Includes forestry, fishing, and animal husbandry.
Source: Based on Departement van Economische Zaken, *Volkstelling, 1930* (Population Census, 1930), 8 vols. (Batavia, 1930–1936).

in Sumatra, about 290,000 were Javanese and 30,000 Sundanese. For the country as a whole, manufacturing accounted for only 10.6 per cent of the total working population, with about one-third of these, or around 680,000 persons, being employed in the textile industry. Most of the enterprises in the textile industry, however, were small-scale or home industries. Thus, in Java most of the 500,000 workers in the textile industry were women employed in *batik* enterprises. In the urban areas in Java about one-quarter of the working population were in manufacturing industries, and around 14 per cent in trade. In the other islands only 17.6 per cent of the urban workers were employed in manufacturing. Although Indonesia is an archipelago, only 1.3 per cent of the total working population worked in fisheries, which were prominent mainly in Riau, Bangka, and Maluku.

Many persons did, in fact, have more than one occupation. Thus, many peasants were also traders, and a significant number were also seasonal workers in the sugar industry and in other plantations. Since most of the peasants who were also traders preferred their occupation to be classified as agriculture rather than trade, the census data on trade did not accurately reflect its importance as a means of livelihood for the population. Moreover, many women workers in the agricultural sector were engaged in home-based and small-scale industries during off-seasons. Data on secondary activities had been collected during the census, but due to deficiencies they were not even processed. One serious difficulty recognized by the census report was the fact that the census classifications of economic activities were not well understood by many enumerators, who as a result interpreted some concepts differently.[33]

With respect to marital status, the census report stated that among the Indonesians 74.7 per cent of the adult males and 68.1 per cent of the adult females were married. However, the number of married adult females was higher than the number of married adult males. The difference, amounting to 424,588 persons, was in part due to the existence of polygamy. For Indonesia as a whole, 2.5 per cent of the men had more than one wife. The largest percentage was in West Sumatra (almost 10 per cent) and in Timor. About 10 per cent of the men with more than one wife were married to three or four women. For the whole of Indonesia the percentage of single adult males was 17.0, and of adult females 7.9. West Java had respectively 10.6 and 4.3 per cent, while North Sulawesi had the highest percentages—29.1 and 22.0. The percentage of divorced adult males was 4.2 versus 7.6 for adult females, or, in absolute numbers, 0.7 million males and 1.4 million females. This large difference is due to the fact that many of the divorced males had remarried (or already had a second wife) so that in the census they were not classified as being divorced. As with polygamy, the highest percentage of divorced persons was in West Sumatra: 9.8 per cent of the adult males and 14.2 per cent of the adult females.

With regard to literacy among the Indonesians, the census reported that only 7.4 per cent of the adult population (13.2 per cent of the males and 2.3 per cent of the females) were able to read and write in any character. High percentages of literacy among the adult population were found in South Sumatra—

[33] *Volkstelling, 1930*, VIII, 56.

Lampung (40.3), Bengkulu (19.4), and Palembang (18.2)—
and also in North Sulawesi (29.0) and in Maluku (18.6). In
Java, 6.0 per cent of the adult population were literate (11.4 per
cent of the males and 1.3 per cent of the females), and in Bali
and Lombok 3.9 per cent (respectively 7.8 and 0.4 per cent of
the males and females).

Migration and Population Resettlement

By using the information in the 1930 population census on
place (or region) of residence, and place (or region) of birth,
inferences can be drawn regarding the extent of internal migration. In addition, by relating place of residence to ethnic origin,
some indication is given as to the direction and magnitude of
internal migration. Comparisons between place of birth and
place of residence are actually of only limited value in estimating
the extent of migration, however, since persons who have lived
in other regions may have returned and settled in their place of
birth. Should this type of population movement be frequent, any
inferences drawn from the census data may considerably underestimate the magnitude of migration. Relating place of residence
with ethnic origin is even more hazardous, since descendants of
immigrants who were born in their parents' present place of
residence may be classified together with their parents as immigrants. In addition, some of the immigrants belonging to a certain ethnic group may have been born or have lived outside the
regions of origin of that ethnic group. Moreover, neither of
these methods of establishing migration records takes into account the possibility of migration by stages. Still another weak-
ness is the fact that the date of the population movements is not
ascertained. To some extent this defect can be neutralized if the
data include information on ages, but this is not the case with the
1930 census data.

Despite all these drawbacks, however, inferences drawn from
the census data do give some valuable information on the direction and magnitude of internal migration. The conclusions ar-

rived at are in most cases in conformity with, and therefore supported by, the computed differential growth rates between the regions in Java. Thus, the high annual rate of increase of the residency of Besuki in East Java between 1920 and 1930 (32.9 per 1,000 persons) is consistent with the information that about one-quarter of its population was born in other regions. Also, the exceptionally low annual rate of increase of the residency of Kedu in Central Java during the same period (3.2 per 1,000 persons) conforms with the fact that more of the people born in Kedu had left the region to live elsewhere than was the case in any other region.

Besides Besuki, a region of Java that received many immigrants was the residency of Djakarta. Regions of out-migration were Kedu and Jogjakarta in Central Java, and Madura, Kediri, and Madiun in East Java. In the other islands, regions of in-migration were East Sumatra, Lampung, Riau, and Djambi (all in Sumatra), while regions of out-migration were Tapanuli in North Sumatra, West Sumatra, South Sulawesi, and South Kalimantan.

A further inference concerning the major directions of internal migration during the earlier decades of this century can be drawn from the census data. Within the island of Java there was migration from the densely populated regions of Central and East Java to neighboring regions with lower population densities, particularly to Besuki at the eastern tip of Java. Almost one-third of the population of Besuki born outside the region came from Madura, while many others originated from Kediri, Malang, Jogjakarta, and other regions with high population densities. Much of the migration into the residency of Djakarta came from the surrounding regions in West Java: Bogor, Bandung, and Tjirebon.

Population movements within Sumatra primarily took place from Tapanuli (in northwestern Sumatra) and West Sumatra into East Sumatra. About 60 per cent of the persons who left Tapanuli settled in East Sumatra. The population of West Sumatra exhibited a high degree of mobility, many of them leaving their region of birth and settling in East Sumatra and other parts of the island.

Interisland migration occurred primarily from Java to East Sumatra and to Lampung (the southernmost region of Sumatra), from South Kalimantan to parts of Sumatra, and into South Kalimantan from South Sulawesi. Information on the rapid population increase in East Sumatra and Lampung is consistent with the conclusion drawn from data on place of birth: about 31 per cent of the population of East Sumatra and 26 per cent of that of Lampung were born in Java. Around one-sixth of the inhabitants of East Sumatra born elsewhere originated from Kedu, about 10 per cent from Kediri, and many from Jogjakarta, Banjumas, and other regions of Java. As has been pointed out earlier, these population movements were related to the development of plantation agriculture in East Sumatra. In Lampung around 25 per cent of the population born elsewhere came from Banten in West Java, on the opposite side of the Strait of Sunda, and about 20 per cent from Kedu. Population movements also occurred between Sumatra and Kalimantan. Around 30 per cent of the inhabitants of Riau who were born in other regions, and 25 per cent of those in Djambi, originated from South Kalimantan. In turn, in-migration took place into South Kalimantan from South Sulawesi.

Naturally, there were some population movements in the opposite direction, but they were very small. Thus, the census reported that almost 1,400 persons in Kedu were born in East Sumatra. These were probably children of migrants from Kedu to East Sumatra who had returned to Kedu with their parents. Before 1930 the number of migrants who went back to their original regions was minimal, but during the thirties, with the severe impact of the depression, a large stream of migrants left East Sumatra and returned to Java.

According to the census data, many of the inhabitants of West

Java who were born elsewhere came from West Sumatra, Minahasa, and Maluku. In Central Java the largest number of persons
born in other regions originated from Maluku, and in East Java
from Minahasa and Maluku. In terms of the total population,
however, the number of Java's inhabitants who were born in the
other islands constituted only a very small percentage, and the
percentage of those born in Java who left for the other islands
was also very small. Throughout all the other islands only
around one million persons were known to have been born in
Java, which was less than 3 per cent of Java's 1930 population.
In total, out of the 60.7 million persons in Indonesia only 6.6
million were enumerated outside their region of birth.

The large number of people originating from Java who lived
in Lampung (in South Sumatra) at the time of the census was
partly a result of the resettlement program, better known as
colonization (*kolonisatie*), started in 1905.[34] This was a govern-
ment-sponsored and government-organized program aimed at
lessening Java's population pressures by resettling Javanese peasants in agricultural settlements in South Sumatra and other regions. During the first twenty-five years of the program very
little was achieved. At the end of that period the total number of
people who had been settled amounted to only around thirty
thousand. The scheme had many deficiencies that were corrected when a more intensive program was developed during the
1930's. These shortcomings included the lack of soil investigation, mapping, and land-use planning. The originators of the
program assumed that the Javanese, who had been peasants for
generations, would have the necessary skills to clear the jungle
and develop irrigated ricefields. Actually, they had lost this skill,
for in Java clearing the jungle to develop irrigated fields had
been carried out centuries before, and the contemporary Javanese peasants were used to working in well-established fields.

[34] For an excellent account of this resettlement program, see Karl J.
Pelzer, *Pioneer Settlement in the Asiatic Tropics* (New York, 1948).

As a consequence, after a while many of these resettled peasants had to be moved to other areas, since their fields suffered either from floods or from water shortage. Very little attention was paid to the peasants' health, so that contagious diseases spread rapidly with consequent high death rates. In addition, the process of selecting future settlers was inadequate: they accepted as migrants not only people who were already too old, but also sick persons and criminals.

After 1931 a number of improvements were introduced, culminating in the establishment in 1937 of a special commission in charge of this program. Under the commission the annual number of migrants increased to 14,700 in 1935 and 52,800 in 1940. Before a settlement was established, surveys were made on property rights to land, and on soil fertility, climate, topography, water supply, and related items, which were the ingredients for land-development plans. The selection of prospective migrants was based on the "ten commandments." Among other things, they pointed out that a person should be selected only if he was a real peasant ("non-peasants will be a burden for others"), physically strong, young of age ("to slow down Java's population growth"), with a family ("the cornerstone of law and order"), but not recently married ("source of difficulties"). He should not have many children nor a pregnant wife, and he should not be a former plantation worker ("incites unrest"). In no case should a bachelor be accepted, since "one day he certainly will get into trouble with somebody else's wife." The resettling of whole villages was to be permitted, and in that case all other conditions could be disregarded.

The settlements that the government developed were almost identical to villages in Java. This official policy was based on the notion that Javanese peasants would not and could not live in communities that differed from those with which they were already familiar. To do otherwise, it was felt, would only lead to undesirable tensions and disorder. Therefore, the colonial government directed all its efforts toward the maintenance of Javanese patterns; not only in the method of cultivation (intensive agriculture on irrigated fields) and the kinds of crops (rice and other foodcrops), but also in the physical layout of the settlements, the organization of the village government, and even the style of the houses. All traditions, customs, and social institutions were preserved, and the settlements were named after Javanese towns and villages.

Such a policy of preservation might have been attractive to the peasants from Java. However, this policy ensured that the inherent weaknesses of the Javanese communities were also preserved. Thus, instead of the resettlement program being used as an opportunity to encourage planned social change through developing new forms of viable and dynamic communities, it became merely a program for establishing "tiny Javas" or "tiny Kedus" in the other islands. In these tradition-bound peasant communities operating on a limited base, the members were constantly in chronic need of credit, and this led to the actual control not only of the produce of the land but in many cases also of the use of the land itself being transferred to creditors, followed by the rise of absentee ownership. These developments were further aggravated by the fact that the lands allotted for settlements were never the best, since such lands were reserved by the government for plantations. Moreover, these "tiny Javas" were clearly separated from the local settlements of the indigenous population. With both groups being encouraged to preserve traditional social and cultural institutions that were clearly barriers to change, there was little chance of relationships developing between the two.

CHAPTER 6

"Children Who Could Not Yet Walk" and the Consistency of Mortality Patterns, 1930–1940

The period of depression in the thirties had a major effect on the Indonesian economy. The colonial government adopted a deflationary monetary policy that increased the impact of the declining exports, and it also introduced restrictive schemes for export products. In the case of rubber production, the burden of this restriction was mainly borne by the Indonesian small holders, since the colonial government felt obliged to protect the interest of Dutch and other foreign investors. In spite of its many protective policies, however, the government felt it necessary to carry out wholesale cuts in wages and employment, resulting in the return of thousands of workers to Java from plantations and mines in the other Indonesian islands. In Java itself many workers left the plantations to return to their villages. These population shifts aggravated even further the already very serious conditions in the rural areas, and in many regions rural debts and harvest mortgages assumed huge proportions.[1]

Although the collapse of Java's sugar industry made more land available for food production, the majority of the peasants

---

[1] On the impact of the depression on the economy, see G. Gonggrijp, *Schets ener Economische Geschiedenis van Nederlands Indië* (Sketch of an Economic History of the Netherlands Indies), 3rd ed. (Haarlem, 1949), pp. 211–242.

were obliged to sell a larger proportion of their crops in order to be able to pay taxes, buy other necessities, and repay debts. The need for cash was felt even more acutely by the subsistence peasants since the reduction in their tax was far less than the decrease in their income. Thus, the serious impact of the depression on the subsistence village economy was further increased by the government's monetary and tax policies.

The depression and resulting government policies had their consequences for the population of Indonesia. In fairness to the colonial government, however, it must be pointed out that during the thirties more was done in the field of health improvement than in previous periods. Public health measures were introduced in many regions, although they were still on a limited scale in comparison with the size of the population and the extent of the area. In addition, a modest attempt was begun to stimulate small-scale and medium-scale industries, and more attention was paid to agricultural extension activities and the provision of credit facilities. However, the nature of these programs was such that they benefited a thin layer rather than the masses of the rural population.

During this period both official sources and individual studies provided some data on vital rates, but they were even more scarce than data on total populations. As with other countries that had a comparable degree of development in statistics, the information on mortality was somewhat more reliable than that on births. In some government documents, figures on births were considered inaccurate, and estimates on crude birth rates were based on death statistics and assumptions about rates of natural increase. In the year 1937 a birth and death registration system was introduced by the Public Health Service in the regency of Purwokerto in Central Java.[2] This system was based on the results of initial trials conducted in 1929 in Jogjakarta. The village heads issued uniform birth certificates (pink for

[2] J. L. Hydrick, *Intensive Rural Hygiene Work in the Netherlands Indies* (New York, 1944), pp. 63–64.

girls, blue for boys), made out in triplicate: one for the parents, one retained by the village head, and one sent to the regency office. Death certificates were also issued by the village heads. This use of certificates, together with a good deal of propaganda, resulted in some improvement in the registration system. It was reported that the number of registered births in Purwokerto showed a crude birth rate of around 40 per 1,000 persons. The same system was soon introduced into most of the province of Central Java, and also into Djakarta.

The Minimum Crude Birth Rate on the Basis of the 1930 Census Data

The 1930 census reported that there were at that time in Java, 2,244,418 "children who could not yet walk" (Indonesians only), of which 1,116,373 were boys and 1,128,045 were girls. The procedure employed to calculate the crude birth rate from these data consists of estimating the number of children who were less than one year old and from this figure calculating the corresponding number of births in one year. As has been pointed out earlier, the census reports assume that the category of "children who could not yet walk" consisted of persons aged less than fifteen or eighteen months, but the only basis given for such an assumption is that it was said to be the opinion of "experts."

Three alternative combinations of assumptions are used to arrive at estimates of the number of persons aged less than one year: (1) If it is assumed that the "children who could not yet walk" were all less than one year old, then the number of persons aged less than one year in Java was 2.24 million. This is the maximum possible number. (2) If it is assumed that the children who could not yet walk were all less than fifteen months old, and that in addition none of the persons born died before the age of fifteen months, then the number of persons aged less than one year was 4/5 of 2.24 million, or 1.79 million, comprising 0.89 million males and 0.90 females. This is the minimum number if none of the "children who could not yet walk" was older than fifteen

Table 21. Alternative estimates of number of births and crude birth rates, based on three estimates of the number of persons aged less than one year, Java, 1930

Expectation of life at birth	2.24 mill. under 1 yr.		1.79 mill. under 1 yr.		1.49 mill. under 1 yr.	
	No. of births *	Crude birth rate †	No. of births *	Crude birth rate †	No. of births *	Crude birth rate †
20 years	2.89	70.68	2.31	56.39	1.92	46.93
25 years	2.78	67.94	2.22	54.41	1.85	45.29
30 years	2.71	66.23	2.16	52.82	1.80	43.97
35 years	2.64	64.54	2.10	51.48	1.75	42.85
40 years	2.58	63.07	2.06	50.30	1.71	41.87

* In millions.
† Per 1,000 persons.
Source: Based on United Nations, *Methods for Population Projections by Sex and Age* (Population Studies, no. 25; New York, 1956), pp. 72–81.

months. (3) If it is assumed that the children who could not yet walk were all less than eighteen months old, and that in addition none of the persons born died before the age of eighteen months, then the number of persons aged less than one year was ⅔ of 2.24 million, or 1.49 million, comprising 0.74 million males and 0.75 million females. This is the minimum number of persons aged less than one year.

The established procedure for arriving at alternative annual numbers of births from alternative estimates of the number of persons aged less than one year is to apply to them a suitable life table for each of the sexes. Adding together the results for each of the sexes gives the estimated total number of births. Since no life table exists for Java's population, a selection has been made from the model life tables developed by the United Nations Secretariat.[3] Five abridged life tables are chosen, exhibiting mortality patterns that correspond to expectations of life at birth of respectively 20, 25, 30, 35, and 40 years.[4] Table 21 shows the resulting alternative estimates of the number of births and of the

[3] United Nations, *Methods for Population Projections by Sex and Age* (Population Studies, no. 25; New York, 1956), pp. 72–81.
[4] Since the L_x columns in the U.N. life tables refer to quinquennial periods, the values of L_o have been approximated as follows:
$$L_o = 0.3\, l_o + 0.7\, l_1.$$

crude birth rates, given a total population (Indonesians only) for Java of 40.89 million in 1930. Depending on the alternative estimates of the number of persons aged less than one year, the estimates of the number of births ranged from 1.71 million to 2.89 million, and the corresponding crude birth rates from 41.87 to 70.68 per 1,000 persons. Since from data on other populations it is known that crude birth rates higher than 50 per 1,000 persons have rarely been observed where the data were known to be accurate, it seems more plausible to conclude that, assuming a fair degree of accuracy in the census statistics, the number of children aged less than one year at the time of the census was probably between 1.49 million and 1.79 million and that the crude birth rate in Java was very likely higher than 40 per 1,000 persons.

This estimate appears to be in agreement with several other findings. Using the data for Indonesia as a whole, Keyfitz arrived at the following conclusion:

If the 3,246,000 infants were "at most 15 to 18 months of age," then at the very most they were born over a period of one and one half years, that is to say over 2,000,000 of them are the survivors of the births of one year. The births themselves would be 2,500,000 if infant mortality was 20 per cent.[5]

Given a total population (Indonesians only) of 59.14 million for Indonesia in 1930, Keyfitz' estimate results in a crude birth rate of 42.27 per 1,000 persons. A study by Wertheim arrived at the conclusion that: "Altogether, a general birth rate of ±40% for Indonesia does not look improbable." [6] Also dealing with the data for Indonesia as a whole, Van Wijngaarden, in an appendix to Wertheim's article, summed up his calculations as follows: "If 20% of the children die in the first 18 months of life, if at a given

---

[5] N. Keyfitz, "The Population of Indonesia," *Ekonomi dan Keuangan Indonesia*, VI, no. 10 (Oct. 1953), 649.

[6] W. F. Wertheim, "A Forty Per Cent Test :A Useful Demographic Tool," *Ekonomi dan Keuangan Indonesia*, VIII, no. 3 (March 1955), 177.

moment the number of children under 18 months of age amounted to 3 ¼ million, then the number of births per annum amounts to 2.15 million at least, 2.8 million at most." [7] The first figure was based on the assumption that the 20 per cent deaths occurred immediately after birth, the second on the assumption that the deaths occurred at the moment of reaching the age of eighteen months. These upper and lower limits imply a crude birth rate between 36.35 and 47.34 per 1,000 persons. An earlier study by van Gelderen arrived at an estimated crude birth rate of 38 per 1,000 persons.

Other Estimates of Crude Birth Rates

Among the estimates of vital rates that have been most often quoted in the past are probably those of van Gelderen as published in "The Numerical Evolution of Population with Particular Reference to the Population of Java." [8] Unfortunately, these estimates were more often than not taken for granted without any proper effort at appraisal. Van Gelderen's data and assumptions were as follows: the total population in 1930 was 40.9 million, the crude death rate based on registered deaths was about 20 per 1,000 persons, the infant mortality rate was 200 per 1,000 births, the registered deaths included only one-half of the actual number of infant deaths, and the annual rate of increase was 15 per 1,000 persons. On this basis he arrived at an estimate of a crude birth rate of 38 and a crude death rate of 23 per 1,000 persons.

An appraisal was made of van Gelderen's figures by comparing his estimates of the number of births with the number of births as calculated from the reported number of "children who could not yet walk" in the 1930 census. This comparison indi-

[7] *Ibid.*, p. 186, App. B.
[8] Comitato Italiano per lo Studio dei Problemi della Popolazione, Corrado Gini, ed., *Proceedings of the International Congress for Studies on Population (Rome, Sept. 7–10, 1931)* (Rome, 1933–34), I, pp. 275–287.

cates that the number of births and consequently also the crude birth rate as computed from the data and conjectural assumptions of van Gelderen are too low. Another test of internal consistency has also been carried out by comparing van Gelderen's infant mortality rate of 200 per 1,000 births with the death rate of persons aged one year and over as computed from his data, since from studies of other populations it is known that a positive correlation exists between infant mortality and mortality during the remainder of the life span. The result of the test shows that if the assumption of an infant mortality rate of 200 per 1,000 births is to be maintained, the crude death rate and the crude birth rate would be higher than 24 and 39 per 1,000 persons respectively. Finally, if an additional assumption of the death rate of persons aged one year and over is incorporated, the resulting crude birth rate is 42.7 and the crude death rate 27.7 per 1,000 persons.[9]

As has been pointed out earlier, Wertheim came to the conclusion that the crude birth rate in prewar Indonesia was probably 40 per 1,000 persons or higher. Briefly, Wertheim's estimate was arrived at in the following way: Starting with the fact that in most low-income countries the proportion of persons aged less than fifteen years has empirically been found to be around 40 per cent of the total population, and given that the Indonesian population as reported in the 1930 census could be regarded as conforming to a population of which 40 per cent were aged less than fifteen years, and furthermore assuming that the fertility level stayed constant and that the population was subject to a mortality pattern that was based on certain conjectures as to the levels of infant and child mortality, he arrived at the conclusion that the crude birth rate was very probably higher than 40 per 1,000 persons.

[9] See Widjojo Nitisastro, "Migration, Population Growth, and Economic Development in Indonesia: A Study of the Economic Consequences of Alternative Patterns of Inter-island Migration" (Ph.D. diss., University of California, Berkeley, 1961), pp. 120–126.

Wertheim's assumption that the number of persons aged less than fifteen years was around 40 per cent of the total population was probably fairly accurate. According to the 1930 census, the proportion of persons considered to be other than adults was 41.1 per cent in Java. For males the percentage was 44.2, and for females 38. This difference was no doubt partly due to the arbitrary classifications of persons into adults and nonadults. As has been pointed out earlier, the census report indicated that girls were considered as adults at younger ages (14–15) and boys (16–17). In general, the data for the different regions indicated that the proportion of children among males was higher than among females. This is consistent with the findings for those other countries where no effort was made in the censuses to arrive at a more reliable age distribution.[10]

To draw inferences concerning the fertility level of a population of which 40 per cent are less than fifteen years old, a mortality pattern conforming to such an age structure has to be used. When an attempt was made to establish such a pattern, it was found that, depending on the assumed ratios of increase, populations with several different patterns of mortality can have a proportion of at least 40 per cent of persons aged less than fifteen years.[11] Thus, in the case of populations with high levels of mortality, as is common with most low-income economies, if the existing growth rate is very small, the proportion of persons aged less than fifteen years is not necessarily 40 per cent or higher. On the other hand, even if the mortality level is comparatively low, as long as the growth rate is very high, it is still quite likely that such a population would have a proportion of 40 per cent or higher of those aged less than fifteen years.

An appraisal of Wertheim's assumptions and calculations shows that, in accord with other computations already presented,

[10] United Nations, *Methods of Appraisal of Quality of Basic Data for Population Estimates* (Population Studies, no. 23; New York, 1955), p. 33.

[11] Widjojo, *op. cit.*, pp. 134–136.

the crude birth rate around 1930 was indeed very probably higher than 40 per 1,000 persons. In a little less cumbersome, if not more conventional, computation for estimating crude birth rates using Wertheim's assumptions, it was found that given a rate of increase of 10, 20, and 30 per 1,000 persons, the corresponding crude birth rates are 44.7, 47.9, and 51.2 per 1,000 persons.[12]

The crude birth rate of a sample of the population of Djakarta was reported by J. W. Tesch, who was in charge of the daily operations of a pilot study on health conditions in a ward of that city.[13] For the years 1938–1940, the crude birth rate was reported to be 35.1, 38.3, and 37.0 per 1,000 persons. In each of these years, however, the number of births was smaller than the number of persons aged less than one year, which was an indication of net in-migration of infants. Since infants very likely accompany their mothers or parents, this in-migration had an impact on the age structure of the population. Moreover, Tesch reported that many adult males living in the city had left their families in the villages and that it was rather common for expectant mothers to return to their district of origin, which was only partly compensated for by the fact that others came from the villages to the city for confinement. It seems plausible, then, to draw the conclusion that the computed crude birth rate of around 37 per 1,000 persons was a consequence of the sex-age composition of an immigrant population and that it underestimated the actual fertility of the population.

Data on Mortality

The existing mortality statistics during the colonial era were somewhat better than the statistics on births, as was the case with most other countries, but nevertheless even these figures were of

[12] *Ibid.*, pp. 127–128.
[13] J. W. Tesch, "The Hygiene Study Ward Centre at Batavia: Planning and Preliminary Results (1937–1941)," *Acta Leidensia Edita Cura et Sumptibus Scholae Medicinae Tropicae*, Vol. XIX (1948).

questionable reliability. Although since 1911 there had been a system for registering deaths, the quality of the results was poor. In some of the larger cities the data on the number of deaths were more reliable than in rural areas because an examination of deaths was required before burial, and some estimates of infant mortality rates based on these data have been published. Outside of the cities, however, there is virtually no reliable data. In one area of West Java that suffered from the plague the resulting compulsory death examination enabled a mortality study to be made óf a rural area. It was not until the middle of the thirties that a serious effort was made to compile birth and death statistics in any region of Central Java.

Table 22 shows the total population, the number of deaths, and the crude death rates for Indonesians, as published in the official reports. Using the 1920 census population and the mean of the number of reported deaths in the years 1919–1921, the crude death rate for 1920 appears as 24.3 per 1,000 persons. Using the same procedure for 1929–1931, the crude death rate for 1930 is found to be 17.9. It is quite possible that the mortality level around 1920 was indeed higher than that of 1930, primarily as a consequence of the severe influenza epidemic. The actual crude death rates for both of these years must have been higher than the official figures, however, since it is known that the registration system at that time was very deficient.

An improved registration system was introduced during the thirties, and although limited to certain regions, it had an impact on the recorded number of deaths, as can be seen by comparing the death rates in different years. Using the mean figures for the numbers of deaths in three consecutive years for the years 1925, 1930, 1935, and 1940, the annual levels of increase in mortality during 1925–1930, 1930–1935, and 1935–1940 can be computed as respectively 0.75, 1.59, and 3.06 per cent. Since the annual rate of population growth between the two censuses was 17.6 per 1,000 persons, the large discrepancies between the growth rates of the total population and of the number of deaths could

Table 22. Total population, number of deaths, and crude death rate, Java, 1916–1940 (Indonesians only)

Year	Total population	No. of deaths	Crude death rate (per 1,000)
1916	32,963,861	586,757	17.8
1917	33,357,941	673,830	20.2
1918	33,619,766	1,227,121	36.5
1919	33,456,646	930,095	27.8
1920	33,087,264	764,316	23.1
1921	34,399,477	815,268	23.7
1922	34,480,630	689,613	20.0
1923	34,838,353	634,058	18.2
1924	35,070,939	655,827	18.7
1925	35,505,233	706,554	19.9
1926	35,889,883	753,688	21.0
1927	36,173,984	676,454	18.7
1928	36,439,100	717,850	19.7
1929	37,046,865	733,528	19.8
1930	40,890,244	740,113	18.1
1931	40,619,432	722,756	17.8
1932	40,933,713	720,928	17.6
1933	40,891,093	706,311	17.3
1934	40,891,093	785,409	19.2
1935 *		802,081	
1936		790,422	
1937		852,486	
1938		846,331	
1939		881,496	
1940		965,706	

* In the *Indisch Verslag, 1936* (The Hague, 1936), it was pointed out that the population figure of the 1930 census was used for the years 1930–1934. Moreover, since 1935 was the year exactly in between the 1930 census and the expected census of 1940, it was decided that after that year only the actual number of deaths (and births) would be published, without figures on total population and crude death rates. Actually, only for the years 1933 and 1934 was the exact figure of the 1930 census used. The figures used for the earlier years were probably based on the preliminary outcomes of the census.

Source: *Koloniaal Verslag* (The Hague) for 1917–1930 and *Indisch Verslag* for 1931–1941.

mean either that the mortality level was decreasing sharply between 1925 and 1930, was more or less constant between 1930 and 1935, and was again increasing very steeply between 1935 and 1940 or, alternatively, that there was an improved coverage in the registration of deaths. The latter possibility seems to be more plausible.

A number of studies were undertaken, primarily based on the death statistics in urban centers, to estimate infant mortality rates. Although it is impossible to assign any specific value to estimates of the crude death rate based on the infant mortality rate, there is some relationship between the two, and for want of more reliable information, a knowledge of the level of infant mortality might give some indication of the general mortality conditions.

One troublesome problem with infant mortality rates is that they depend not only on the number of infant deaths, but also on the fertility level. Where the information on births is deficient, the computed infant mortality rate might be far off, even if there is a very accurate registration of infant deaths. Moreover, omissions of one are usually accompanied by omissions of the other, with a resulting underestimate or overestimate of the computed infant mortality rate. In addition, there is the problem that since the conventional infant mortality rates refer to births and deaths occurring in the same calendar year, there is no perfect matching of births and deaths. Where the infant mortality rates pertain to small geographical units with extensive migration to and from adjacent areas, such as in urban centers, the lack of perfect matching between births and deaths is further complicated by the discrepancies in place of occurrence.

Almost all studies of infant mortality refer to the large cities. This is because of the greater reliability of the mortality data, resulting from the post mortem examinations required in most of these cities. The information included a specification of sex, age, ethnic group, and probable cause of death. The legal character of the required examination is indeed a reason to expect *a priori* that the data on deaths were superior to those on births, for which there were no such legal requirements, although such legal compulsion does not necessarily mean that the registration was complete or nearly complete. Nevertheless, the data on deaths as used in these infant mortality studies are actually the best available and are more reliable than the denominator in computing the infant mortality rates.

Infant Mortality and Life Expectancy

An attempt will now be made to arrive at some estimate of the infant mortality rate of Djakarta in 1930, based on the returns of the 1930 census. During the years 1929–1931 the annual number of deaths of children aged less than one year in Djakarta was reported to be 3,822.[14] The 1930 census report indicated that in Djakarta there were 16,901 "children who could not yet walk," 8,422 males and 8,479 females. By the same procedure that was used in calculating the number of births for Java as a whole, it appears that the maximum number of persons in Djakarta aged less than one year was 16,901, while the minimum number was ⅔ of 16,901, or 11,267. Given the same alternative model life tables, the number of births can be estimated as between 12,951 and 21,748. The actual number of births, however, is not necessarily within these limits, for unlike the computation for Java as a whole, the impact of migration on the population of Djakarta cannot be assumed away. Estimation of the number of births is based upon the number of persons who were born outside the city and arrived there before they were one year old and excludes those born in the city who left for other places during their first year of life.

As the total population (Indonesians only) of Djakarta was 325,978 persons, the minimum and maximum estimates of the number of births imply a crude birth rate ranging from 39.7 to

[14] W. Brand, "Sterfte te Batavia, 1929–1931" (Mortality in Batavia, 1929–1931), *Geneeskundig Tijdschrift voor Nederlandsch-Indië* LXXX (1940), p. 1470.

66.7 per 1,000 persons. The estimates of the number of births give an infant mortality of between 176 and 294 per 1,000 births. A number of studies on infant mortality in Djakarta have been conducted. One of them, by G. B. Walch-Sorgdrager, was based on the records of children born at the Budi-Kemulaan maternity hospital.[15] In it the infant mortality rate was found to be 231 per 1,000 births. This was actually a special type of infant mortality rate in which there was perfect matching between births and deaths.

Another study on infant mortality in Djakarta was carried out by J. H. de Haas for the years 1934–1937.[16] For each of the four years, he arrived at an estimate of around 300 infant deaths per 1,000 births, which seems to be too high due to his low estimate of the number of births. In turn, this was a consequence of the low estimate of the population numbers in those years as compared to the 1930 census population, and also a consequence of his not taking into account an important change in the boundaries of the city in 1935.[17] The estimated crude birth rate of 35 per 1,000 persons used by de Haas is not improbable, not because, as de Haas suggested, urban conditions must necessarily

[15] G. B. Walch-Sorgdrager, "Onderzoek naar de Kinderen, Die in 1929 te Batavia Geboren zijn met Behulp van Vroedvrouwen van Boedi Kemoeliaán (1e Gedeelte)" (Investigation of the Children Who Were Born in 1929 in Batavia with the Assistance of Trained Midwives of Boedi Kemoeliaan, [1st Part]) Geneeskundig Tijdschrift voor Nederlandsch-Indië, LXXI (1931), 841–861.

[16] J. H. de Haas, "Over de Zuigelingensterfte in de Stad Batavia in 1934" (On Infant Mortality in the City of Batavia in 1934), Geneeskundig Tijdschrift voor Nederlandsch-Indië, LXXVI (1936), 2186–2203; J. H. de Haas, "Zuigelingensterfte in Batavia, II: Bewerking der Gegevens over 1935 en 1936" (Infant Mortality in Batavia, II: Compilations of Data for 1935 and 1936), Geneeskundig Tijdschrift voor Nederlandsch-Indië, LXXVIII (1938), 1467–1512; and J. H. de Haas, "Sterfte naar Leeftijdsgroepen in Batavia, in het Bijzonder op den Kinderleeftijd" (Mortality by Age Group in Batavia, Especially during Childhood), Geneeskundig Tijdschrift voor Nederlandsch-Indië, LXXIX (1939), 707–726.

[17] Widjojo, op. cit., pp. 153–154.

result in lower fertility than rural areas, but because of the sex-age structure of the population, which was heavily affected by net in-migration.

Some idea of probable infant mortality rates for 1936 in Djakarta can be arrived at by using alternative assumptions regarding the rate of increase among the Indonesian inhabitants. A comparison of the census returns of 1920 and 1930 shows that the number of Indonesian inhabitants of the city of Djakarta increased by 5.8 per cent annually, while the population of the residency of Djakarta increased by 2.9 per cent. Using a range of assumed annual rates of increase of between 1 and 5 per cent from 1930 to 1936,[18] an annual crude birth rate of 35 per 1,000 persons, and a mean annual number of 4,087 infant deaths in 1935–1937, the resulting infant mortality rates as conventionally computed range from 211 to 268 per 1,000 births (see Table 23). It should be noted that these infant mortality

Table 23. Alternative infant mortality rates based on alternative assumptions of annual rates of population increase between 1930 and 1936, Djakarta, 1936 (Indonesians only) *

Annual rate of population increase (per 1,000)	No. of persons	No. of births	Infant mortality rate (per 1,000)
10	434,984	15,224	268
20	461,886	16,166	253
30	490,447	17,166	238
40	520,774	18,227	224
50	552,977	19,354	211

* Total population in 1930 was 409,655 (since a change in the boundaries of Djakarta took place in 1935 and the neighboring Djatinegara became part of Djakarta, the sum of the populations of Djakarta and Djatinegara, which were respectively 325,978 and 83,677 persons, is used as the 1930 base population in this calculation); the mean annual number of infant deaths in 1935–1937 was 4,087; the crude birth rate is assumed to be 35 per 1,000 persons.

[18] As a result of the depression during the thirties, the net in-migration into the cities was very likely smaller than during the preceding decade, and as a consequence the rate of population increase in the cities was probably lower than in previous years.

rates are not exactly of the same type as those computed for 1930 on the basis of the number of "children who could not yet walk." Unlike the latter, the present set of rates refer to deaths and births in the same geographic area for the same year.

For the years 1938–1940, Tesch presented data on infant mortality rates, which were respectively 206, 208, and 209 per 1,000 births.[19] Since the deaths included children who were born during the preceding year, and since a number of those born in a particular year reached the age of one year only in the subse-

Table 24. Estimated age-specific death rates, Tanah-Tinggi, Djakarta, 1938–1940 (average)

Age group	No. of persons	No. of deaths	Age-specific death rate (per 1,000)
1–4	2,187	102	46.6
5–14	4,562	23	5.0
15–19	2,079	7	3.4
20–49	10,822	78	7.2
50 +	1,503	72	47.9
Total, age 1 and over	22,026	439	19.9

Source: Based on data in J. W. Tesch, "The Hygiene Study Ward Centre at Batavia: Planning and Preliminary Results (1937–1941)," Acta Leidensia edita cura et sumptibus Scholae Medicinae Tropicae, XIX (1948), 75.

quent year, a simple adjustment can be carried out by combining the data for the three years, giving an infant mortality rate of 211 per 1,000 births. Another problem relates to migration: the deaths include infants born in other places and the births include those who moved to other places before reaching the age of one year. By relating births and deaths of the same cohort, Tesch arrived at an infant mortality rate of 185 per 1,000 births.

Some effort to arrive at age-specific death rates is shown in Table 24, using information supplied by Tesch on the proportional distribution of deaths, the total number of deaths, and the

[19] Tesch, op. cit., p. 71.

age distribution of the population of the pilot study ward. The resulting age-specific death rate for the age group 1–4 years appears to be 46.6 per 1,000 persons.

For the years 1929–1931, the mean annual number of deaths among Indonesians in Djakarta was reported to be 8,406. Given a total census population of 325,978 persons, the crude death rate was 25.8 per 1,000 persons. Since the figures for the total population of 1930 were probably quite accurate, while the death statistics were probably far from complete, the actual crude death rate is probably higher, and the figure of 25.8 can be considered as an absolute minimum. The mean annual number of deaths in Djakarta during the period 1935–1937 was 11,143. Based on alternative assumptions of the annual growth rate of the population of the city, the minimum and maximum estimates of the total population in 1936 are respectively 434,984 and 552,997. This amounts to a crude death rate of between 20.1 and 25.6 per 1,000 persons. The latter figure is based on the assumption that the city population increased by only 1 per cent annually, which is quite unlikely.

A comparison of the age distributions of all deaths for the different years is shown in Table 25. If these data can be relied on, they indicate a decline in the proportion of infant deaths from 45.5 per cent of the total number of deaths in 1929–1931 to about 36.4 in 1935–1937. This proportional decrease continued between 1935 and 1937. However, this lower proportion of infant deaths does not necessarily mean a lower infant mortality rate or a lower level of general mortality. A change in age distribution or, more specifically, a decrease in the proportion of persons aged less than one year would result in a lower proportion of infant deaths without any actual decline in infant mortality rate. A decrease in net in-migration (or an increase in net out-migration) of infants, or an actual decrease in the annual number of births, due, for example, to shifts in the sex-age distribution of persons of reproductive age, would lead to such a decline in the proportion of infants. Only if it has been established that these factors were nonexistent or that they were of

Table 25. Age distribution of deaths, Djakarta, 1929–1931, 1935, 1936, 1937, and 1936–1938

Age group	Average, 1929–1931 *		1935		1936		1937		Average, 1936–1938 (sample) (%)
	No.	%	No.	%	No.	%	No.	%	
0–1	3,822	45.5	4,199	38.2	4,037	37.2	4,025	34.8	36.1
1–4	1,804	21.5	2,219	20.2	2,422	22.3	2,638	22.8	23.3
5–14			523	4.8	535	4.9	609	5.3	5.3
15–19			119	1.8	203	1.9	254	2.2	1.7
20–49	1,844	21.9	2,029	18.5	1,952	18.0	2,181	18.8	17.7
50+	936	11.1	1,828	16.6	1,703	15.7	1,878	16.2	16.4
Total, all ages	8,406	100.0	10,993	100.0	10,852	100.0	11,585	100.0	100.0

* The actual age groupings as reported by Brand were: less than 1, 1–15, 16–50, and larger than 50. Unlike the other years, the data on 1929–1931 do not include the number of deaths in Djatinegara.

Source: W. Brand, "Sterfte te Batavia, 1929–1931" (Mortality in Batavia, 1929–1931), Geneeskundig Tijdschrift voor Nederlandsch-Indië, LXXX (1940), 1470; J. H. de Haas, "Sterfte naar Leeftijdsgroepen in Batavia, in het Bijzonder op den Kinderleeftijd" (Mortality by Age Group, Especially during Childhood), Geneeskundig Tijdschrift voor Nederlandsch-Indië, LXXIX (1939), 710–711; J. W. Tesch, "The Hygiene Study Ward Centre at Batavia: Planning and Preliminary Results (1937–1941)," Acta Leidensia edita cura et sumptibus Scholae Medicinae Tropicae, XIX (1948), 75.

inconsequential magnitude, would it be justified to infer a decrease in the infant mortality rate, and probably also in the general mortality level. The number of infant deaths per 1,000 deaths among all age groups can not be used in an identical way to the number of infant deaths per 1,000 births, and, in more general terms, a proportional distribution of deaths by age is no substitute for an age-specific death rate.

The city of Bandung reputedly maintained a good register of its Indonesian inhabitants. Births, deaths, arrivals, departures, and changes of address in the city were reported to the city hall, and in addition a number of city employees were assigned to make house-to-house visits to record changes in the household composition. As was the case with Djakarta, there were also compulsory examinations of deaths before burial. From these data W. Brand computed the infant mortality rates during the 1930's.[20] Although it is probable that both the crude birth rate and the infant mortality rate in his study were underestimates due to the under-registration of births and infant deaths, the adjusted infant mortality rates for the different years illustrate some tendency toward a mortality decline in that city during the period 1931–1938. For this purpose a very simple adjustment has been applied by combining data for several consecutive years.[21] The results are shown in Table 26.

Although most studies of infant mortality in Indonesia were concerned with urban populations, an exception is the one carried out in a rural region of West Java by Liem Tjay Tie and J. H. de Haas.[22] The area studied consisted of five out of thirty-

[20] W. Brand, "Differential Mortality in the Town of Bandung," *The Indonesian Town* (The Hague, 1958), p. 256.

[21] Other types of adjustments have also been applied to the data (see Widjojo, *op. cit.*, pp. 178–180).

[22] Liem Tjay Tie and J. H. de Haas, "Over de Zuigelingensterfte in enige Onderdistricten van het Regentschap Tasikmalaja (West Java) in 1935, 1936, en 1937" (Concerning Infant Mortality in some Subdistricts of Tasikmalaja Regency [West Java] in 1935, 1936, and 1937), *Geneeskundig Tijdschrift voor Nederlandsch-Indië*, LXXIX (1939), 5015–5038.

Table 26. Unadjusted and adjusted infant mortality rates per 1,000 persons, Bandung, 1931–1938 (Indonesians only)

| Year | Infant mortality rate | |
	Unadjusted	Adjusted
1931	117.3	
1932	170.8	145.5
1933	145.1	161.6
1934	166.9	155.0
1935	152.3	154.0
1936	143.1	148.5
1937	150.0	142.5
1938	134.6	

Source: W. Brand, "Differential Mortality in the Town of Bandung," *The Indonesian Town* (The Hague, 1958), p. 256. Adjusted rates added.

three subdistricts of the regency of Tasikmalaja. The total number of births was estimated from the number of smallpox vaccinations on children aged three to four months. The then existing plague epidemic required that employees of the plague control service examine deaths of all persons aged three months and older. Based on the information that migration was negligible, and assuming that the natural rate of increase since 1930 remained constant, the crude birth rate was estimated at 39 and the crude death rate at 29 per 1,000 persons, while the infant mortality rate was found to be about 180 per 1,000 births.

Some tests of internal consistency have been applied to the data and results of this study by relating the estimated infant mortality rate to the death rate of persons aged one year and over. When compared with the general tendencies among other populations, the estimated infant mortality rate of 180 per 1,000 births was found to be too low. Another test, relating the estimated infant mortality rate to the proportion of infant deaths during the first week and the first month, as reported in the study, strengthen this conclusion.[23]

In comparing the mortality levels of Tasikmalaja and of Dja-

[23] See Widjojo, *op. cit.*, pp. 186–187, 189–190.

karta, Liem and de Haas pointed out that the higher rate for the
latter was due to the "unfavorable effect of the tropical city
milieu," resulting from "overcrowding." The infant mortality
rate for Djakarta might or might not have been higher than for
the rural areas, but it seems that there was a general tendency to
emphasize the distressing conditions in urban centers, with the
consequence that figures showing a lower infant mortality rate
for rural areas were too readily accepted, the rationalization
being the existence of a "rural atmosphere." [24] Actually, not only
do large sections of the urban centers ecologically resemble rural
villages, but "overcrowding" in the sense of living close to one
another was, and is, certainly not an exclusively urban feature,
since in the vast majority of villages in Java, houses are built very
close to each other. It is not disputed that the number of persons
per square mile is higher in urban centers, since otherwise they
would not have been designated as urban, but a comparison of
the number of persons per square mile of the area actually used
for habitation would no doubt reduce the contrast to more
realistic proportions. Moreover, many factors of the conditions
in the rural areas completely neutralize the lesser degree of
"overcrowding." Nevertheless, a higher infant mortality rate in
urban centers is far from improbable, not because of the absence
of a "rural atmosphere," but because of the relatively small
proportion of children and the fact that the process of net
in-migration of infants increased the number of them exposed to
the risks of infant death.

From this lengthy analysis of the existing scanty data on vital
rates in Java during the thirties, several conclusions may be
drawn. In prewar Java the crude birth rate was very probably
higher than 40 per 1,000 persons, while the mortality level seems
to be consistent with a mortality pattern corresponding to an

[24] In addition to Liem and de Haas, other writers, such as Brand and
Wertheim, seem also to subscribe to this view (W. Brand, "Sterfte te
Batavia, 1929–1931," *op. cit.*, p. 1470, and W. F. Wertheim, *Indonesian
Society in Transition* [The Hague, 1959], pp. 190–191).

expectation of life at birth of thirty or thirty-five years. Without disputing the probability that a higher infant mortality rate existed in the urban centers than in the rural regions, the estimated infant mortality rate of 300 per 1,000 births for Djakarta seems to be too high, while the computed infant mortality rate of 180 for the Tasikmalaja rural region is very probably an underestimate. An infant mortality rate ranging from 225 to 250 per 1,000 births seems to be plausible.

Almost no data on vital statistics exist for the other Indonesian islands with a very few exceptions, among which the residency of Sumatra's east coast is the most important. The existence of data for this region is related to the development of large-scale plantations during the last decades of the nineteenth century. The plantations' major problem of labor scarcity was solved by bringing workers over from Java. In order to ensure best use of their precious labor resources, the plantations conducted a well-organized health program. A number of medical doctors connected with this program compiled and published vital statistics on the plantation laborers and their families. In two of these plantations for the year 1926, M. Straub reported crude birth rates of 46.8 and 41.9 per 1,000 persons.[25] The crude death rate was reportedly 26 or 27 per 1,000 persons, while the infant mortality rate in several plantations ranged from 160 to 370 per 1,000 births. From Straub's account it seems that the plantations kept quite accurate records of the workers and their families, so that the published figures are probably fairly reliable. H. Heinemann, another medical doctor, reported that on a number of plantations there was compulsory registration of births. He also stated that there was a more rapid population increase following the transfer of the workers from jointly occupied barracks to separate houses for each family.[26] Van Driel reported that the

[25] M. Straub, *Kindersterfte ter Oostkust van Sumatra* (Child Mortality on the East Coast of Sumatra) (Amsterdam, 1927), pp. 27–28, 30.

[26] H. Heinemann, "Het Hygienisch Werk der Senembah-Maatschappi gedurende de Laatste Jaren" (The Work of the Senembah

crude birth rate among workers (that is, exclusive of their family members) was around 10 per 1,000 persons between 1927–1932.[27] Since nearly all the workers in these plantations originated from Java, and since the efforts at improving health conditions in the plantations were more advanced than in other regions, the available data on vital rates for this area were probably not representative of the rest of the population in the other Indonesian islands.

Corporation in the Field of Hygiene during Recent Years), *Geneeskundig Tijdschrift voor Nederlandsch-Indië*, LXXV (1935), 527–528. Also M. Straub, "Kindersterfte als Biologisch Verschijnsel en het Bevolkingsvraagstuk ter Oostkust van Sumatra" (Child Mortality as a Biological Phenomenon and the Population Problem on the East Coast of Sumatra), *Geneeskundig Tijdschrift voor Nederlandsch-Indië*, LXX (1930), 28–29.

[27] B. M. van Driel, "De Sterfte der Ondernemingsarbeiders in de Buitengewesten van Nederlandsch Indië in 1931 en 1932" (The Mortality of Plantation Workers in the Outer Provinces of the Netherlands Indies in 1931 and 1932), *Geneeskundig Tijdschrift voor Nederlandsch-Indië*, LXXV (1935), 1911.

CHAPTER 7

The Impact of Wars, 1940-1950

During most of this period, vital rates underwent abrupt changes as a result of the Japanese occupation from 1942 to 1945 and the war of independence from 1945 to the end of 1949. Under the occupation the harsh and arbitrary mobilization of available manpower and foodcrops for the Japanese war effort brought about a rapid decline in the people's living conditions. Village societies were shaken by the exorbitant compulsory deliveries of crops, by the conscription of hundreds of thousands of men and women for forced labor in other regions of Indonesia and on the Asian mainland, by the virtual disappearance of such essential commodities as textiles and agricultural tools, and by the total disregard by the Japanese administration of any measures to cope with famine and other calamities. Tremendous social dislocations and population displacements resulted, which in turn had significant repercussions on the course of fertility and mortality.

On August 17, 1945, the Republic of Indonesia was proclaimed, and a few weeks later, with the landing of the British army soon followed by the return of Dutch troops, the four-year-long war of independence began. During the subsequent year the Dutch succeeded in occupying several areas, but the greater part of Java and Sumatra remained completely under the control of the Indonesian government. Full-scale attacks were launched by the Dutch in 1947 and 1948 with the objective of crushing the Indonesian Republic and regaining control of the areas producing export crops and oil. Although the Dutch armed forces succeeded in occupying a number of the larger cities, they were, however, never able to establish their control over most of the surrounding rural areas, which formed the bases for vigorous guerrilla warfare. Large-scale population movements accompanied the war: as soon as Dutch troops moved to occupy a city, many of its inhabitants left for the hinterland or other areas controlled by the Indonesian government. The impact of the war of independence on the fertility and mortality levels of the population was further strengthened by lack of medical supplies, since the Dutch blockade of the surrounding seas prevented these from reaching the regions under Republican control.

It is very probable that the changes in vital rates during the forties brought about a decrease in the rate of population growth. The population might not have increased at all during some of these years, and the possibility that an actual population decrease occurred cannot be excluded. There is no doubt that these changes also had an important impact on the present age structure of the population and its future rate of growth. As can be expected, however, the dearth of data for this period is even greater than for the earlier decades. The prewar registration system was continued by some local officials, but few data were compiled for larger administrative divisions and most of these were lost during the wars. In order to maintain tight control over the population and mobilize the available manpower for the war effort, the Japanese divided all villages into units of around twenty households with a population register maintained in each of these units. In addition, local officials had to approve all population movements and records were kept of arrivals and departures. All these regulations would have provided much information on population changes, but unfortunately only a fraction of the data were ever recovered.

The official 1940 population estimate for Indonesia as a whole was 70.4 million, for Java 48.4 million, and for the other Indonesian islands 22.0 million. These estimates were based on the assumption of a constant rate of increase after the census of 1930, and a further assumption of identical growth rates for Java and for the other islands. The official estimates for 1950, which were based on information supplied by local authorities, reported a population of 77.2 million for the whole of Indonesia: 50.5 million for Java and 26.7 million for the islands other than Java. These estimates imply an annual rate of increase during the forties of 9.2 per 1,000 persons for Indonesia as a whole, 4.1 per 1,000 persons for Java, and 19.5 per 1,000 persons for the other islands. The estimates for the Indonesian islands other than Java thus appear quite implausible. While it might well be true that during this period Java suffered even more severely from food shortages and population displacements than some of the other islands, it is nevertheless unlikely that the annual rate of population increase in the other islands could have been almost thirty per cent greater than their estimated rate of growth of around 15 per 1,000 persons during the thirties. It seems more likely that, like Java, the other Indonesian islands suffered a decline in their rate of population increase during the decade of the forties.

Estimates on Vital Rates in Java

Some data on vital rates for a number of regions of Java in the years 1943 and 1944 indicate a decrease in the number of births and an increase in the number of deaths so great that the estimated crude death rates surpassed the estimated crude birth rates.[1] Thus, the crude birth rate for the residency of Kedu in

[1] The data are given in Benedict R. O'G. Anderson, "Japan—The Light of Asia" in Josef Silverstein *et al.*, *Southeast Asia in World War II: Four Essays* (New Haven, 1966), p. 48. He cites "Tjatatan stenografis sidang Sanyo Kaigi ke-empat pada tanggal 8 bulan 1 2605" (Stenographic Report of the Fourth Session of the Sanyo Kaigi on the 8th of the 1st month of 2605 [February 3, 1945]), *Indische Collectie—Rijksinstituut voor Oorlogsdocumentatie* (Collection on the Indies—Royal Institute for War Documentation) (Amsterdam), doc. no. 036627, p. 3(a).

Central Java reportedly decreased from 31.5 per 1,000 persons for the first quarter of 1944 to 25.8 for the third quarter of the same year, while during the same period the crude death rate reportedly increased from 29.5 to 39.2 per 1,000 persons. For the residency of Pati, also in Central Java, the reported crude birth rate of 38.6 for 1939 decreased to 25.0 for the second quarter of 1944, while the crude death rate reportedly increased from 23.0 for the fourth quarter of 1943 to 38.0 for the second quarter of 1944. For the third quarter of 1944, the crude death rate of the regency of Purworedjo was 42.7 per 1,000 persons and that for Wanosobo was 53.7 (both regencies are in the residency of Kedu). These data were compiled during the Japanese occupation by the Department of Health probably from local reports based on returns of the registration system continued from before the war. While the reliability of these data is at least as questionable as the prewar data, they nevertheless seem to reflect the general tendency of declining fertility and increasing mortality during the first half of the forties.

In 1946 an article appeared by E. de Vries, entitled "Birth and Death during the Japanese Occupation." [2] In this de Vries reported some official statistics on births and deaths for the residency of Djakarta between January 1943 and May 1945. For Djakarta, what de Vries called the "normal crude birth and death rates"—the average rates as computed from official prewar statistics—were 28 and 16 per 1,000 persons respectively. The statistics for the years of the Japanese occupation indicated a decrease in the birth rate and an increase in the death rate, and in May 1945 the crude birth rate was reportedly 15 and the crude death rate 28 per 1,000 persons. Citing a magazine article as his source,[3] de Vries also supplied figures for the years 1943 and 1944 on births and deaths for all regions of Java. While not

[2] E. de Vries, "Geboorte en Sterfte onder de Japansche Bezetting" (Birth and Death during the Japanese Occupation), *Economisch Weekblad voor Nederlandsch-Indië*, 7th year, XII (1946), 60–61.

[3] *Mak'moer*, Vol. I, no. 2, Jan. 10, 1946, p. 49.

indicating the actual procedure of compiling these data, de Vries asserted that the population figures, on which the rates were based, were obtained from "administrative counts." For Java as a whole the crude birth rate in 1944 was found to be 25 and the crude death rate 33 per 1,000 persons. For the different regions the crude birth rate ranged from 16 to 30, and the crude death rate from 19 to 50. On the basis of the same data and applying the reported rates for Djakarta in 1945 to Java as a whole, W. Brand drew the inference that Java's population in 1946 was probably the same as it had been in 1941, since the increase in the years 1941–1943 had been canceled out by the decrease between 1944 and 1946.[4]

As the reliability of the information on which de Vries and Brand based their conjectures is not known, the figures they provide are consequently of only very limited value. As has been pointed out, however, living conditions deteriorated markedly during the Japanese occupation. The food supply for the civilian population was squeezed beyond the bare minimum, and large numbers of the people were compelled to become forced laborers in distant lands, many of them never returning to Indonesia. The result was a rapid increase in mortality, especially among infants and toddlers, matched by a decrease in fertility. Although the extent of these vital changes is not known, their existence can be seen from the age composition reported in the 1961 population census and also from other postwar data on the age composition of sample populations. These data show that the birth cohorts of the forties were comparatively small, indicating lower fertility, higher infant mortality, or both.

Thus, as shown in Table 27, the 1961 population census indicates that for Java as a whole the 20–24 years age group consisted of 5.1 million persons, the 15–19 years age group 4.8 million, the 10–14 years age group 5.1 million, and the 5–9 years

---

[4] W. Brand, "Het Bevolkingsvraagstuk op Java" (The Population Problem in Java), *Mensch en Maatschappij*, 23rd year, no. 1 (1947), pp. 35–36.

Table 27. Survivors of births of different years, Java, 1961

Age in 1961	Year of birth	No. of persons (in thous.)	% of total population
5–9	1952–1956	9,803	15.6
10–14	1947–1951	5,134	8.2
15–19	1942–1946	4,831	7.7
20–24	1937–1941	5,058	8.0

Source: Based on Biro Pusat Statistik, *Sensus Penduduk, 1961—
Seluruh Indonesia (Angka2 Sementara Hasil Pengolahan 1% Sample)*
(Population Census, 1961—All Indonesia [Preliminary Figures, 1
Per Cent Sample Tabulation]) (Djakarta, 1963).

age group 9.8 million. These persons were survivors of those
born between 1937–1941, 1942–1946, 1947–1951, and
1952–1956, respectively. The data show that the number of
survivors from those born between 1943 and 1946 was smaller
—or at the most as large as—the number of survivors from those
who were born five years earlier. On the other hand, the survivors of the births of 1947–1951 were only about 52 per cent of
the survivors of those born five years later. Allowing for some
inaccuracy in the census figures, the data still show clearly that
the number of survivors from births of the forties is exceptionally small when compared with the number of survivors of
preceding and succeeding periods.

Similar conclusions can also be drawn from the labor force
sample survey conducted in Java in 1958. As shown in Table 28,

Table 28. Survivors of births of different years, Java, 1958

Age in 1961	Year of birth	No. of persons (in thous.)	% of total population
5–9	1949–1953	7,980	14.3
10–14	1944–1948	4,721	8.4
15–19	1939–1943	4,701	8.4
20–24	1934–1938	4,362	8.0

Source: Based on Departemen Perburuhan, Republik Indonesia,
*Laporan Penjelidikan Angkatan Kerdja Berdasarkan Sample di Djawa
dan Madura* (Report on the Labor Force Sample Survey in Java
and Madura) (Djakarta, 1961).

the number of survivors of the births of 1944–1948 was around
60 per cent of the survivors of those born in 1949–1953. The
percentage differences between these figures and the census data
is due to the fact that the labor force sample covers the survivors
of births between 1949 and 1953, thus including those born
during the late forties, and the survivors of births between
1939–1943, including births before the Japanese occupation.

Other data on this period were provided by H. de Meel, who
referred to estimates of Scholte, which were actually conjectural.[5] According to Scholte, the rates of increase of Java's
population during the years 1942–1948 were successively 15.0,
7.5, 0.0, −10.0, −10.0, 0.0, and 0.0 per 1,000 persons. Primarily
on this basis de Meel conjectured that the total population was
50.1 million in 1942, 50.0 million in 1945, 49.3 million in 1948,
and 50.4 million in 1951. These guesses are rather questionable,
as their underlying assumption seems to be that the situation
during the second half of the forties was worse than that of the
previous years. Such an assumption is of doubtful validity.
While it is true that there were more casualties resulting directly
from the independence war, living conditions for the majority of
peasants had definitely improved over those prevailing during
the Japanese occupation. With the termination of the exorbitant
shipments of food to the Japanese armies, the people's food
supply increased. As to the level of food production, despite the
fact that the Dutch armed forces occupied the urban centers,
actual food production in the rural areas was apparently not
severely affected. At any rate, there was more food available for
the population than during the Japanese occupation. Therefore,
the assumption that during the latter half of the forties population growth was even smaller than during the first half appears
questionable. The impressions and observations of persons familiar with the events of the period indicate that at least as far as

[5] H. de Meel, "Demographic Dilemma in Indonesia," *Pacific Affairs*,
XXIV (1951), 266–283.

famine was concerned, the years 1944 and early 1945 were the worst of the decade.

Estimated Population Growth in the Indonesian Islands Other than Java

The events of the forties also had an impact on the fertility and mortality levels, and therefore on the growth of the population, of the other Indonesian islands. The various islands suffered to different degrees. In comparison with some of the other islands, Java may have suffered more from tremendous population displacements and severe food shortages, but it is possible that some other regions suffered at least equally. The 1961 census results give some indication of the extent of the changes in vital rates. As is shown in Table 29, the survivors of the births of 1947–1951 are much fewer than the survivors of those born in 1952–1956. On the other hand, the number of survivors of the

Table 29. Survivors of births of different years by region, Indonesia, 1961

Age in 1961	Yr. of birth	Java No. of persons *	% †	Sumatra No. of persons *	% †	Kalimantan No. of persons *	% †
5– 9	1952–1956	9.8	15.6	2.6	16.5	0.7	16.1
10–14	1947–1951	5.1	8.2	1.4	9.1	0.4	9.6
15–19	1942–1946	4.8	7.7	1.3	8.4	0.4	9.2
20–24	1937–1941	5.1	8.0	1.3	8.4	0.3	8.6

Age in 1961	Yr. of birth	Sulawesi No. of persons *	% †	Other islands No. of persons *	% †	Indonesia No. of persons *	% †
5– 9	1952–1956	1.2	17.3	1.0	16.2	15.3	15.9
10–14	1947–1951	0.7	9.4	0.5	8.4	8.2	8.5
15–19	1942–1946	0.7	9.2	0.5	8.3	7.7	8.0
20–24	1937–1941	0.6	8.2	0.5	7.5	7.8	8.1

* In millions.
† Percentage of total population of each region.
Source: Based on Biro Pusat Statistik, *Sensus Penduduk, 1961—Seluruh Indonesia* (*Angka2 Sementara Hasil Pengolahan 1% Sample*) (Population Census, 1961—All Indonesia [Preliminary Figures, 1 Per Cent Sample Tabulation]) (Djakarta, 1963).

births of 1942–1946 are similar to the survivors of those born during the previous five years. Thus, these data indicate that during the forties, as in Java, the other Indonesian islands also underwent an increase in mortality, a decrease in fertility, or both. A closer examination of the data, however, reveals certain differences between Java and the other islands. For Java, the proportion of persons aged 10–14 years—that is, those born in 1947–1951—is smaller than for any of the other islands. This also applies to those aged 15–19 years, that is, those born in 1942–1946. Moreover, unlike Java, the percentage of survivors from births between 1942 and 1946 in the other islands is higher than, or at least equal to, that of the survivors of births between 1937 and 1941, although the percentages of the two age groups are very similar. On the basis of these data the following inference seems to be plausible: during the decade 1940–1950, mortality levels in the Indonesian islands other than Java increased, very probably with a parallel decrease in fertility, resulting in a decline in the rate of population increase as compared to the preceding decade. The impact of the wars was, however, less severe in most of these islands than in Java, and therefore their rate of population growth during the forties was probably somewhat higher than Java's.

CHAPTER 8

The Population
of the Fifties

While the Japanese occupation and the war of independence caused abrupt changes in vital rates during the forties, the succeeding decade saw a gradual reversal in the course of fertility and mortality as these returned to their prewar levels. Food and such other essentials as textiles became more readily available, and the tremendous social dislocations and population displacements of the forties were eventually ended, although unrest and upheavals still prevailed in a number of regions.

Apart from the improvement in the food situation, another important factor that contributed toward population growth was the vigorous health campaign conducted throughout the fifties. The campaign to eradicate malaria was particularly successful and was in large part responsible for the rapid decline in the mortality level. At the same time the low fertility rate of the forties was restored to its prewar level. As a result there was a tremendous population upsurge during the fifties, particularly among the very young age groups.

Population Size and Population Growth

The official population estimate for Indonesia as a whole in 1950 was 77.2 million: for Java 50.5 million and for the other Indonesian islands 26.7 million.[1] These estimates were compiled

[1] *Statistical Pocketbook of Indonesia, 1963* (Djakarta, 1963), p. 11.

from local reports, based on information supplied by the village heads, who kept population registers and maintained records on births, deaths, and migration. In the early fifties, the concepts and procedures used in compiling these were not uniform, and although the methods improved during the decade, the breadth and accuracy of the data continued to vary substantially from one area to another. In general, the population records for most regions of Java were more reliable than for the rest of the country. But even in areas of Java the population registers were often quite deficient. Therefore, the regional figures for the period 1950–1960 are less than satisfactory, and the reliability of the population estimates for the country as a whole are consequently questionable.

The 1961 census gave a total population of 97.0 million for the whole of Indonesia, 63.0 million for Java, and 34.0 million for the rest of the country. Based on the 1950 population estimates and the 1961 census figures, new official population estimates for the different years of the fifties were calculated and published.[2] These calculations were based on some simple assumptions: it was assumed that in 1951 the population of Indonesia as a whole increased by around 20 per 1,000 persons a year and that the rate of population increase grew annually to a level of 23.0 per 1,000 persons in 1961; for Java the population growth in 1951 was assumed to be 19.3 per 1,000 persons, reaching 22.4 per 1,000 persons by 1961; for the rest of the country the rate of population growth was assumed to increase from 20.9 per 1,000 persons in 1951 to 24.1 per 1,000 persons in 1961. From these assumptions resulted the population estimates for the years between 1950 and 1960 shown in Table 30. In using these official population figures of the fifties, the underlying simple assumptions must always be fully allowed for. For example, if they are to be used as deflators or to calculate the per capita output or per capita

[2] *Ibid.*, p. 11.

consumption of certain commodities, it has to be remembered that these assumptions discounted the possibility of a constant rate of population growth during any part of the decade.

It is actually quite reasonable to assume that there was a continuous increase in the rate of population growth during the fifties, since the rate of fertility had returned to its prewar level

Table 30. Official estimates of total population, Indonesia, 1950–1962 (in thousands)

Year (end)	Java	Other islands	Indonesia
1950	50,456	26,751	77,207
1951	51,430	27,311	78,741
1952	52,437	27,892	80,329
1953	53,480	28,493	81,973
1954	54,560	29,116	83,676
1955	55,679	29,761	85,440
1956	56,837	30,430	87,267
1957	58,037	31,123	89,160
1958	59,280	31,842	91,122
1959	60,567	32,586	93,153
1960	61,901	33,358	95,259
1961 (census)	62,993	34,026	97,019
1961	63,289	34,161	97,450
1962	64,597	34,983	99,580

Source: Statistical Pocketbook of Indonesia, 1963 (Djakarta, 1963), p. 11 (1961 census figures revised).

while a continuous decline in the general level of mortality resulted from the intensive public health campaign. The success of this campaign not only was due to the great resources poured into its programs, but more importantly was a result of its positive public reception. With independence and the ensuing large-scale efforts in the field of public education there was an increasing awareness of alternative opportunities, which led to rising demands for more and better facilities in both education and public health.

In 1930, Java had about 68 per cent of the total population of Indonesia, while in 1961 this proportion dropped to around 65 per cent. It thus appears that the population of the other islands was increasing more rapidly than that of Java. One notable feature of the Indonesian population is its very unequal distribution. Thus, as shown in Table 31, while almost 85 per cent of the total area had an average population density in 1952 of less than 50 persons per square kilometer, only 8.25 per cent had a density of 200 persons or more. On the other hand, almost 60 per cent of the total population lived in areas with an average population density of 200 persons or more per square kilometer, while at the

Table 31. Average population densities, Indonesia, 1952

Average population density per sq. km.	Area (as % of total area)	Population (as % of total population)
600 +	.45	6.2
400–599	1.9	16.9
200–399	5.9	35.9
100–199	2.9	7.6
50–99	4.1	5.0
0–49	84.5	19.4

Source: The Population of Indonesia: A Statement Prepared by the Indonesian Participants to the United Nations Seminar on Population in Asia and the Far East (Bandung, 1955), p. 2.

same time only about 20 per cent were in areas with an average population density of less than 50 persons. Although Java has a higher population density than most of the other islands, its rural population is not evenly distributed. As Karl Pelzer has pointed out, the differences in population densities in Java are related to the fertility of the soil and are an example of the relation between geology, soils, irrigation, and population.[3]

In addition to the unequal distribution, there is the phenomenon of growth differentials between the different regions. Part of the growth differentials is undoubtedly due to differences in natural increase, but part is also the result of migration within the country. There is very little information, however, regarding the direction and extent of internal migration. Some indication of its existence can be obtained by comparing the

[3] Karl J. Pelzer, "Physical and Human Resource Patterns" in *Indonesia*, ed. Ruth T. McVey (New Haven, 1963), pp. 17–19.

population growth of different regencies, using the population figures for 1930 and the estimates for 1952–1954.[4] For this period of around twenty-three years, 17 out of a total of 161 regencies had an increase of more than 60 per cent, 35 regencies had an increase of between 0 and 20 per cent, and 11 regencies showed population decreases. Most of the regions with high increases were in Sumatra (primarily South Sumatra, resulting from the settlement of people from Java), while almost all the regencies with population decreases were in Central and East Java.

During this period the urban areas experienced a rapid population growth. The population of Djakarta increased from 533,000 in 1930 to around 1.8 million in 1955, while the population of other cities also increased, although not as rapidly as in the capital. A sample survey was conducted by the Institute of Economic and Social Research of the University of Indonesia in 1954 on the process of urbanization of the city of Djakarta.[5] In his report on this survey, H. J. Heeren pointed out that one-third of the 1954 population of Djakarta had arrived in the city within the previous four years. Thus, about 100,000 persons moved annually into the capital. About 60 per cent of these came from West Java and 30 per cent from Central Java, particularly from Pekalongan, Tegal, and Jogjakarta, while only 7 per cent came from the other islands. The larger part of the migrants moved directly to the city, without intermediary stages. About one-third of the migrants had been peasants, and in the city most of them were employed in manufacturing industries and transportation. With respect to their distribution in the city, it was reported that migrants with similar occupations or those origi-

[4] *The Population of Indonesia: A Statement Prepared by the Indonesian Participants to the United Nations Seminar on Population in Asia and the Far East* (Bandung, 1955), p. 8.

[5] Lembaga Penjelidikan Ekonomi dan Masjarakat, Universitet Indonesia, "Urbanisasi Djakarta" (Urbanisation of Djakarta) (a report of the Institute of Economic and Social Research, Faculty of Economics, University of Indonesia), in *Ekonomi dan Keuangan Indonesia*, VIII, no. 3 (March 1955), 107–151.

nating from the same region tended to live in the same areas. On the other hand, it was found that many of the second-generation migrants already called themselves Djakartanese rather than Sundanese or Javanese.

The Transmigration Scheme

The reactions of the Republican government of the fifties toward the discrepancies in population distribution were quite similar to those of the prewar government. After 1950, resettlement to the other islands, now called transmigration, was considered desirable both as a means of providing employment opportunities for Java's landless peasants and as a method of furnishing other islands with the necessary labor force.

The procedure of resettlement was that after the necessary surveys had been completed, the areas designated for settlements were cleared, and roads, irrigation works, and temporary housing units were built. The prospective settlers, who in the meantime were registered and selected by government agencies in Java, received free transportation to the settlements and two hectares of partly cleared land. Until the first harvest (six or eight months) they also received food, clothing, household utensils, seeds, and simple agricultural equipment, all of which they were ultimately obliged to pay for. Most of these settlements were located in South Sumatra; the rest were spread over Central Sumatra, Kalimantan, Sulawesi, and Maluku. The annual number of these government-organized settlers increased from ten thousand to fifty thousand persons during the 1950's.

Despite the emphasis placed by the government on transmigration, budgets for financing this scheme were always limited. But the main problem seemed to be the organization rather than the financing of the program. Resettlement is a many-sided venture. While the government assumed a central role in every aspect of resettlement, there was for years no definite delineation of responsibilities of the different government agencies with regard to the scheme. The Department of Transmigration set up

in 1950 never had sole responsibility for the entire undertaking
—in the sense that a "regional development authority" might
have had. Furthermore, its coordination with other agencies such
as those responsible for the building of roads and irrigation
works was far from satisfactory. This organizational deficiency
resulted in bottlenecks and wasteful duplications. Among the
more serious consequences were shortage of irrigation works
and transportation facilities. Since most of the settlements were
designed on the basis of wet cultivation, proper irrigation played
a decisive role. Transportation facilities were insufficient not
only between Java and the other islands, but also locally between new and older settlements and between the newly settled
areas and the more populous areas of the same region. There
were instances where settlements had to be abandoned because
deficiencies in initial soil surveys led to an erroneous choice of
the areas. In other cases, settlers moved to other areas because
inadequate water supplies resulted in meager crops. On the other
hand, there were settlements with abundant food crops that the
settlers were not able to sell because of the lack of proper
marketing facilities.

There were several ways in which this transmigration differed
from the prewar colonization. For example, while the prewar
policy had been to separate the Javanese settlements from the
locally populated areas, there was now a provision that new
settlements were open to migrants from Java as well as to the
indigenous population from the surrounding areas. Instead of
separate elementary schools for the different population groups
each with their own language, there was now only one type of
school, which used the Indonesian language. Where prewar
colonists received only one hectare of land, transmigrants now
received two hectares of land for each family. Despite these
changes, there were in fact more similarities than differences
between the two programs. Although the official policy referred
to the need of "balanced" development between agriculture and
industry for the settlements, actually all postwar settlements

were based on agriculture and almost all on wet cultivation, as are the majority of villages on Java. Almost all features of the prewar settlements (method of cultivation, kind of crop, physical layout, village government, traditions and institutions) were followed in the new settlements.

Some of the other migrants were called "spontaneous transmigrants." These were the people who migrated from Java to the settlement areas in South Sumatra entirely at their own expense instead of being moved by the government. Some were relatives of older settlers. Initially they stayed with their relatives and worked for them. Meanwhile they also worked on land that they received from the government, and after the first harvest they were entirely on their own. It has been estimated that some 20,000 to 30,000 persons migrated annually in this way from Java to South Sumatra.[6] The greatest difficulty they faced seems to have been lack of adequate transportation facilities from the populous regions of Central and East Java to the settlements in South Sumatra. The migrants had to stop over in Djakarta, a delay that added considerably to their financial burden, and many of them had to find employment there to meet the extra cost or else return to their villages. This situation clearly had an adverse effect on the willingness of others to follow them.

Data on Sex-Age Composition

Knowledge concerning the sex-age composition of the population in this decade is available from the results of a number of surveys. For Java the official estimate of the 1957 population based on local reports gives a sex ratio of 93.4 males per 100 females, as compared to 95.5 in 1930. This preponderance of females existed in all major administrative divisions, with the exception of the Djakarta area, where the sex ratio was 102.2

[6] Djoko Santoso and Ali Wardhana, *Some Aspects of Spontaneous Transmigration in Indonesia* (a report by the Institute for Economic and Social Research) (Djakarta, 1957), p. 10.

males to 100 females. This is very likely due to a higher proportion of male immigrants into the city.

With regard to age distribution, K. Horstmann has concluded
that because of the events of the forties the proportion of children in certain age groups was probably exceptionally low.[7] A
number of studies bear out this conclusion, including three sample surveys carried out in a demonstration and study center for
public health in Djakarta during 1956–1957 [8] (see Table 32). In
each of these surveys the proportion of children aged 10–14
years was around 9 per cent of the total population, while the
age groups 5–9 and 15–19 years represented about 12 and 10 to
11 per cent respectively. Since the persons aged 10–14 years
were the survivors of the birth cohorts 1942–1947, this dent in
the age pyramid is an indication of either a lessening of fertility
or an increase in infant mortality, or both, during that period.
The proportion of persons aged less than 15 years was consequently less or certainly not much higher than 40 per cent.
These three surveys show this proportion as respectively 38.4,
39.2, and 40.9 per cent.

In the three surveys in Djakarta the age group 15–20 years
also showed some dent in the age pyramid, but in this case there
is an asymmetry between males and females: in each of the three
populations the dent is more pronounced for the males than for
the females, probably because of age differentials in net in-migration into the city. It is quite likely that a greater number of
female immigrants were younger than the male immigrants. The

[7] K. Horstmann, "The Exceptionally Small Number of Children in
Indonesia," *Ekonomi dan Keuangan Indonesia*, IX, no. 12 (Dec. 1956),
209–212.

[8] R. Mochtar and R. Soedarjono, "A General Public Health Survey
within the Demonstration and Study Centre for Public Health &
Preventive Medicine in Djakarta-City," *Madjalah Kedokteran Indone-
sia*, VII, no. 12 (Dec. 1957), 375–399; R. Mochtar, "A General Public
Health Survey in the Tanah Tinggi Ward, Djakarta, March 1957,"
Madjalah Kedokteran Indonesia, VIII, no. 12, Dec. 1958), 349–391; R.
Mochtar and Hertonobroto, "A Public Health Study in Djakarta"
(mimeo., n.d.).

Age group	Subdistrict Senen				Block D (Tanah-Tinggi)				Subdistrict Salemba			
	Male	Female	Both sexes No.	%	Male	Female	Both sexes No.	%	Male	Female	Both sexes No.	%
0–4	2,866	1,793	3,659	16.8	762	696	1,458	18.5	1,239	1,263	2,502	18.3
5–9	1,341	1,347	2,668	12.2	475	451	926	11.8	874	864	1,738	12.7
10–14	1,028	1,029	2,057	9.4	348	349	697	8.9	596	553	1,149	8.4
15–19	1,166	1,270	2,436	11.2	354	434	788	10.0	716	724	1,440	10.5
20–24	1,115	1,219	2,334	10.7	356	468	824	10.5	665	739	1,404	10.3
25–29	1,021	1,094	2,115	9.7	375	438	813	10.3	713	792	1,505	11.0
30–34	860	797	1,657	7.6	355	303	658	8.3	616	488	1,104	8.1
35–39	775	632	1,407	6.5	324	275	599	7.6	533	406	939	6.9
40–44	512	505	1,017	4.7	215	159	374	4.7	335	301	636	4.6
45–49	395	357	752	3.4	128	90	218	2.8	224	186	410	3.0
50–54	342	330	672	3.1	103	86	189	2.4	185	151	336	2.5
55–59	184	160	344	1.6	76	42	118	1.5	91	78	169	1.2
60–64	127	171	298	1.4	47	53	100	1.3	102	88	190	1.4
65–69	60	69	129	0.6	25	29	54	0.7	31	38	69	0.5
70–74	56	83	139	0.6	11	21	32	0.4	17	29	46	0.3
75–79	11	22	33	0.1	6	5	11	0.1	8	6	14	0.1
80–84	9	19	28	0.1	3	7	10	0.1	6	13	19	0.1
85+	3	17	20	0.1	4	2	6	0.1	7	8	15	0.1
Unknown	1	2	3		2	1	3					
Total, all ages	10,872	10,896	21,768	100.0	3,969	3,909	7,878	100.0	6,958	6,727	13,685	100.0

Source: R. Mochtar and R. Soedarjono, "A General Public Health Survey within the Demonstration and Study Centre for Public Health & Preventive Medicine in Djakarta-City," *Madjalah Kedokteran Indonesia*, VII, no. 12 (Dec. 1957), 381; R. Mochtar, "A General Public Health Survey in Tanah Tinggi Ward, Djakarta, March 1957," *Madjalah Kedokteran Indonesia*, VIII, no. 12 (Dec. 1958), 368; R. Mochtar and Hertonobroto, "A Public Health Study in Djakarta" (mimeo, n.d.), table 1.

large number of persons aged less than five years is no doubt an indication of the upsurge of fertility and the decline in mortality during the fifties. The high degree of migration into the city is also indicated by the fact that far more than half of the population included in the survey of the subdistrict of Salemba was reported to have arrived in the city not earlier than 1950. The labor force sample survey conducted in Java by the Department of Labor [9] also provided data on sex-age composi-

Table 33. Estimated population by sex and age, based on labor force sample survey, Java, 1958 (in thousands)

Age group	Male	Female	Both sexes
0–1	632	557	1,189
1–4	3,948	4,044	7,992
5–9	3,945	4,035	7,980
10–14	2,592	2,129	4,721
15–19	2,433	2,268	4,701
20–24	1,773	2,589	4,362
25–29	2,287	3,216	5,503
30–34	2,106	2,303	4,409
35–39	2,277	1,957	4,234
40–44	1,499	1,613	3,112
45–49	1,267	1,235	2,502
50–54	1,033	1,058	2,091
55–59	725	609	1,334
60–64	563	624	1,187
65+	593	654	1,247
Total, all ages	27,673	28,891	56,564

Source: Departemen Perburuhan, Republik Indonesia, Laporan Penjelidikan Angkatan Kerdja Berdasarkan Sample di Djawa dan Madura (Report on the Labor Force Sample Survey in Java and Madura) (Djakarta, 1961), table 3.

tion. By applying the results of this sample survey to Java as a whole, its total population was estimated at 56.6 million in 1958. As shown in Table 33, there was a large difference between the number of persons aged 5–9 years (almost 8 million) and those aged 10–14 years (4.7 million), further bearing out the results of

[9] Departemen Perburuhan, Republik Indonesia, Laporan Penjelidikan Angkatan Kerdja Berdasarkan Sample di Djawa dan Madura (Report on the Labor Force Sample Survey in Java and Madura) (Djakarta, 1961).

the other surveys with regard to the impact of the events of the forties on fertility and on infant and child mortality.[10] Another study carried out during 1954 and 1955 by the Institute of Economic and Social Research in twenty-three Javanese villages showed that 33.7 to 45.2 per cent of the villagers were less than fifteen years old.[11] The 15–59 age group comprised 51.2 to 64.2 per cent of the population, while those aged 60 years and older ranged between 0.1 to 3.5 per cent. In most of these villages there were between 60 and 90 persons aged either less than fifteen or sixty and over, as against every 100 persons aged between fifteen and fifty-nine. It was found that in most villages there were more women than men. This was true for the total population as well as for those aged fifteen years or over. In two villages the ratio was between 907 and 999 per thousand females, and in six villages there were more men than women. This preponderance of females over males is consistent with the results of the labor force sample survey, which shows a sex ratio of 958 men per 1,000 women. The 1961 population census gives a sex ratio of 957 males per 1,000 females for Java, and 973 for the whole country.

The Labor Force Sample Survey in Java

In the latter part of 1958 the Department of Labor conducted a labor force sample survey in Java.[12] It was preceded by a

[10] The rather large number of persons aged 25–29 years as compared to the preceding and succeeding age groups may very well be an indication of deficiencies in age reporting, since information on age is always subject to certain errors. Also, the very low sex ratio for the 20–24 years age group (68.5 males per 100 females) may point to over- or under-enumeration in that age group, or to misreporting of ages.

[11] J. E. Ismael, *Keadaan Penduduk di Duapuluhtiga Desa di Djawa* (The Population of Twenty-three Villages in Java), Institute of Economic and Social Research, Faculty of Economics, University of Indonesia (Djakarta, 1960), pp. 11–12, 15–17.

[12] Departemen Perburuhan, Republik Indonesia, *op. cit.* Reports on the preceding surveys include: Direktorat Tenaga Kerdja Kementerian Perburuhan, Republik Indonesia "Laporan Penjelidikan Angkatan

number of local surveys on the labor force starting in 1956 in the city and regency of Sukabumi (West Java), the city of Bandung (West Java), the district of Wurjantoro (Central Java), the city of Menado and the regency of Minahasa (Sulawesi). The survey, which covered the whole island of Java, had among its objectives estimating the size and composition of the working-age population, the components of the labor force employed in different economic activities, and the degree of unemployment and underemployment. For this purpose a sample of 12,000 households was drawn, consisting of 10,700 households in the rural areas and 1,300 households in urban centers. The results were then applied to the total population of Java, which was calculated to be 56.56 million, out of which 48.34 million were estimated to live in the rural areas and the remaining 8.22 million in the urban areas. It was furthermore estimated that there were 11.37 million households in the rural areas and 1.71 million in the urban centers. Thus, the average number of persons in a rural household was 4.3, as against 4.8 in an urban household. The larger size of the urban household can also be seen from the actual survey, which shows that in rural areas households comprising five persons or less accounted for 76.6 per cent of the total number of households, while the percentage for urban households was 67.5. The percentage of rural households comprising six persons or less was in each case larger than the corresponding percentage of urban households, while for households of seven persons or more it was always smaller. This difference may be indicative of the ongoing process of urbanization, as the survey report suggests, but in addition it may also be

Kerdja Berdasarkan Sample Daerah Kota Besar dan Kabupaten Suka-
bumi" (Report on the Labor Force Sample Survey in the City and
Regency of Sukabumi), in *Ekonomi dan Keuangan Indonesia*, XI nos.
3–4 (March–April 1958), 115–157; Kementerian Perburuhan, Republik
Indonesia, *Laporan Penjelidikan Angkatan Kerdja Berdasarkan Sample
Kotabesar Bandung* (Report on the Labor Force Sample Survey in the
City of Bandung) (Djakarta, 1958).

a very rough indication of lower mortality levels in urban areas, which would result in larger households.

In comparing the data on the rural and urban labor forces, it has to be remembered that the time period involved was one year for the rural areas and one week for the urban areas, which suggests that these data are not quite comparable. For the rural areas of Java the labor force was estimated at 24.15 million persons (13.52 million males and 10.63 million females), which amounted to almost 50 per cent of the total rural population, or 76.3 per cent of the rural population aged twelve years and

Table 34. Estimated rural labor force by sex and age group, Java, 1958
(in millions and percentages)

	Male		Female		Both sexes	
Age group	No. (in mills.)	% of male labor force	No. (in mills.)	% of female labor force	No. (in mills.)	% of total labor force
12–14	0.56	4.1	0.31	2.9	0.87	3.6
15–24	2.66	19.7	2.38	22.4	5.04	20.9
25–44	6.95	51.4	5.60	52.7	12.55	52.0
45+	3.35	24.8	2.34	22.0	5.69	23.6
Total, age 12 and over	13.52	100.0	10.63	100.0	24.15	100.0

Source: Departemen Perburuhan, Republik Indonesia, Laporan Penjelidikan Angkatan Kerdja Berdasarkan Sample di Djawa dan Madura (Report on the Labor Force Sample Survey in Java and Madura) (Djakarta, 1961), table 7.

older. To the labor force belonged 57.12 per cent of the male population and 43.09 per cent of the female population. The age distribution of the rural labor force is shown in Table 34. A little more than half of the total labor force belonged to the age group 25–44 years, while only less than 4 per cent were between 12 and 14 years old. As is to be expected, the majority (70 per cent) of the rural labor force were engaged in agriculture and related activities, about 11 per cent were in trade, and manufacturing came third with around 8 per cent (see Table 35). According to the survey, about one-fourth of the labor force had two occupations, mainly in the field of agriculture, while the remainder had only one occupation.

The survey gave a total of 2.82 million persons belonging to the urban labor force, amounting to about one-third of the urban population. Out of this number two million were male and the rest female. The male labor force accounted for about half of the total male urban population, while, unlike its counterpart in the rural areas, the female labor force consisted of only 20 per cent of the female population of the urban areas. Almost

Table 35. Estimated rural and urban labor force by economic activity, Java, 1958

Economic activity	Rural		Urban	
	No. of persons (in mills.)	% of labor force	No. of persons (in mills.)	% of labor force
Agriculture *	16.81	70.2	0.12	4.6
Mining	0.04	0.2		
Manufacturing	2.00	8.3	0.61	23.3
Construction †	0.27	1.1	0.13	5.0
Trade	2.72	11.4	0.73	27.9
Transportation	0.25	1.0	0.21	8.0
Services	1.86	7.8	0.82	31.3
Total, all activities	23.95	100.0	2.62	100.0

* Includes forestry, fishing, and animal husbandry
† Includes electricity
Source: Departemen Perburuhan, Republik Indonesia, *Laporan Penjelidikan Angkatan Kerdja Berdasarkan Sample di Djawa dan Madura* (Report on the Labor Force Sample Survey in Java and Madura) (Djakarta, 1961), tables 9 and 21.

55 per cent of the urban labor force belonged to the 25–44 years age group and only 1 per cent were between 12 and 14 years old. As can be seen from Table 34, about one-third of the labor force was engaged in services, more than one-fourth in trade and related activities, a little less than one-fourth in manufacturing, and about 8 per cent in transportation.

The survey report also contains data on the extent of unemployment and underemployment. In the rural areas it was reported that only 0.83 per cent of the labor force was unemployed, most of these being new entrants into the labor force, while in the urban areas unemployment amounted to 7 per cent of the labor force, with half of them belonging to the 15–24 age group. This information, however, is only of limited value. As in most agricultural economies, the usual concept of unemployment is quite meaningless, since the actual problem is rather underemployment. In this respect the survey also provides some information. In the rural areas it reported that 15.74 million persons aged twelve years and over worked during the peak season in an agricultural year. Out of this number, more than seven million worked seven or more hours a day, and 1.27 million worked only one to three hours a day. In contrast, during the slack season of the agricultural year, out of the 13.3 million workers only 0.47 million worked seven hours or more a day, 4.7 million between four and six hours, and more than 8 million worked only between one and three hours a day. On the basis of these data, the report inferred that unemployment in agriculture amounted to about one-third of the potential man-hour resources—that is, one-third of the total number of man-hours of work by the agricultural labor force during the peak season, assuming they were at work for seven hours a day and 305 days a year.

Data on Vital Rates: Fertility and Mortality

In 1950 the registration of births and deaths, which was discontinued during the forties, resumed, and it was reported that in 1952 data on vital statistics were collected in nearly all regencies of Java.[13] In principle, the procedure followed was similar to that of the thirties. The village heads were in charge of issuing birth and death certificates, with copies for the village records and for the higher administrative offices.[14] From the published

[13] R. Mochtar, *Health Education and Rural Health Problems in Indonesia* (Djakarta, 1953), p. 32.
[14] Nathan Keyfitz and Widjojo Nitisastro, *Soal Penduduk dan Pembangunan Indonesia* (Population Problems and the Development of Indonesia) (Djakarta, 1955), pp. 41, 48.

materials, for 1958 the crude birth rate for the different regions ranged from 11.7 to 51.1 per 1,000 persons, while the crude death rates were between 4.4 and 21.3. That the reliability of these data is limited can be seen from the warnings at the beginning of every issue of these reports, wherein it was stated that "the annual birth and death rates are not based on the actual number of such occurrences within a year, but on the numbers recorded by the village heads within that year," that "the registration in each regency is approximately 50 per cent of the actual number of births and deaths," that "crude birth rates of less than 30 and crude death rates of less than 15 per 1,000 persons are to be considered unreliable," and so on.[15] Since both components of these rates, the numerator and the denominator, are of limited reliability, it is not always certain that the higher rates are more dependable. Under-registration of births and deaths and also of the total population might result in rates that are seemingly plausible. Nevertheless, data for a number of regencies, among which is Wonosobo, have a reputation for accuracy. In 1958 the crude birth rate for Wonosobo was 51.1 and the crude death rate 21.3 per 1,000 persons. During the same year only five other regencies were reported to have crude birth rates of 40 or more, of which the highest was 43.1. Thus, even for these areas with high crude birth rates the Wonosobo figure was exceptional. All six of these regencies are located in Central Java, where the improved registration system had already been in vogue for some time, one other reason for attaching greater credence to the results. The crude death rate for Wonosobo in 1958 was found to be 21.3, but despite their plausible birth rates some of the other five regencies showed crude death rates that appear too low: 10.2, 12.3, 13.6. Since, as is pointed out in the reports on vital statistics, crude death rates of less than 15 are to

[15] E.g., Bagian Statistik, Kementerian Kesehatan, Republik Indonesia, *Laporan Kelahiran & Kematian, Tahunan, 1958, Daerah Djawa dan Madura* (Report on Births and Deaths, Yearly, 1958, Java and Madura) (Djakarta, 1959).

be considered questionable, and since it is known from the registration of other populations that the coverage of death registration is usually more complete than that of births, it appears that even in these regencies the available data were still quite defective. There seems to be no doubt that as a result of the concerted efforts in health improvement the mortality level decreased during this decade, but it seems unlikely that it reached as low a level as is indicated by the data. With the exception of Wonosobo, none of the regencies was reported to have a crude death rate of 20 or more in 1958. Only fourteen out of about a hundred regencies were reported to have a crude death rate of 15 or more.

The reports on mortality and fertility also contained data on infant mortality rates, which for 1958 ranged from 21.3 to 178.4 per 1,000 births. The highest infant mortality rates, those of Djakarta (170.6) and Surabaja (178.4), were accompanied by very low crude birth rates (23.8 for Djakarta and 23.4 for Surabaja), which probably explain the high levels of infant mortality. For Wonosobo the infant mortality rate was 148.1 per 1,000 births.

The three studies on health conditions in Djakarta made some estimates of the fertility and mortality levels. The area included in these studies comprised the subdistricts of Senen and Salemba. The first study took a 25 per cent sample of the population of Senen, and the second surveyed the total population of a limited area within Salemba. Each subdistrict comprised a number of *kelurahan* (wards), which in turn were divided into several *kampung* (blocks). The area studied was block D of the Tanah Tinggi ward, which was the area covered by the prewar study on hygiene reported by Tesch. The third survey was a 10 per cent sample of the whole population of the Salemba subdistrict.

Information on past births and deaths was supplied by the sample households. It was reported that in the Salemba subdistrict the annual crude birth and death rates were 40.4 and 12.8 respectively. The rates found in the other surveys are shown in

Table 36. Leaving sampling problems aside, the reliability of the reported vital events depends very much on the probing techniques used in the interviews. When the rates found in the surveys are compared with those computed from the registration data of the civil service, it can be seen that in all three surveys the crude birth rates are higher than those computed from the registration data, while at the same time the crude death rates

Table 36. Crude birth rates and crude death rates per 1,000 persons, computed from survey and from registration data, two subdistricts in Djakarta, 1956, 1957

	Crude birth rate		Crude death rate	
Subdistrict	Survey data *	Registration data *	Survey data *	Registration data *
Senen	42.1	32.3	12.5	16.2
Salemba	40.4	28.9	12.8	15.4
(Block D)	(38.0)	(32.4)	(16.0)	(21.1)

* For Senen the survey data refer to 1956, and the registration data to 1955. For Salemba, and also Block D, the survey data refer to 1957, the registration data to 1956.

Source: R. Mochtar and R. Soedarjono, "A General Public Health Survey within the Demonstration and Study Centre for Public Health & Preventive Medicine in Djakarta-City," *Madjalah Kedokteran Indonesia,* VII, no. 12 (Dec. 1957), 383; R. Mochtar, "A General Public Health Survey in Tanah Tinggi Ward, Djakarta, March 1957," *Madjalah Kedokteran Indonesia,* VIII, no. 12 (Dec. 1958), 377; R. Mochtar and Hertonobroto, "A Public Health Study in Djakarta" (mimeo., n.d.), table 13.

reported in the surveys are consistently lower. As has been noted earlier, death registration in the cities was accompanied by a compulsory death examination. It seems very likely that this factor resulted in the death registration's being more reliable than the information in the surveys on the number of deaths, although this does not imply that death registration was anywhere near complete.

Another fertility index supplied in these surveys was the child-woman ratio, that is, the number of children under five per woman of childbearing age (15–44 years). For the subdistrict of

Senen the ratio was 0.66, for the subdistrict of Salemba 0.73. These ratios would indicate that the fertility level in Senen was somewhat lower than in Salemba. From a comparison of the crude birth rates shown in the surveys, however, it appears that the reverse was the case (Senen, 42.1; Salemba, 40.4). These conflicting results are partly due to the fact that the child-woman ratio is not a true index of fertility. The numerator consists of children who are survivors of births in the past. In other words, this ratio includes the effects of infant and child mortality. Thus, if between two populations one has a higher fertility level but also a higher level of infant and child mortality, this population might exhibit a lower child-woman ratio than the other.

In his report on the population of twenty-three Javanese villages, J. E. Ismael stated that the child-woman ratio in most of these villages ranged from 600 to 1,000 children per 1,000 women at reproductive ages, that the fertility of completed marriages was between 4,000 and 6,000 children per 1,000 ever-married women aged forty years and over, and that the average number of children born to ever-married women ranged from 2.4 to 5.5.[16]

On the basis of the available data on vital registration, de Haas inferred that most probably the crude birth rate during the fifties was about 40 per 1,000 persons, the crude death rate 15 to 20 per 1,000 persons, and the infant mortality rate 100 to 200 per 1,000 births. He pointed out that his estimate of the rate of natural increase (20 to 25 per 1,000 persons) was higher than the official estimates (15 to 20 per 1,000 persons) because of his impression that "the death rate seems to be lower than before the

---

[16] Ismael, *op. cit.*, pp. 8–10. The population of one of these villages is also described in Widjojo Nitisastro, "Some Data on the Population of Djabres—A Village in Central-Java: A Report of the Institute for Economic and Social Research, Faculty of Economics, University of Indonesia," in *Ekonomi dan Keuangan Indonesia*, IX, no. 12 (Dec. 1956), 759–784.

war, while the birth rate has not changed or has become somewhat higher." [17]

In estimating the vital rates for this period, it seems that satisfactory results cannot be obtained by relying merely on the existing vital registration, although throughout the decade many improvements were made in both the coverage and the accuracy of this data. As Tan Goan Tiang has rightly pointed out, collection of vital statistics, particularly on births, is a continuous activity that demands accuracy and constant attention, unlike a census, which is an "einmalig" activity within a certain period. [18] Particularly where the degree of accuracy of both the numerator and the denominator of the ratios is not known, data on vital rates based on the collection of statistics need to be supplemented by other methods. The availability of the 1961 population census data now makes it possible to draw inferences concerning the level of fertility during the fifties. While the use of census data should be considered as a substitute for vital statistics based on accurate registration, they have the advantage of consistency and coherence with the general structure and the dynamics of the population.

In the absence of a significant amount of in-migration and out-migration, the age structure of a population in a certain year is a logical reflection of the course of fertility and mortality in preceding periods. Thus, on the basis of the age distribution of the 1961 population Kartono Gunawan made estimates of the fertility level in preceding years. Applying the theory of stable and quasi-stable populations and using the United Nations model life tables, he developed a number of hypothetical age structures

[17] J. H. de Haas, *Maternal and Child Health Survey in Indonesia* (*Java, Bali and Sumatra*) (n.p., 1955), pp. 8–9.

[18] Tan Goan Tiang, "Peranan Fertilitas Dalam Perkembangan Penduduk dan Pembangunan Ekonomi" (The Role of Fertility in Population Growth and Economic Development), in Institute of Economic and Social Research, Faculty of Economics, University of Indonesia, *Workshop Masalah Penduduk* (Workshop on Population Problems) (Djakarta, 1964).

with alternative levels of mortality—as reflected by the expectation of life at birth—and alternative rates of population growth. Thus, for each combination of expectation of life at birth and rate of population increase there is a corresponding definite age structure and certain level of fertility. For example, a combination of an expectation of life at birth of 42.5 years and a rate of population growth of respectively 15, 20, 25, and 30 per 1,000 persons has a corresponding birth rate of respectively 36.9, 41.7, 46.8, and 53.0 per 1,000 persons, and each of these combinations results in a certain age distribution of the population. By comparing the age distribution of the 1961 population with these hypothetical age structures for various levels of expectation of life at birth, a choice is then made as to the most appropriate rate of population increase. For this rate of increase there is also a corresponding fertility level. Thus, by comparing the age structure of the actual population with the hypothetical age distributions, the most appropriate or consistent fertility level is found. Whenever no perfect matching is achieved (in the sense of identical proportions of persons under certain ages)—as is to be expected in most cases—intrapolations are used to arrive at the appropriate fertility level. This method led Kartono Gunawan to arrive at an estimate of the birth rate of 45 to 46 per 1,000 persons.[19]

The 1961 population census included data on the number of children by single year of age, from under one year to fourteen years. Using the information on children two to six years old and assuming an age bias of six to eighteen months, Vaino Kannisto made estimates of the crude birth rates for each of the years from 1956 to 1960 by applying survivorship ratios corresponding to the United Nations model life tables. The estimates for each of these years consistently exceeded 40 per 1,000 per-

---

[19] Kartono Gunawan, "Taksiran Tingkat Kelahiran di Indonesia Berdasarkan Hasil-hasil Sementara Sensus 1961" (An Estimate of the Fertility level in Indonesia on the Basis of the Preliminary Results of the 1961 Census), in *Workshop Masalah Penduduk*.

sons and were closer to a figure of 43 per 1,000 persons.[20] In order to estimate crude birth rates for the different regions, Kannisto established the ratio of children two to seven years old to the total population of the different regions. Taking the ratio of the country as a whole to correspond to a crude birth rate of 43 per 1,000 persons, estimates of the crude birth rates of the different regions were found by converting the respective ratios into crude birth rates of the same proportion. The results indicate that during the fifties Java had a lower crude birth rate than the rest of the country (42.0 as against 45.0) and that rural areas had higher crude birth rates than urban centers (43.8 as against 38.5).

Another attempt to arrive at estimates of the fertility rates during the decade of the fifties was carried out by Si Gde Made Mamas, of the Central Bureau of Statistics.[21] By applying the reverse-survival method to the 0–4 and 5–9 years age groups as reported in the census, he estimated the sex-age adjusted birth rates for the periods 1956–1961 and 1951–1956.[22] The 0–4 years age group in 1961 represented the survivors of births in 1956–1961, while persons who were five to nine years old in 1961 were survivors of those born in 1951–1956. As was expected, Mamas' study showed that given alternative assumptions

[20] Vaino Kannisto, "Population Increase in Indonesia," Central Bureau of Statistics (Djakarta, 1963).

[21] Si Gde Made Mamas, "The Estimation of Vital Rates of Indonesia from the 1961 Census of Population" (mimeo., submitted to the Demographic Training and Research Centre as part of the training program, 1963–64, Bombay) (Bombay, 1964).

[22] The sex-age adjusted birth rate is the number of births per 1,000 of a weighted aggregate of numbers of women in the various five-year age groups from 15 to 44 (United Nations, *Methods for Population Projections by Sex and Age* [Population Studies, no. 25; New York, 1956], p. 42). It is a device to eliminate the effects of changes in the age structure on the measurement of fertility. Since, as is known, the age structure of a population depends much less on variations in mortality than on variations in fertility, it is to be expected that given alternative assumptions as to the level of mortality in the fifties, the corresponding levels of mortality will be quite similar.

of the level of mortality in terms of an expectation of life at birth of respectively 40, 42.5, and 45 years for the period 1956–1961, the corresponding levels of fertility in terms of the sex-age adjusted birth rate were 43.4, 42.7, and 42.0. For the period 1951–1956 the alternative assumptions of an expectation of life at birth of 35, 37.5, and 40 years resulted in a corresponding sex-age adjusted birth rate of 48.9, 48.2, and 47.0. Thus, it was found that in every combination of assumptions for the two periods the corresponding sex-age adjusted birth rates for 1956–1961 were always smaller than for 1951–1956, the former being about 43.0, the latter around 48.0. This implies one of two possibilities: either there was indeed a decline in mortality during the fifties or the difference was due to an underenumeration of the age group 0–4 years in the census. Although the first possibility cannot be completely discounted, it seems that the second is more likely. One well-known characteristic of censuses in many countries is the underenumeration of children under five years of age, in contrast to those aged five to nine years, who are usually enumerated more accurately even when the age data in general are defective.

Conclusions from the available population data for the period 1950–1960 can be summed up as follows. After 1950 the fertility level returned to its prewar level with a sex-age adjusted birth rate of between 43.0 and 48.0, while mortality steadily decreased. As a result there was a continual acceleration in the rate of population increase during the whole period. The sudden changes in the vital rates during the forties resulted in a relatively small number of persons in some of the younger age groups. As soon as this birth cohort entered the productive ages, there would probably be an increase in the burden of young dependency. Also, the entry of this cohort into the most reproductive years of childbearing would result in a lessening of the crude birth rate, which might give the impression that there has been a decline in the actual level of fertility. On the other hand, the rapid population upsurge in the fifties must have its impact on the structure and growth of the population in succeeding decades. Following closely on the very small birth cohorts of the forties, the entry of the very large cohorts of the fifties into the school-going ages and later into the working ages will have wide implications.

CHAPTER 9

Java's Population Structure and Growth, 1930-1960: An Estimate

The scanty data on vital rates in Java during the period 1930–1960 support several inferences. In the thirties the crude birth rate in Java was very likely higher than 40 per 1,000 persons, while the mortality level seems to be consistent with a life expectancy of thirty to thirty-five years.[1] Moreover, an infant mortality rate ranging from 225 to 250 per 1,000 births was found to be in agreement with other indicators of the fertility and mortality levels. In the decade of the forties, vital rates underwent abrupt changes as a result of the Japanese occupation and the war of independence.[2] There was a decline in fertility, while mortality increased sharply, resulting in a lower rate of population growth. During parts of this period the population may not have increased at all, and even the possibility of a population decrease cannot be excluded. Estimates of the probable levels of fertility and mortality for this period are conjectural, but the available evidence suggests either a fertility decline or a mortality increase or very probably both. With the end of the war of independence, fertility resumed its prewar level, and the possibility of an even higher level of fertility because of family reunions and the upsurge in marriages, many of which had been postponed during the preceding period, is not to be discounted. At the same time, the vigorous efforts in the field of public health had a tremendous impact on the level of mortality,

[1] See Chapter 6.   [2] See Chapter 7.

which showed a continuous decline. Not only was the public health program enthusiastically received, but actually it could not keep pace with the rising demands for better health services resulting from the awareness of the existence of better alternatives that independence and large-scale mass education had brought about.

A rough estimate of the growth and structure of Java's population during the period 1930–1960 has been attempted using certain assumptions that are in conformity with those inferences.[3] The approximation has been developed only for the island of Java since information on changes in vital rates for that thirty-year period in the other Indonesian islands is even more scarce. Moreover, the period covered in the approximation has been confined to thirty years because estimates on earlier periods would be even more conjectural. The method used consists first in applying the concept of stable population as an approximation to the 1930 population of Java and then estimating the size and structure of the populations of succeeding years on the basis of certain assumptions and by using five-year intervals. An alternative procedure would be to employ backward projections by applying the reverse-survival method to the 1961 population census. As has been pointed out earlier, the findings of the 1961 census substantiate the inferences drawn concerning the course of fertility and mortality in preceding decades. Thus, the age structure of the 1961 population clearly reflected the abrupt changes in vital rates during the forties and the tremendous upsurge of births in the fifties.

The Concepts of Stable and Quasi-stable Populations

The age structure of the 1930 population of Java is estimated by using the concept of stable population. A stable population is a hypothetical model of a population with constant levels of

[3] Widjojo Nitisastro, "Migration, Population Growth, and Economic Development in Indonesia: A Study of the Economic Consequences of Alternative Patterns of Inter-island Migration" (Ph.D. diss., University of California, Berkeley, 1961), ch. 10.

fertility and mortality for an indefinite period in the past. Given constant fertility and mortality levels for a sufficiently long period, it has been shown that such a population, which is assumed to have no in- or out-migration, will show a constant rate of increase, a constant birth rate, a constant death rate, and a constant age distribution. Thus, estimates on age structure can be derived from information concerning fertility and mortality, or concerning fertility and rate of increase, or concerning mortality and rate of increase. Likewise, any one of the characteristics can be derived from data on the other two, provided that fertility and mortality have remained constant for a sufficiently long period. Many actual populations have a constant age distribution, and it has been shown that the age structure of such a population appears identical to that of a stable population. Thus, in a population with a constant age structure the same relationship exists between age distribution, fertility, mortality, and the rate of natural increase as in a stable population. Moreover, even when mortality decreased considerably, the resulting population was found to maintain similar characteristics to the stable population, so long as fertility remained fairly constant.[4]

Although a mortality decline has a slight effect on the age distribution, nevertheless the demographic characteristics of the resulting population still resemble those of the stable population. Fertility as measured by the crude birth rate is partly a function of the age structure, and the small impact of mortality decline on the latter results in only slight changes in the crude birth rate.

The impact of a decline in mortality depends on which age groups are most affected by the increased probability of surviving. Many patterns of mortality decline are possible, but one is known to be prevalent. Since the probability of surviving at age 0 is low, a general mortality decline results in a high increase in the probability of surviving at that age. Similarly, it also results

[4] The discussion here refers to the outstanding work of Alfred J. Lotka, J. Bourgeois-Pichat, Ansley J. Cole, and other demographers. The Population Branch of the United Nations Secretariat has developed schemes based on stable and quasi-stable population models.

in a high increase in the probability of surviving at ages above fifty or sixty years. The opposite is the case for the 5–50-year age group. At those ages the probability of surviving is high in comparison to other ages. Therefore, a general mortality decline results in a low increase in the probability of surviving for the 5–50-year age group. The overall effect of an increase in survivorship depends on whether the younger or the older group is most affected. Typically, the two groups neutralize each other, and as a result the mortality decline has a small overall effect on the age distribution.

Populations with constant fertility and declining mortality have been called quasi-stable populations. Their close similarity to stable populations can be illustrated by an example. It is assumed that there is a quasi-stable population with the following properties: a constant level of fertility (gross reproduction rate of 3.0) and a mortality decline over forty years at a rate of increase in life expectation at birth of 2.5 years per five-year period, starting with an expectation of life at birth of thirty years and reaching fifty years at the end of the period. From the results in Table 37 it can be inferred that the age distribution and

Table 37. A comparison of quasi-stable and stable populations

	(1) Population type	(2) 0–14	(3) 15–59	(4) 60+	(5) Annual crude birth rate (per 1,000)	(6) Annual crude death rate (per 1,000)	(7) Annual crude rate of natural increase (per 1,000)
		% of total population of age group					
Initial stable population *		41.3	54.6	4.1	47.7	33.7	14.0
Quasi-stable population †		43.2	51.7	5.1	43.5	15.9	27.6
Stable population ‡		44.6	50.9	4.5	44.9	15.8	29.1

*With a gross reproduction rate of 3 and an expectation of life at birth of 30 years.
†With a gross reproduction rate of 3 and an expectation of life at birth of 50 years (and initially 30 years).
‡With a gross reproduction rate of 3 and an expectation of life at birth of 50 years.
Source: Based on tables 21 and 22 of United Nations, The Future Growth of World Population (Population Studies, no. 28; New York, 1958), pp. 42–43.

the crude birth rate of the quasi-stable population at the end of the forty-year period (line 2) differ little from those of the initial stable population (line 1). They resemble even more closely the characteristics of a stable population with the same levels of fertility and mortality (line 3). Thus, in a population with constant fertility and declining mortality, there are approximately the same relationships between age distribution, fertility rate, mortality rate, and rate of natural increase, as in a stable population. Thus, populations with either constant levels of fertility and mortality or constant fertility and declining mortality can be roughly approximated by stable populations.

An Estimate of the Age Structure of the 1930 Population

On the basis of the preceding discussion on stable and quasi-stable populations, and given the information available on Java's population, it seems safe to assume that the fertility and mortality characteristics of the pre-1930 population—a combination of either fairly constant fertility and mortality or constant fertility and very slowly declining mortality—resulted in a 1930 population possessing the demographic characteristics of a stable population. Thus, the age structure of Java's 1930 population can be approximated by the age distribution of a stable population. In order to derive a stable population, data from a stationary population are needed and can be obtained from a life table. Since there is no life table for the population of Java in 1930, a model abridged life table has been selected from the collection of model life tables developed by the Population Branch of the United Nations Secretariat. The collection of life tables is the result of a study of mortality patterns by sex and age. On the basis of an analysis of a wide selection of actual life tables covering many countries and many periods of time, it has been observed that there exist very close correlations between the probabilities of dying for pairs of adjacent age groups. Therefore, if the probability of dying for an age group is known, the probability of dying for adjacent age groups can be computed from the estimated regression equation, and so a life table can be developed. The U.N. collection consists of life tables ranging from very high to very low mortality patterns corresponding to an expectation of life at birth of 20, 22.5, and 25 years onwards.[5]

In analyzing the vital data of the thirties it was estimated that the mortality pattern corresponded to a life expectancy at birth of thirty to thirty-five years. On that basis it is assumed that separate model abridged life tables for males and females for a population with an expectation of life at birth of thirty years represent the mortality conditions of the 1930 population of Java. It is further assumed that the annual rate of population growth was 12 per 1,000 persons, and that the sex ratio at birth was 1.05 males per female birth. From these data a model stationary population was developed, from which a model stable population was derived, as shown in Table 38. In turn, the model stable population was transformed into a stable population of Java for 1930 by simple prorating, on the assumption that the total population census figure of 41,718 million persons was quite accurate.

The age distribution of the populations as shown in Table 38 is incomplete in that it omits persons aged eighty-five years and over. This is because the age grouping in the model life tables ends at eighty-five years. The exclusion of this age group, however, has a negligible effect because the low expectation of life at birth means that there are very few persons in that age group. Also, the sex ratio for the 1930 stable population is higher than the corresponding ratio in the census population: 1.026 males per female as against 0.959 males per female. This is because in prorating the model stable population into the 1930 stable population, each sex-age category of the former was multiplied by the ratio of the totals of the two populations. If sufficient reliance

[5] United Nations, *Age and Sex Patterns of Mortality* (Population Studies, no. 22; New York, 1955).

(1) Age group (x to $x + n$)	(2) Mid-point ($x + 2.5$)	(3) $e^{-r(x+2.5)}$ ($r = 0.012$)	Model stationary population *		Model stable population †		Stable population for Java, 1930 ‡ (in thousands)		
			(4) Male	(5) Female	(6) Male	(7) Female	(8) Male	(9) Female	(10) Both sexes
0–4	2.5	0.97045	370,535	362,113	359,586	351,413	3,330	3,254	6,584
5–9	7.5	0.91393	317,814	310,320	290,460	283,611	2,690	2,626	5,316
10–14	12.5	0.86071	303,718	295,548	261,413	254,381	2,421	2,356	4,777
15–19	17.5	0.81058	291,254	281,920	236,085	228,519	2,186	2,116	4,302
20–24	22.5	0.76338	275,066	264,718	209,980	202,080	1,945	1,871	3,816
25–29	27.5	0.71892	256,536	245,095	184,429	176,204	1,708	1,632	3,340
30–34	32.5	0.67706	237,158	224,635	160,570	152,091	1,487	1,409	2,896
35–39	37.5	0.63763	216,533	203,900	138,068	130,013	1,279	1,204	2,483
40–44	42.5	0.60050	193,956	183,288	116,471	110,064	1,079	1,019	2,098
45–49	47.5	0.56553	169,160	162,668	95,665	91,994	886	852	1,738
50–54	52.5	0.53259	142,774	141,298	76,040	75,254	704	697	1,401
55–59	57.5	0.50158	115,453	118,795	57,909	59,585	536	552	1,088
60–64	62.5	0.47237	88,045	94,812	41,590	44,786	385	415	800
65–69	67.5	0.44486	61,732	69,735	27,462	31,022	254	287	541
70–74	72.5	0.41895	37,900	45,240	15,878	18,953	147	176	323
75–79	77.5	0.39455	19,036	24,115	7,511	9,515	70	88	158
80–84	82.5	0.37158	7,090	9,548	2,635	3,548	24	33	57
Total, all ages					2,281,752	2,223,033	21,131	20,587	41,718

* Derived from the model abridged life table corresponding to an expectation of life at birth of 30 years in United Nations, *Methods for Population Projections by Age and Sex* (Population Studies, no. 25; New York, 1956), pp. 78–79. The females are indicated by the entries of the $_5L_x$ column of the life table, while for males the entries were multiplied by 1.05, the assumed sex ratio at birth.

† The model stable population is derived from the model stationary population: (6) = (3) × (4) and (7) = (3) × (5).

‡ The stable population for Java is derived from the model stable population by prorating: each sex-age group of the model stable population is multiplied by the ratio of the total census population (41,718,000) and the total number of the model stable population.

could be placed on the sex ratio as shown in the census population, it would be possible to prorate each sex separately.

Assumptions on the Course of Vital Events

It is assumed that between 1930 and 1940 a reduction in mortality resulted in an increase in life expectancy of 2.5 years every five years, so that between 1930 and 1935 the expectation of life at birth is assumed to be 32.5 years, and for 1935–1940, 35.0 years. Fertility is assumed to be constant for both periods. The estimated population of 1935 contains the survivors of the population of 1930. Their number is calculated by multiplying each sex-age group of the 1930 population with the survival ratios of the model abridged life table corresponding to an expectation of life at birth of thirty years. The 0–4 years age group of 1935 is the product of the total number of births during the period 1930–1935 and the survival ratio from birth, calculated separately for each of the sexes. From the 1935 population the estimate of the 1940 population is arrived at by applying a similar procedure using the corresponding life table.

It is necessary to make a separate calculation of the number of births during the periods 1930–1935 and 1935–1940. This calculation is based on an estimate of the sex-age adjusted birth rate, defined as the number of births per 1,000 of a weighted aggregate of numbers of women in the various five-year age groups from 15 to 44 years. It is a standardized birth rate, the weights being proportional to the averages of the age-specific birth rates of a large number of populations. This type of birth rate is based on the observation that for populations with widely differing conditions of fertility, the percentages of births to women in a given age group are quite similar. The use of these weights eliminates the effects of changes in sex-age composition on the number of the estimated births.

It is assumed that the fertility level during the periods 1930–1935 and 1935–1940 stayed constant at the level of 1930. To estimate the sex-age adjusted birth rate of the 1930 population, the number of births in that year is derived from the crude birth rate, which in this case is the intrinsic birth rate of the estimated stable population of 1930. This is identical to the intrinsic birth rate of the model stable population—45.51 per 1,000 persons—and is also the birth rate of the 1930 stable population.

Given a total population of 41.718 million, the estimated birth rate gives a total number of 1.899 million births. Together with the weighted sum of the 1930 female population aged fifteen to forty-four years, the number of births gives an estimate of the sex-age adjusted birth rate of 46.40 births per 1,000 persons in 1930. This is then used as the assumed sex-age adjusted birth rate for the two following five-year periods, from which the total number of births in a five-year period can be estimated. Using the assumed sex ratio at birth, the number of births of each sex can be calculated.

As a consequence of World War II and the war for independence, it is assumed that the decade 1940–1950 witnessed an abrupt conversion of the mortality trend. During the first half of the decade, life expectancy is assumed to have decreased to an even lower level than that of 1930, while at the same time fertility decreased from a sex-age adjusted birth rate of 46.40 to 40.00 births per 1,000 persons. These levels of fertility and mortality are assumed to have continued through the second half of the decade. The impact of the second world war was not actually felt until 1942, but for purposes of simplification the changes in vital rates are assumed to begin in 1940. In addition, a number of writers have speculated on the differences between the vital rates for the two halves of the decade. As was shown in Chapter 7, these conjectures are very questionable, and in the present study the more simple assumption of identical levels for both halves has been chosen. For the decade 1950–1960 it is assumed that fertility returned to its former level, while at the same time the level of mortality decreased, so that life expectancy at birth reached 35.0 years in 1950–1955 and 37.5 years in

1955–1960. On the basis of these assumptions the implied mean annual crude birth rate for each period is estimated, and by using the population figures at different points in time the annual rate of natural increase implied in the assumptions can be found.

The Results

Table 39 shows the assumed expectation of life at birth and the annual sex-age adjusted birth rates for the five-year periods between 1930 and 1960, together with the implied annual crude

Table 39. Assumed annual sex-age adjusted birth rate and expectation of life at birth used in estimating population of Java, 1930–1960, and implied annual crude birth rate, crude rate of natural increase, and crude death rate, per 1,000

(1) Period	(2) Annual sex-age adjusted birth rate	(3) Expecta-tion of life at birth	(4) Annual crude birth rate	(5) Annual crude rate of natural increase	(6) Annual crude death rate
Until 1930	46.40	30.0	45.51	12.00	33.51
1930–1935	46.40	32.5	45.32	15.24	30.08
1935–1940	46.40	35.0	44.85	17.02	27.83
1940–1945	40.00	27.5	39.03	3.90	35.13
1945–1950	40.00	27.5	40.25	5.28	34.97
1950–1955	46.40	35.0	47.31	19.04	28.27
1955–1960	46.40	37.5	46.58	20.42	26.16

birth rates, rates of natural increase, and crude death rates. The assumptions imply that the annual rate of natural increase rose from 12 to 17 per 1,000 persons during the prewar years, was very low during the forties, and reached a level of 20 in the fifties. The fluctuations in the crude birth rate during the thirties and fifties—even though fertility is assumed to be constant—reflect the changes in the sex-age composition of the population.

The increased number of deaths during the forties is assumed to affect all age groups in conformity with the typical pattern of mortality for a population with a life expectancy of 27.5 years, rather than assuming that particular age groups were more affected by the increased mortality rate. It is considered that the indirect effect of the wars through economic dislocation had a larger impact on survivorship than their direct effects. This assumption underlines the already predominant effect of the assumed fertility decline during that period on the course and composition of the future populations.

Table 40 shows the estimated population of Java by sex and five-year age groups from 1930 to 1960. The total population increased from 41.718 to 62.518 million during the thirty-year period, which means an annual rate of increase of 12.69 per 1,000 persons. The annual rate of increase of the total population and of its component parts in the five-year periods is shown in Figure 1. The lower rate of total increase during the forties is shown to be largely due to the decrease in the absolute numbers of the 0–14 years age group during that period and, to a lesser extent, to the deceleration in the growth rates of the older age groups. Taken as a whole, the working-age group (15–59 years) underwent little, if any, decline in its growth rate during that period. A disaggregation into fifteen-year age groups, however, shows a lessening of the rates of increase for the middle-aged and the older working-age population.

During the fifties the restoration of fertility to its former level combined with the increases in survivorship resulted in an upsurge in the rate of population increase. This applied to all population components, but the 0–14 year age group in particular underwent a rapid acceleration in its growth rate. Between 1955 and 1960, however, there was a decline in the growth rate of the working-age population taken as an aggregate. A closer examination reveals that this was due to a slight decrease in the number of those aged 15–29 years, as a consequence of the vital changes during the forties. As soon as the 1940–1945 birth cohorts reached the age of fifteen, there was an increase in the proportion of the 0–14 year age group and a resulting increase in its rate of growth, paralleled by a slightly negative rate of increase among those aged 15–29 years.

Table 41 gives the numbers and proportions of the broad age groups for the thirty-year period. Figure 2 compares the relative sex-age distribution in five-year age groups for the populations

Table 40. Estimated population of Java by sex and age, 1930–1960 (in thousands)

(1) Age group	(2) 1930	(3) 1935	(4) 1940	(5) 1945	(6) 1950	(7) 1955	(8) 1960
Male							
0–4	3,330	3,648	4,018	3,391	3,578	4,858	5,412
5–9	2,690	3,084	3,235	3,377	2,850	3,173	4,369
10–14	2,421	2,492	2,976	3,074	3,208	2,751	3,075
15–19	2,186	2,331	2,409	2,841	2,935	3,101	2,668
20–24	1,945	2,074	2,222	2,264	2,670	2,798	2,969
25–29	1,708	1,824	1,957	2,060	2,099	2,519	2,654
30–34	1,487	1,591	1,711	1,795	1,889	1,969	2,378
35–39	1,279	1,371	1,480	1,546	1,622	1,757	1,846
40–44	1,079	1,160	1,257	1,308	1,366	1,487	1,627
45–49	886	956	1,042	1,078	1,121	1,227	1,351
50–54	704	761	835	862	892	979	1,086
55–59	536	581	640	660	682	750	836
60–64	385	418	463	476	491	543	608
65–69	254	277	307	316	325	361	408
70–74	147	160	180	183	188	211	240
75–79	70	76	86	87	89	101	117
80–84	24	27	31	31	31	36	43
85+		5	7	6	6	8	10
Total, males	21,131	22,836	24,856	25,399	26,042	28,629	31,697
Female							
0–4	3,254	3,570	3,923	3,310	3,493	4,742	5,273
5–9	2,626	2,841	3,167	3,290	2,776	3,098	4,266
10–14	2,356	2,515	2,735	2,997	3,113	2,672	2,996
15–19	2,116	2,258	2,421	2,595	2,843	2,997	2,583
20–24	1,871	1,999	2,144	2,259	2,421	2,699	2,859
25–29	1,632	1,745	1,876	1,970	2,075	2,273	2,548
30–34	1,409	1,509	1,627	1,703	1,788	1,934	2,134
35–39	1,204	1,293	1,398	1,459	1,527	1,657	1,807
40–44	1,019	1,096	1,190	1,239	1,293	1,405	1,539
45–49	852	917	998	1,039	1,082	1,178	1,293
50–54	697	752	820	852	887	968	1,065
55–59	552	597	653	676	702	771	852
60–64	415	450	495	510	528	582	648
65–69	287	312	346	355	366	406	455
70–74	176	191	213	218	224	250	284
75–79	88	97	109	110	112	127	146
80–84	33	37	42	41	41	49	57
85+		7	11	10	10	12	16
Total, females	20,587	22,186	24,168	24,633	25,281	27,820	30,821

Table 40 (continued)

(1) Age group	(2) 1930	(3) 1935	(4) 1940	(5) 1945	(6) 1950	(7) 1955	(8) 1960
Both sexes							
0–4	6,584	7,218	7,941	6,701	7,071	9,600	10,685
5–9	5,316	5,925	6,402	6,667	5,626	6,271	8,635
10–14	4,777	5,007	5,711	6,071	6,321	5,423	6,071
15–19	4,302	4,589	4,830	5,436	5,778	6,098	5,251
20–24	3,816	4,073	4,366	4,523	5,091	5,497	5,828
25–29	3,340	3,569	3,833	4,030	4,174	4,792	5,202
30–34	2,896	3,100	3,338	3,498	3,677	3,903	4,512
35–39	2,483	2,664	2,878	3,005	3,149	3,414	3,653
40–44	2,098	2,256	2,447	2,547	2,659	2,892	3,166
45–49	1,738	1,873	2,040	2,117	2,203	2,405	2,644
50–54	1,401	1,513	1,655	1,714	1,779	1,947	2,151
55–59	1,088	1,178	1,293	1,336	1,384	1,521	1,688
60–64	800	868	958	986	1,019	1,125	1,256
65–69	541	589	653	671	691	767	863
70–74	323	351	393	401	412	461	524
75–79	158	173	195	197	201	228	263
80–84	57	64	73	72	72	85	100
85+		12	18	16	16	20	26
Total, both sexes	41,718	45,022	49,024	49,988	51,323	56,449	62,518

of 1930, 1940, 1950, and 1960. The increase in survivorship during the thirties resulted in a slight increase in the base population of 1940. The changes in fertility and survivorship between 1940 and 1950 can be seen in the small proportion of those aged 5–10 years in 1950, and of those aged 15–20 (and to a lesser extent 10–15) in 1960, in comparison with the adjacent age groups.

Figure 3 describes the course of the changing proportions of the different age groups. It shows the moderate increase in child dependency during the thirties, its sharp decrease during the forties, and its sharp increase during the fifties. The decline in the proportion of the 15–59 year age group from 57.5 to 54.5 per cent between 1955 and 1960 was the result of the proportional, and absolute, decline in the number of persons between fifteen and twenty-nine years. Using one category for the total working-age population conceals the fact that the number of persons aged 30–44 years underwent a slight proportional increase.

As the 1940–1950 birth cohorts grow older, changes can be

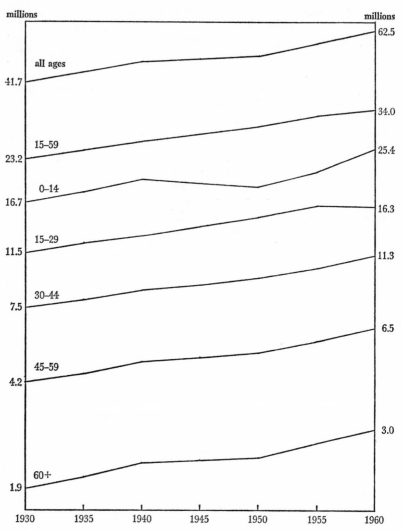

Figure 1. Growth of estimated population by broad age group, Java, 1930–1960

expected in the proportions of the different components of the working-age population. Since, as they become of working age they at the same time enter the reproductive ages, these changes will also affect the number of births and the proportion of younger children.

Table 41. Estimated population of Java by broad age group, 1930–1960

Age group	1930		1935		1940		1945		1950		1955		1960	
	No. (in thous.)	% of pop.	No. (in thous.)	% of pop.	No. (in thous.)	% of pop.	No. (in thous.)	% of pop.	No. (in thous.)	% of pop.	No. (in thous.)	% of pop.	No. (in thous.)	% of pop.
0–14	16,677	39.98	18,150	40.31	20,054	40.91	19,439	38.89	19,018	37.06	21,294	37.72	25,391	40.61
15–29	11,458	27.47	12,231	27.17	13,029	26.58	13,989	27.99	15,043	29.31	16,387	29.03	16,281	26.04
30–44	7,477	17.92	8,020	17.81	8,663	17.67	9,050	18.10	9,485	18.48	10,209	18.09	11,331	18.12
45–59	4,227	10.13	4,564	10.14	4,988	10.17	5,167	10.34	5,366	10.46	5,873	10.40	6,483	10.37
Total, 15–59	23,162	55.52	24,815	55.12	26,680	54.42	28,206	56.43	29,894	58.25	32,469	57.52	34,095	54.53
60+	1,879	4.50	2,057	4.57	2,290	4.67	2,343	4.69	2,411	4.70	2,686	4.76	3,032	4.85
Total, all ages	41,718	100.00	45,022	100.00	49,024	100.00	49,988	100.00	51,323	100.00	56,449	100.00	62,518	100.00

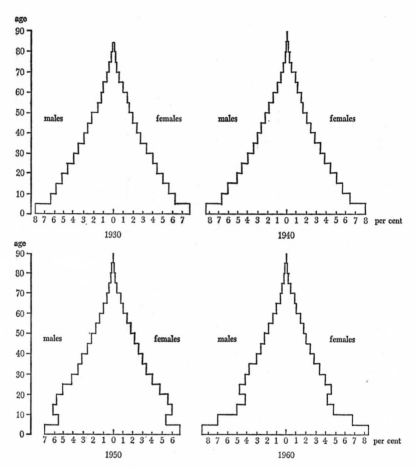

Figure 2. Estimated population of Java by sex and age, 1930–1960 (percentage of total population)

Table 42 compares the estimated population of 1960 with the census population of 1961. The figures from the estimate of the total population and those of the census are rather close to each other: the estimated 1960 population of Java is 62.518 million, while the census reports a total population of 62.993 million for 1961. The male population is estimated at 31.7 million for 1960, while the 1961 census figure is 30.8 million. The corresponding figures for females are 30.8 and 32.2 million. The difference in

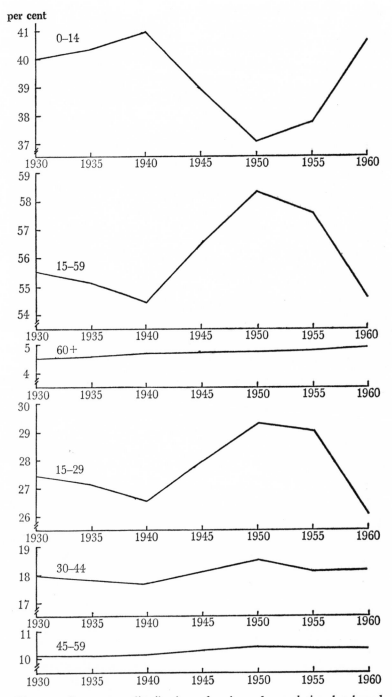

Figure 3. Percentage distribution of estimated population by broad age group, Java, 1930–1960

Table 42. Estimated population, 1960, and census population, 1961, Java

Sex and age group	Estimated population, 1960 No. (in thous.)	%	Census population, 1961 No. (in thous.)	%
Male				
0–4	5,412	17.1	5,413	17.6
5–9	4,369	13.8	4,896	15.9
10–14	3,075	9.7	2,731	8.9
15–19	2,668	8.4	2,420	7.9
20–24	2,969	9.4	2,200	7.1
25–34	5,032	15.9	4,915	16.0
35–44	3,473	10.8	3,830	12.4
45–54	2,437	7.7	2,393	7.8
55–64	1,444	4.5	1,261	4.1
65–74	648	2.0	489	1.6
75+	170	0.5	212	0.7
Unknown			40	0.1
Total, males	31,697	100.0	30,801	100.0
Female				
0–4	5,273	17.1	5,512	17.1
5–9	4,266	13.8	4,907	15.2
10–14	2,996	9.7	2,403	7.5
15–19	2,583	8.4	2,412	7.5
20–24	2,859	9.3	2,858	8.9
25–34	4,682	15.2	5,910	18.4
35–44	3,346	10.9	3,652	11.3
45–54	2,358	7.7	2,433	7.6
55–64	1,500	4.9	1,287	4.0
65–74	739	2.4	535	1.7
75+	219	0.7	246	0.8
Unknown			36	0.1
Total, females	30,821	100.0	32,192	100.0
Both sexes				
0–4	10,685	17.1	10,926	17.3
5–9	8,635	13.8	9,803	15.6
10–14	6,071	9.7	5,134	8.2
15–19	5,251	8.4	4,831	7.7
20–24	5,828	9.3	5,058	8.0
25–34	9,714	15.5	10,825	17.2
35–44	6,819	10.9	7,482	11.9
45–54	4,795	7.7	4,826	7.7
55–64	2,944	4.7	2,548	4.0
65–74	1,387	2.2	1,025	1.6
75+	389	0.6	457	0.7
Unknown			77	0.1
Total, both sexes	62,518	100.0	62,993	100.0

the sex ratios—102.8 males per 100 females for 1960 in the estimate as against 95.7 for 1961 in the census—is due to the fact that the model stable population used in the 1930 approximation was prorated for the population as a whole and not for each sex separately, and also because it has been constantly assumed that the sex ratio at birth is 105 males per 100 females.

There is a close resemblance between the age distribution in the two sets of figures. In both populations the age group 10–14 and even more markedly that of 15–19 are smaller than the adjacent age groups. In contrast, the age groups 5–9 and 0–4 years are quite large in both populations as a logical consequence of the rise in the fertility level during the fifties and the continuous increase in life expectancy.

There are also a number of differences between the two populations. In the census population there is a greater difference between the age group 0–9 years and the age group 10–19 years. In the estimated population of 1960 the age group 0–9 years constituted 30.9 per cent of the total population, while in the census the 0–9 age group was larger, both in relative and in absolute terms. This indicates that the restoration of the fertility level and the decline in mortality during the fifties had a greater impact than had been assumed in estimating the 1960 population. At the same time the lower number and percentage of those aged 10–19 years in the census population also imply that the sudden changes in vital events during the forties had a greater effect than was assumed in the 1960 approximation. On the other hand, when the two sets of figures are compared, it should not be assumed that the information on the age structure in the 1961 population census is completely accurate, since there is certain to have been under- and overenumeration of certain age groups and misstatements of ages. For example, one common feature of many censuses is the underenumeration of the 0–4 years age group. But if this did occur in the 1961 census, it implies that the population upsurge in the fifties was even greater than was assumed in the 1960 population estimate.

CHAPTER 10

The 1961
Population Census

The 1961 census of Indonesia gave a total population of
97,018,829 persons for the whole country, including an estimate
of 758,000 persons for West Irian, which at the time of the
census had not yet been liberated. Indonesia was thus the fifth
largest country in the world in terms of population, after the
People's Republic of China (669 million in 1958), the Republic
of India (438 million in 1961), the Union of Soviet Socialist
Republics (214 million in 1960), and the United States of America (182 million in 1961). Two other countries with populations
close to Indonesia's are Japan (93.82 million in 1960) and Pakistan (93.81 million in 1961). It is estimated that in 1963 the
population of Indonesia exceeded the 100 million mark, and that
it was approximately 106 million in 1965 and about 110 million
in 1967.

The first population census in the Republic of Indonesia was
conducted sixteen years after the proclamation of independence
in 1945 and thirty-one years after the last census of the colonial
era in 1930. During the time that elapsed between the two
censuses important events took place which had an impact on
the growth and composition of the present population and
which will also have consequences for the future population of
Indonesia. The following is a brief description of the population
of Indonesia in the early sixties—including its geographical distribution, its sex and age composition, and its economic and

social characteristics—preceded by some discussion of the 1961 population census and of a number of subsequent surveys that have added to the continuing stream of demographic data.

The 1961 population census of Indonesia was the first census in the modern sense of the term ever carried out in the Indonesian archipelago. Even the 1930 population census—which was the last and the best of the colonial era—did not fully meet the requirements of modern censuses, as was reflected in its primitive treatment of age classification[1] and its lack of coverage of the populations outside of Java. The 1961 population census was a milestone in the population history of the nation and provided the country with badly needed information for planning its future course of development. In the face of what seemed to be insurmountable difficulties, the census was carried out successfully throughout the sprawling archipelago, in large part because of the dedication of hundreds of thousands of census workers and its cooperative reception by the entire population.

In addition, and complementary to the census, a postenumeration survey was conducted in the same year and demographic surveys were carried out during each of the subsequent three years. The objective of the postenumeration survey was to provide an estimate of the coverage and accuracy of the census, while the later surveys, by making use of the same enumeration districts as the postenumeration survey, were aimed at gathering information to estimate fertility and mortality levels and the rate of population increase, and in addition also provide data on internal migration. Two rounds of the National Sample Surveys were also carried out, the first in 1963–1964 and limited to Java, and the latter in 1964–1965 covering the whole territory of Indonesia. These National Sample Surveys were aimed at gathering information on the economic and social conditions of the population which was needed for planned development efforts, and they also included demographic information. The popula-

---

[1] See Chapters 5 and 6.

tion census, the postenumeration survey, the demographic surveys, and the National Sample Surveys provide demographic
material that had been lacking in Indonesian statistics for a long
time. Analytical studies on the basis of the material obtained in
the census and the surveys are at present being carried out in a
number of institutions, including the Central Bureau of Statistics, the Institute of Demographic Research and Training at the
Faculty of Economics of the University of Indonesia, and the
National Institute of Economic and Social Research of the
Council of Sciences of Indonesia. Apart from the population
census, the early years of the sixties also witnessed heightened
statistical activities in other fields with the holding of an agricultural census and an industrial census. The results of the demographic studies, combined with the analyses of the data provided
by the agricultural and industrial censuses, will result in an even
stronger foundation of necessary data needed for charting the
course of future planned development of the country.

The 1961 Population Census

The first population census in the Republic of Indonesia was
conducted on October 31, 1961. Its legal basis was contained in
the Census Law of 1960, No. 6, and the Ordinance of the
Government of the Republic of Indonesia, 1960, No. 49, on the
Execution of the 1961 Population Census. The census covered
the whole area of the Republic of Indonesia. No enumeration
was carried out in West Irian, which at the time of the census
was still occupied by Dutch forces, but the census total does
include an estimate for its population of about 700,000 persons.
The census referred to a combination of the *de jure* and *de facto*
population. Excluded from the census were members of foreign
diplomatic and military personnel and their families.

With respect to the organization of the census, the planning
and administrative organization was assigned to the Central Bureau of Statistics. In each province a census office was set up and
the governor of the province was appointed ex-officio director

of the census operations in his region. At the provincial census office a number of officials were appointed who received special training at the Central Bureau of Statistics. They in turn gave intensive training to the census officials at the regency level, who passed their knowledge and expertise to the census officials at the subdistrict level. The latter then trained the supervisors and enumerators. In most cases the enumerators were carefully selected from among schoolteachers, agriculture extension workers, and other workers of extension services. In total there were 350,000 enumerators and 50,000 supervisors, which implies on an average around 280 persons per enumerator. About 200,000 enumeration districts were set up, each consisting of about 100 households with a population of about 500 persons. In the preparatory stage much attention was given to preparing careful maps of the enumeration districts. About three years before the census, experimental surveys were carried out as part of the preparatory work. The total field operation of the census took place between February and October 1961. The first stage of house-listing and verification took up most of this time, and the actual population enumeration was carried out in the month of October. The only exceptions were a few areas in South Sulawesi, where security considerations necessitated the enumeration's being conducted in December 1961. During the enumeration the enumerators first visited and canvased the households; then steps were taken to verify the information. There was a final check of the enumeration between October 19 and 31, when the enumerators revisited all the households to find out all new births, deaths, and other changes that had taken place since the household was canvased.

Two schedules were used in the census, an individual schedule and a household schedule. For all ages the topics in the individual schedule consisted of name, relationship to head of household, sex, age, marital status, nationality, religion, language, place of birth, education, and school attendance. In addition, for those aged ten years and over, the following characteristics were included: literacy, type of activity, primary occupation, industry, status in industry, secondary occupation, and the number of births to every married woman. The household schedules carried a number of topics applying separately to industrial establishments, institutional households, and private households, and also information on the type of house and on agriculture.

Less than two months after completion of the census, in December 1961, the provisional results were released. Six months later provisional census figures for each regency and municipality in the whole country were published.[2] The information contained separate figures for each of the sexes. In January 1963 the final tabulation of the population data of Djakarta Raya was released.[3] It contained a complete set of final tables based on a 100 per cent tabulation. Similar publications for East Java and Jogjakarta were later released, to be followed by other provinces. With respect to processing, all urban schedules and 10 per cent of the schedules from the rural areas were processed mechanically in the Central Bureau of Statistics, while 90 per cent of the rural schedules were tabulated manually in the provinces. In order to provide the government and public with the urgently needed data, a 1 per cent sample tabulation was carried out and the results published.[4] The enumeration districts were used as sampling units, being the smallest units for the field operation of the census. Since all census data for the urban areas

---

[2] Biro Pusat Statistik, *Sensus Penduduk, 1961, Republik Indonesia* (Population Census, 1961, Republic of Indonesia) (Djakarta, 1962).

[3] Biro Pusat Statistik, *Sensus Penduduk, 1961, D.C.I. Djakarta Raya* (Population Census, 1961, D.C.I. Djakarta Raya) (Djakarta, 1963).

[4] Biro Pusat Statistik, *Sensus Penduduk, 1961—Seluruh Indonesia* (*Angka2 Sementara Hasil Pengolahan 1% Sample*) (Population Census, 1961—All Indonesia [Preliminary Figures, 1 Per Cent Sample Tabulation]) (Djakarta, 1963). It was followed by a more comprehensive publication: Biro Pusat Statistik, *Sensus Penduduk, 1961—Seluruh Indonesia* (*Angka2 Sementara Hasil Pengolahan 1% Sample—Diperluas*) (Population Census, 1961—All Indonesia [Preliminary Figures 1 Per Cent Sample Tabulation—Extended]) (Djakarta, 1963).

were processed centrally at the Central Bureau of Statistics, the sample urban enumeration districts were selected systematically with a random start and with a sampling interval of 100 from the list of urban enumeration districts. For the rural areas only 10 per cent of the census data were forwarded to the Central Bureau of Statistics to be processed centrally. The 1 per cent sample for the rural areas was selected secondarily out of the 10 per cent rural enumeration districts. The ratio estimates of the sample were then applied to the census totals for each of the regions, with a breakdown for rural and urban areas.[5] The following presentation on the characteristics of the Indonesian population in the early sixties will be based on the results of this 1 per cent sample tabulation.

Geographical Distribution

The census figure of 97 million for the total population in 1961 implies that the population density of the country as a whole in that year was 51 persons per square kilometer. This figure shows how meaningless averages can be. In the census, Java's total population numbered 62,993,056 persons, which implies a population density of 477 persons per square kilometer. The 1961 figures for the other islands are as follows: Sumatra, 15,739,363 persons; Kalimantan, 4,101,475 persons; Sulawesi, 7,079,349 persons; and the other islands, 7,105,586 persons. The respective population densities are thus 33.0, 7.6, 37.0, and 12.5 persons per square kilometer. As is shown in Table 43, the population densities in the different provinces of Java, apart from Djakarta, range between 380 and 707 persons per square kilometer. Bali is also densely populated (321 persons per square kilometer), while West Irian and East Kalimantan have popula-

---

[5] For a discussion of the sample procedure and the reliability of the estimates, see Kozo Ueda, *Analysis of the Results of the One Per Cent Sample Tabulation of the Population Census of Indonesia, 1961*, Statistical Research and Development Centre, Central Bureau of Statistics, (Djakarta, 1964).

Table 43. Total population and area by region, Indonesia, 1961

Region	Total population (in thous.)	Area (sq. km.)	Persons per sq. km.
Djakarta Raya	2,907	577	5,038
West Java	17,615	46,300	380
Central Java	18,407	34,206	538
Jogjakarta	2,241	3,169	707
East Java	21,823	47,922	455
Total, Java	62,993	132,174	477
South Sumatra	4,847	158,163	31
Riau	1,235	94,562	13
Djambi	744	44,924	17
West Sumatra	2,319	49,778	47
North Sumatra	4,965	70,787	70
Atjeh	1,629	55,392	29
Total, Sumatra	15,739	473,606	33
West Kalimantan	1,581	146,760	11
Central Kalimantan	497	152,600	3.3
South Kalimantan	1,473	37,660	39
East Kalimantan	551	202,440	2.7
Total, Kalimantan	4,102	539,460	7.6
North Sulawesi	2,003	88,578	23
South Sulawesi	5,076	100,457	51
Total, Sulawesi	7,079	189,035	37
Bali	1,783	5,561	321
West Nusa Tenggara	1,808	20,177	90
East Nusa Tenggara	1,967	47,876	41
Total, Bali and Nusa Tenggara	5,558	73,614	76
Maluku	790	74,505	11
West Irian	758	421,951	1.8
Total, Indonesia	97,019	1,904,345	51

Source: Biro Pusat Statistik, *Sensus Penduduk, 1961, Republik Indonesia* (Population Census, 1961, Republic of Indonesia) (Djakarta, 1962). (Data for Djakarta Raya, Java, and Indonesia have been revised.)

tion densities of respectively 1.8 and 2.7 persons per square kilometer.

This wide disparity in population density is one of the main features of the population of Indonesia (see Figure 4). The island

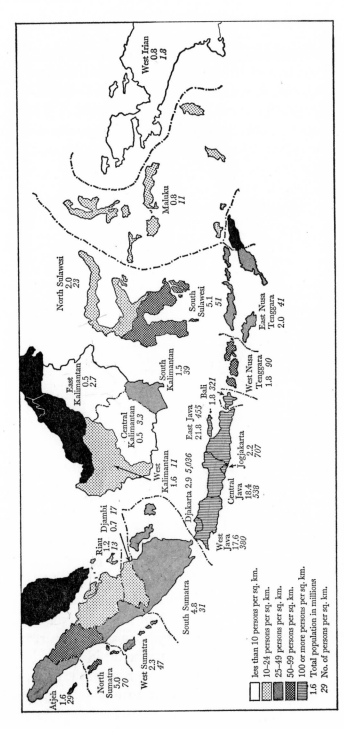

Figure 4. Population density, Indonesia, 1961

less than 10 persons per sq. km.
10–24 persons per sq. km.
25–49 persons per sq. km.
50–99 persons per sq. km.
100 or more persons per sq. km.
1.6 Total population in millions
29 No. of persons per sq. km.

West Irian
0.8
1.8

Maluku
0.8
11

North Sulawesi
2.0
23

South Sulawesi
5.1
51

East Nusa Tenggara
2.0
41

East Kalimantan
0.5
2.7

Central Kalimantan
0.5 3.3

South Kalimantan
1.5
39

West Kalimantan
1.6 11

Bali
1.8 321

East Java
21.8 455

West Nusa Tenggara
1.8 90

Jogjakarta
2.2
707

Central Java
18.4
538

West Java
17.6
380

Djakarta 2.9 5,036

Riau
1.2
13

Djambi
0.7 17

South Sumatra
4.8
31

West Sumatra
2.3
47

North Sumatra
5.0
70

Atjeh
1.6
29

of Java, which accounts for only 7 per cent of the total area of the country, is inhabited by 65 per cent of the total population. On the other hand, as is shown in Table 44, only 16 per cent of the total population live in Sumatra, which covers 25 per cent of the total area of Indonesia. Kalimantan with an area of 28 per cent of the whole country accounts for only 4 per cent of the total population.

Table 44. Regional percentages of total population and area, Indonesia, 1930 and 1961

Region	% of total population		% of total area
	1930	1961	
Java	68.0	64.9	6.9
Sumatra	13.6	16.2	24.9
Kalimantan	3.6	4.3	28.3
Sulawesi	7.0	7.3	9.9
Other islands	7.8	7.3	30.0

Source: Based on Departemen van Economische Zaken, *Volkstelling, 1930* (Population Census, 1930), 8 vols. (Batavia, 1930–1936), and Biro Pusat Statistik, *Sensus Penduduk, 1961—Seluruh Indonesia (Angka2 Sementara Hasil Pengolahan 1% Sample)* (Population Census, 1961—All Indonesia [Preliminary Figures, 1 Per Cent Sample Tabulation]) (Djakarta, 1963).

During the thirty-one year period since 1930 the population of the country increased from 60.7 million persons to 97 million persons—an increase of about 60 per cent. As compared to most of the other islands, Java experienced a smaller percentage increase during that period: 51 per cent as against 91 per cent for Sumatra, 89 per cent for Kalimantan, 67 per cent for Sulawesi, and 63 per cent for the other islands. These differential growth rates may indicate differences in levels of fertility and mortality, but may very well be also the result of population movements. These differences can also be seen by comparing the percentage distribution of the total population among the islands in the two census years (see Table 44). Java's proportion of the total population decreased from 68.0 per cent in 1930 to 64.9 per cent in

1961, while the other islands experienced relatively higher increases.

Almost 15 per cent of the total population live in urban areas, and as shown in Table 45 about two-thirds of this urban population are inhabitants of Java. The 1961 census regarded as urban areas all municipalities and all capitals of regencies, as well as a number of places that possessed the main characteristics of an urban area. In 1930 only 7.5 per cent of the population lived in "areas with an urban appearance." As is shown in the discussion on migration, the populations of a number of cities increased from three to six times over their 1930 numbers.

Population by Age and Sex

It has been pointed out that the 1961 census used two types of schedules: the household list and the individual schedule. The first was a basic schedule that provided the necessary information for the actual population count, while the individual schedule contained a number of other items. As has been mentioned, the data for Greater Djakarta have already been completely processed and published, while a 1 per cent sample of the data for the rest of the country has been selected and processed, and the resulting ratio estimates have been applied to the census totals.

The population distribution by sex and age so obtained is shown in Table 46. From this it can be seen how the changes in vital rates between the 1940's and 1950's have resulted in a small 10–19 year age group contrasted with the large number in the 0–9 year age group. As all the 1940–1950 birth cohorts reach working age, they will have an impact on the magnitude and proportion of the working-age population. Since at the same time they also enter the reproductive age, they will also affect the number of births and the proportion of younger children. The entry of the 1950–1960 birth cohorts into the working and reproductive ages will have a reverse effect, as will be discussed in the following chapter.

Table 45. Population in urban and rural areas, Indonesia, 1961

Area	Java		All other islands		Indonesia	
	No. of persons	% of total pop. of Indonesia	No. of persons	% of total pop. of Indonesia	No. of persons	% of total population
Urban	9,807,308	10.1	4,551,064	4.7	14,358,372	14.8
Rural	53,185,748	54.8	29,474,709	30.4	82,660,457	85.2
Urban and rural	62,993,056	64.9	34,025,773	35.1	97,018,829	100.0

Source: Based on Biro Pusat Statistik, *Sensus Penduduk, 1961—Seluruh Indonesia (Angka2 Sementara Hasil Pengolahan 1 % Sample)* (Population Census, 1961—All Indonesia [Preliminary Figures, 1 Per Cent Sample Tabulation]) (Djakarta, 1963).

Table 46. Population by sex and age, Indonesia, 1961

Age group	Male	Female	Both sexes No.	% of population
0–4	8,461,949	8,580,361	17,042,310	17.7
5–9	7,683,534	7,639,422	15,322,956	15.9
10–14	4,318,543	3,860,869	8,179,412	8.5
15–19	3,834,117	3,874,058	7,708,175	8.0
20–24	3,452,362	4,338,603	7,790,965	8.1
25–34	7,333,617	8,542,102	15,875,719	16.5
35–44	5,719,856	5,363,334	11,083,190	11.5
45–54	3,559,007	3,483,325	7,042,332	7.3
55–64	1,897,510	1,850,396	3,747,906	3.9
65–74	795,730	829,027	1,624,757	1.7
75+	377,747	406,609	784,356	0.8
Unknown	59,882	56,869	116,751	0.1
Total, all ages	47,493,854	48,824,975	96,318,829*	100.0

* Excludes the estimated population of West Irian (700,000).
Source: Biro Pusat Statistik, *Sensus Penduduk, 1961—Seluruh Indonesia (Angka2 Sementara Hasil Pengolahan 1% Sample)* (Population Census, 1961—All Indonesia [Preliminary Figures, 1 Per Cent Sample Tabulation]) (Djakarta, 1963).

The percentage distribution of the population by large age groups for the different regions is shown in Table 47, while Table 48 gives a similar distribution for the urban and rural areas. According to these data, 55.3 per cent of the total population in 1961 belonged to the working-age population. The percentage for Java was higher (56.5) than for the country as a whole. The percentage of working-age population in the urban

Table 47. Percentage of population by large age groups and region, Indonesia, 1961

Region	0–14	15–24	25–44	45–64	65+	Unknown
Java	41.1	15.7	29.1	11.7	2.3	0.1
Sumatra	44.8	16.8	25.4	10.1	2.8	0.1
Kalimantan	42.8	17.8	26.8	10.0	2.5	0.1
Sulawesi	44.3	17.4	26.3	9.4	2.5	0.1
Other islands	42.7	15.8	26.3	11.8	3.3	0.1
Average, Indonesia	42.1	16.1	28.0	11.2	2.5	0.1

Source: Based on Biro Pusat Statistik, *Sensus Penduduk, 1961—Seluruh Indonesia (Angka2 Sementara Hasil Pengolahan 1% Sample)* (Population Census, 1961—All Indonesia [Preliminary Figures, 1 Per Cent Sample Tabulation]) (Djakarta, 1963).

Table 48. Percentage of population by large age groups in urban and rural areas,
Indonesia, 1961

Area	0–14	15–24	25–44	45–64	65+	Unknown
Urban	40.1	20.2	27.7	9.7	2.2	0.1
Rural	42.5	15.3	28.1	11.5	2.5	0.1
Combined urban and rural	42.1	16.1	28.0	11.2	2.5	0.1

Source: Based on Biro Pusat Statistik, Sensus Penduduk, 1961—Seluruh Indonesia
(Angka2 Sementara Hasil Pengolahan 1% Sample) (Population Census, 1961—All Indonesia [Preliminary Figures, 1 Per Cent Sample Tabulation]) (Djakarta, 1963).

areas was even higher (57.6). Comparing the proportion of
persons aged 15–24 years in the urban and in the rural areas,
respectively 20.2 and 15.3 per cent, gives an indication of the
influx of younger workers to the urban centers.

About 42 per cent of the total population in 1961 belonged to
the 0–14 years age group. The percentage for Java was smaller
than for the other islands, and that for the urban areas smaller
than for the rural areas. For the population as a whole the
burden of dependency, in terms of the number of persons of
dependent ages per 100 persons of working ages, was 80.8. For
Java the figure was 77.

According to the data in Table 49, there were more females
than males in Indonesia. The sex ratio, in terms of the number of
males per 100 females, was 95. For Java the sex ratio was also

Table 49. Population by sex and region, Indonesia, 1961

Region	Male	Female	Both sexes
Java	30,801,151	32,191,905	62,993,056
Sumatra	7,942,834	7,796,529	15,739,363
Kalimantan	2,066,248	2,035,227	4,101,475
Sulawesi	3,489,797	3,589,552	7,079,349
Other islands	3,539,050	3,566,536	7,105,586
Total, Indonesia	47,839,080	49,179,749	97,018,829

Source: Biro Pusat Statistik, Sensus Penduduk, 1961—Seluruh Indonesia
(Angka2 Sementara Hasil Pengolahan 1% Sample) (Population Census, 1961—
All Indonesia [Preliminary Figures, 1 Per Cent Sample Tabulation]) (Dja-
karta, 1963).

close to 95, while for Sumatra and Kalimantan it was respectively 102 and 101 males per 100 females. The higher sex ratio
for the urban areas as compared to the rural areas, as shown in
Table 50, indicates the movement of male workers from the
rural areas to the cities.

Some impression of the completeness and accuracy of these
data can be gained from the results of the postenumeration
survey and of efforts to apply tests of internal consistency of the

Table 50. Population by sex in urban and rural areas, Indonesia, 1961

Area	Male	Female	Both sexes
Urban	7,182,609	7,175,763	14,358,372
Rural	40,656,471	42,003,986	82,660,457
Total, urban and rural	47,839,080	49,179,749	97,018,829

Source: Biro Pusat Statistik, *Sensus Penduduk, 1961—Seluruh Indonesia*
(*Angka2 Sementara Hasil Pengolahan 1 % Sample*) (Population Census, 1961—
All Indonesia [Preliminary Figures, 1 Per Cent Sample Tabulation]) (Djakarta, 1963).

sex and five-year age distribution. The postenumeration survey
was carried out in the island of Java and the capitals of the
provinces in the other islands. It was found that the net underenumeration was 0.19 per cent for Java and 0.45 per cent for the
provincial capitals in the other islands. As to the sex and five-year
age distribution, however, it has been found that the results of
the 1 per cent sample in terms of age and sex ratios show
somewhat large deviations from expected patterns and that
therefore these data still need further scrutiny. A glance at Table
51 containing the age distribution by single year of the population of Djakarta clearly shows the well-known tendency of "age
heaping" at ages ending with zero or five, particularly at the age
of twenty years and older. In addition, there seems to be a strong
preference for the ages of twelve and eighteen. It has been
reported that, as is usual in population censuses, there was also an
underenumeration of the very young, many overstatements of

Table 51. Population by single year of age, Djakarta Raya, 1961

Age	No. of persons	Age	No. of persons	Age	No. of persons	Age	No. of persons
0	105,565	20	133,472	40	67,751	60	21,764
1	91,353	21	54,167	41	13,232	61	3,984
2	110,080	22	67,778	42	20,258	62	4,041
3	105,827	23	48,703	43	11,791	63	2,574
4	98,517	24	42,954	44	8,592	64	2,144
5	86,399	25	133,134	45	40,863	65	7,432
6	80,792	26	41,875	46	9,617	66	1,674
7	91,140	27	54,041	47	11,144	67	2,055
8	80,204	28	47,944	48	10,198	68	1,618
9	62,395	29	30,286	49	7,218	69	1,043
10	68,691	30	124,649	50	37,050	70	7,704
11	49,535	31	29,022	51	6,520	71	1,012
12	54,873	32	42,227	52	9,513	72	1,453
13	44,634	33	23,447	53	5,762	73	874
14	39,665	34	20,569	54	5,310	74	726
15	45,773	35	90,900	55	15,165	75+	10,406
16	39,879	36	23,762	56	5,869		
17	56,580	37	27,319	57	4,932	Unknown	2,632
18	85,220	38	24,010	58	4,337		
19	61,423	39	16,276	59	3,195		
						Total, all ages	2,906,533

Source: Kozo Ueda, Analysis of the Results of the One Per Cent Sample Tabulation of the Population Census of Indonesia 1961, Statistical Research and Development Centre, Central Bureau of Statistics (Djakarta, 1964).

ages by old people, and understatement of ages by young females.[6]

Economic Characteristics of the Population

The 1961 population census used the labor force concept. To the labor force belonged persons ten years and over who were actually at work for at least two out of the six months preceding the census and those who were not at work but seeking work. As shown in Table 52, there were 63,953,563 persons aged ten years and over, out of which 34,578,234 persons, or 54.1 per cent, belonged to the labor force. Almost 1.9 million persons, or 5.4 per cent of the labor force, were classified as unemployed. It is evident that this figure is of limited value as a measure of the

[6] Ibid.

Table 52. Population (aged ten years and over) by occupation and sex, Indonesia, 1961 (with percentage of total working-age population)

Occupation	Male No.	%	Female No.	%	Both sexes No.	%
Employed	23,805,691	76.0	8,902,923	27.3	32,708,614	51.2
Unemployed	1,203,106	3.8	666,514	2.0	1,869,620	2.9
Total, labor force	25,008,797	79.8	9,569,437	29.3	34,578,234	54.1
Students	3,832,931	12.2	2,539,464	7.8	6,372,395	9.9
Home-house-workers	1,017,245	3.2	18,494,942	56.8	19,512,187	30.5
Others and unknown	1,489,398	4.7	2,001,349	6.1	3,490,747	5.5
Total, all oc-cupations	31,348,371	100.00	32,605,192	100.00	63,953,563	100.00

Source: Based on Biro Pusat Statistik, *Sensus Penduduk, 1961—Seluruh Indonesia* (*Angka2 Sementara Hasil Pengolahan 1% Sample*) (Population Census, 1961—All Indonesia [Preliminary Figures, 1 Per Cent Sample Tabulation]) (Djakarta, 1963).

degree of employment, not only because it does not take under-employment into account, but also because it considers as employed those who only worked for two months or more during the previous six months.

The same table also shows that out of 31,348,371 males aged ten years and over, 25,008,797, or almost 80.0 per cent, belonged to the labor force, and that in turn 1,203,106 males, or 4.8 per cent of the labor force, were classified as being unemployed. In the case of females, only 9,569,437 out of 32,605,192 persons ten years and over, or only about 30 per cent, belonged to the labor force. Out of this number 7.0 per cent were unemployed. Thus, the number of females belonging to the labor force was less than half the number of males. It should be pointed out, however, that particularly in the rural areas the majority of females are both home-houseworkers and are at the same time engaged in economic activity. It is imperative that this point be taken into account when drawing inferences concerning the female labor force on the basis of the census returns.

Almost 10 per cent of the persons ten years and over were

students and 30.5 per cent home-houseworkers. The percentage of male and female students were respectively 12.2 and 7.8 per cent of the corresponding persons ten years and over. As is to be expected, the proportion of home-houseworkers among females was much higher than among males—56.8 as against 3.2 per cent. Table 53, which compares the percentages of the population ten

Table 53. Percentage of population (aged ten years and over) in labor force by sex and region, Indonesia, 1961

Region	Male	Female	Both sexes
Java	80.0	29.1	53.8
Sumatra	78.1	33.4	56.0
Kalimantan	81.9	42.5	62.4
Sulawesi	78.0	17.9	47.1
Other islands	81.8	27.2	54.6
Average, Indonesia	79.8	29.4	54.1

Source: Based on Biro Pusat Statistik, Sensus Penduduk, 1961 —Seluruh Indonesia (Angka2 Sementara Hasil Pengolahan 1% Sample) (Population Census, 1961—All Indonesia [Preliminary Figures, 1 Per Cent Sample Tabulation]) (Djakarta, 1963).

years and over belonging to the labor force in different regions of the country, shows that in the case of both sexes this ranged between 47.1 and 62.4 per cent. For males the dispersion was between 78.0 and 81.9 per cent, while for females between 17.9 and 42.5 per cent. In all three cases the proportion of persons ten years and over belonging to the labor force was highest in Kalimantan and lowest in Sulawesi. The percentage was higher in the rural areas (55.4 per cent) than in urban areas (47.1 per cent) (see Table 54). This phenomenon, applying to both males and females, is due to the fact that in the rural areas relatively more persons enter the working force at a younger age and leave it at an older age than in urban areas.

The reverse is true with respect to the percentage of the unemployed labor force. As is shown in Table 55, this percentage in the urban areas was more than fifty per cent higher than

Table 54. Percentage of population (aged ten years and over) in labor force by sex in urban and rural areas, Indonesia, 1961

Area	Male	Female	Both sexes
Urban	70.6	23.9	47.1
Rural	81.5	30.4	55.4
Combined urban and rural	79.8	29.4	54.1

Source: Based on Biro Pusat Statistik, Sensus Penduduk, 1961 —Seluruh Indonesia (Angka2 Sementara Hasil Pengolahan 1% Sample) (Population Census, 1961—All Indonesia [Preliminary Figures, 1 Per Cent Sample Tabulation]) (Djakarta, 1963).

for the rural areas. The difference is partly due to the fact that overt unemployment in urban centers is more easily discernible and also much more immediately felt by the persons concerned. Both in urban and in rural areas the percentage of unemployed females was higher than that of males. It must be remembered, however, that the census data are of very limited value in analyzing the unemployment situation.

The percentage of the different age groups who belonged to the labor force, as shown in Table 56, ranged between 22.6 to 96.8 per cent for males and between 15.6 and 39.8 per cent for females. The largest percentage for the males was among the 35–44 age group, while for the females it was among the 45–54 age group. There are large differences between the percentages

Table 55. Percentage of labor force unemployed, by sex, in urban and rural areas, Indonesia, 1961

Area	Male	Female	Both sexes
Urban	7.4	11.8	8.5
Rural	4.4	6.3	4.9
Combined urban and rural	4.8	7.0	5.4

Source: Based on Biro Pusat Statistik, Sensus Penduduk, 1961 —Seluruh Indonesia (Angka2 Sementara Hasil Pengolahan 1% Sample) (Population Census, 1961—All Indonesia [Preliminary Figures, 1 Per Cent Sample Tabulation]) (Djakarta, 1963).

Table 56. Percentage of population (aged ten years and over) in labor force by age and sex in urban and rural areas, Indonesia, 1961

Age group	Male Urban	Male Rural	Male Urban and rural	Female Urban	Female Rural	Female Urban and rural
10–14	7.6	25.5	22.6	6.8	17.5	15.6
15–19	45.8	71.6	66.7	24.2	32.0	30.6
20–24	79.4	89.2	87.2	25.4	27.8	27.4
25–34	93.1	94.6	94.4	25.3	27.6	27.2
35–44	96.1	96.9	96.8	30.1	33.8	33.3
45–54	93.3	96.0	95.6	33.3	40.7	39.8
55–64	74.8	91.7	89.6	27.0	41.0	39.1
65–74	58.0	80.7	78.0	19.2	33.5	31.5
75+	42.7	64.1	61.7	12.3	21.7	20.3
Unknown	55.6	88.3	82.2	31.4	57.9	53.2
Average, all ages	70.6	81.5	79.8	23.9	30.4	29.4

Source: Based on Biro Pusat Statistik, *Sensus Penduduk, 1961—Seluruh Indonesia* (*Angka2 Sementara Hasil Pengolahan 1% Sample*) (Population Census, 1961—All Indonesia [Preliminary Figures, 1 Per Cent Sample Tabulation]) (Djakarta, 1963).

for the 10–14 and 15–19 age groups. The difference is related to educational opportunities and is even more pronounced in the urban areas, where only 7.6 per cent of the males aged 10–14 years belonged to the labor force. In both the urban and rural areas and among both males and females the number of persons aged 10–14 years who were students was much larger than those in the labor force: in the urban areas more than ten times and in the rural areas more than two- and-a-half times. Moreover, in the urban areas the number of those aged 15–19 years who were students was about the same as those who belonged to the labor force. In the rural areas the number of students in this age group was less than one-fourth of those belonging to the labor force.

Out of the 34.6 million persons aged ten years and over who belonged to the labor force, about 32.7 million were employed. Table 57 shows their percentage distribution among the different types of industries. For the country as a whole, about 72 per cent of those employed were engaged in agriculture and less than 6 per cent in manufacturing. Trade accounted for less than

Table 57. Percentage of employed persons (aged ten years and over) engaged in different economic activities by region, Indonesia, 1961

Economic activity	Java	Sumatra	Kalimantan	Sulawesi	Other islands	Indonesia
Agriculture *	68.0	78.4	80.2	77.2	83.6	71.9
Mining †	0.1	1.0	0.2	0.2	0.1	0.3
Manufacturing	6.8	2.8	3.2	4.8	4.2	5.7
Construction ‡	2.0	1.5	1.2	1.1	1.2	1.8
Electricity §	0.1	0.3	0.1	0.1	0.1	0.1
Trade §	7.8	5.4	4.9	4.3	3.2	6.7
Transportation ‖	2.3	2.1	1.7	1.9	0.8	2.1
Services	11.0	6.7	6.4	8.1	4.7	9.5
Others and unknown	1.9	1.8	2.1	2.3	2.1	1.9

* Includes forestry and fishing.
† Includes quarrying.
‡ Includes water and gas.
§ Includes banking and insurance.
‖ Includes storage and communication.
Source: Based on Biro Pusat Statistik, Sensus Penduduk, 1961—Seluruh Indonesia (Angka2 Sementara Hasil Pengolahan 1% Sample) (Population Census, 1961—All Indonesia [Preliminary Figures, 1 Per Cent Sample Tabulation]) (Djakarta, 1963).

7 per cent and services 9.5 per cent. The percentage of persons employed in all nonagricultural pursuits, excluding trade and services, amounted to only 10 per cent.

Compared with the other islands, Java had the lowest percentage of persons engaged in agriculture (68 per cent). On the other hand it had the highest percentage employed in manufacturing—6.8 per cent as compared to 2.8 per cent for Sumatra. This was also the case with trade and services. Excluding trade

Table 58. Percentage of employed persons (aged ten years and over) engaged in different economic activities in urban and rural areas, Indonesia, 1961

Economic activity	Urban	Rural	Urban and rural
Agriculture *	11.7	81.0	71.9
Mining †	0.5	0.2	0.3
Manufacturing	15.9	4.1	5.7
Construction	5.9	1.2	1.8
Electricity ‡	0.8	0.1	0.1
Trade §	20.5	4.6	6.7
Transportation ‖	9.7	1.0	2.1
Services	33.1	5.9	9.5
Others and unknown	1.9	1.9	1.9

* Includes forestry and fishing.
† Includes quarrying.
‡ Includes water and gas.
§ Includes banking and insurance.
‖ Includes storage and communication.
Source: Based on Biro Pusat Statistik, Sensus Penduduk, 1961—Seluruh Indonesia (Angka2 Sementara Hasil Pengolahan 1 % Sample) (Population Census, 1961—All Indonesia [Preliminary Figures, 1 Per Cent Sample Tabulation]) (Djakarta, 1963).

and services, in Java the number of persons employed in all other nonagricultural pursuits amounted to 11.3 per cent of the labor force.

Services accounted for about one-third of all employment in the urban areas, followed by trade with 20.5 per cent and manufacturing with about 16 per cent. Thus, manufacturing proper accounted for only about one-sixth of total urban employment, while more than half the employed persons were engaged in trade and services. As is shown in Table 58, almost 12 per cent of the urban population were engaged in agricultural pursuits.

In the rural areas agriculture accounted for 81 per cent of the employed. Less than 5 per cent were engaged in trade and less than 6 per cent in services. It is quite likely that many of the agricultural workers were also engaged in other activities, particularly in trade and in home-industries. Many persons probably considered these their secondary activities. As a consequence, the present census data on trade do not reflect its actual importance in the pattern of employment of the rural population. The

Table 59. Employed persons (aged ten years and over) by economic activity and sex, Indonesia, 1961

	Male		Female		Both sexes	
Economic activity	No.	%	No.	%	No.	%
Agriculture *	17,371,811	72.9	6,144,386	69.0	23,516,197	71.9
Mining †	76,959	0.3	10,435	0.1	87,394	0.3
Manufacturing	1,158,760	4.9	697,392	7.7	1,856,152	5.7
Construction	560,584	2.3	21,456	0.2	582,040	1.8
Electricity ‡	48,104	0.2	2,625	0.02	50,729	0.1
Trade §	1,510,566	6.3	683,412	7.5	2,193,978	6.7
Transportation ‖	666,879	2.8	24,580	0.2	691,459	2.1
Services	2,038,531	8.6	1,056,708	11.6	3,095,239	9.5
Other and unknown	373,497	1.6	261,929	2.9	635,426	1.9
Total, all activities	23,805,691	100.0	8,902,923	100.0	32,708,614	100.0

* Includes forestry and fishing.
† Includes quarrying.
‡ Includes water and gas.
§ Includes banking and insurance.
‖ Includes storage and communication.
Source: Based on Biro Pusat Statistik, *Sensus Penduduk, 1961—Seluruh Indonesia* (*Angka2 Sementara Hasil Pengolahan 1% Sample*) (Population Census, 1961—All Indonesia [Preliminary Figures, 1 Per Cent Sample Tabulation]) (Djakarta, 1963).

census includes information concerning secondary occupations, and the results, which are not yet available, will throw more light on the extent of these multiple activities. Since the census did not ask information concerning the industry in which the person was employed in his secondary occupation, however, comparisons between primary and secondary activities will be concerned with occupations only.

In 1961 about three-fourths of all employed persons aged ten years and over were males. As is shown in Table 59, the percentage of males employed in agriculture was higher than that of females—72.9 as against 67.6 per cent. The same was true in mining and transportation. In all the other industries, particularly manufacturing, trade, and services, there was a larger percentage of females. Almost 8 per cent of the females were engaged in manufacturing as against only about 5 per cent of males. The percentage of persons employed in trade and services was respectively 15 for males and 20 for females.

The group of employed persons included about one million persons aged 10–14 years (3.4 per cent of the total of employed persons of all ages). Two-thirds of them were males and one-third females. As can be expected, most of these young people who were already economically active were engaged in agriculture and related activities. While around 72 per cent of the total of employed persons of all ages were engaged in agriculture, a little more than 87 per cent of those aged 10–14 were in this category. In all other activities their percentage was smaller, sometimes much smaller, than the percentage for persons of all ages engaged in the same groups of industries.

Social Characteristics: Literacy and the Level of Education

According to the census in 1961, 46.7 per cent of the population ten years and over were able to read and write. Those who were able only to read were classed as illiterate. As is shown in Table 60, almost all these literates were able to read and write in Latin characters, while a small number of persons were only able to read and write in other characters, such as Javanese, Arabic, or Chinese. About 60 per cent of males aged ten years and over were literate and a little less than 35 per cent of the females.

A comparison between the degree of literacy in the different regions shows that Sumatra had the largest percentage of persons ten years and over who were able to read and write: 56.6 per cent as against 45.5 per cent in Java. In Sumatra almost 70 per

Table 60. Percentage of population (aged ten years and over) able to read and write in Latin characters and in any characters, by sex, Indonesia, 1961

Sex	Latin characters	Any characters
Male	55.7	59.8
Female	30.7	34.1
Average, both sexes	42.9	46.7

Source: Based on Biro Pusat Statistik, *Sensus Penduduk, 1961— Seluruh Indonesia* (*Angka2 Sementara Hasil Pengolahan 1% Sample*) (Population Census, 1961—All Indonesia [Preliminary Figures, 1 Per Cent Sample Tabulation]) (Djakarta, 1963).

cent of the males and around 44 per cent of the females ten years and over were literate. For Java the percentages were respectively a little less than 60 and around 33. Table 61 shows that the percentage of literates for both sexes in the different regions ranged between 38.8 and 56.6: for males, between 51.0 and 69.3, and for females, between 26.6 and 43.7.

As is to be expected, the proportion of literate persons was larger in the urban areas. Table 62 shows that in 1961 two-thirds of all those aged ten years and over in the urban areas were able to read and write. In the rural areas it was 43 per cent. In the urban areas 80 per cent of the males and about 53 per cent of the

Table 61. Percentage of population (aged ten years and over) able to read and write in any characters, by sex and region, Indonesia, 1961

Region	Male	Female	Both sexes
Java	59.2	32.6	45.5
Sumatra	69.3	43.7	56.6
Kalimantan	58.7	31.0	45.0
Sulawesi	51.9	35.8	43.6
Other islands	51.0	26.6	38.8
Average, Indonesia	59.8	34.1	46.7

Source: Biro Pusat Statistik, *Sensus Penduduk, 1961—Seluruh Indonesia* (*Angka2 Sementara Hasil Pengolahan 1% Sample*) (Population Census, 1961—All Indonesia [Preliminary Figures, 1 Per Cent Sample Tabulation]) (Djakarta, 1963).

Table 62. Percentage of population (aged ten years and over)
able to read and write in any characters, by sex in urban and
rural areas, Indonesia, 1961

Area	Male	Female	Both sexes
Urban	79.9	53.3	66.6
Rural	56.0	30.6	43.0
Combined urban			
and rural	59.8	34.1	46.7

Source: Biro Pusat Statistik, *Sensus Penduduk, 1961—Seluruh
Indonesia* (*Angka2 Sementara Hasil Pengolahan 1% Sample*)
(Population Census, 1961—All Indonesia [Preliminary Fig-
ures, 1 Per Cent Sample Tabulation]) (Djakarta, 1963).

females were literate, while in the rural areas they amounted to
respectively 56 and 31 per cent.

With respect to the distribution of literates by age group,
Table 63 shows that the percentage of literates in the 10–14
years age group was much larger than for the total population.
About 72 per cent of persons of both sexes aged 10–14 years
were able to read and write. For males in this age group the
figure was 76.2 per cent and for females 67.6 per cent. As is to be

Table 63. Percentage of population (aged ten years and over) able
to read and write in any characters, by age group and sex,
Indonesia, 1961

Age group	Male	Female	Both sexes
10–14	76.2	67.6	72.1
15–19	76.6	59.0	67.7
20–24	74.1	44.2	57.5
25–34	61.7	29.9	44.6
35–44	53.0	20.9	37.4
45–54	41.6	11.3	26.6
55–64	31.8	7.7	19.9
65–74	24.2	6.0	14.9
75+	23.5	6.5	14.7
Unknown	53.2	27.1	40.5
Average, age			
10 and over	59.8	34.1	46.7

Source: Based on Biro Pusat Statistik, *Sensus Penduduk, 1961—
Seluruh Indonesia* (*Angka2 Sementara Hasil Pengolahan 1% Sample*)
(Population Census, 1961—All Indonesia [Preliminary Figures, 1
Per Cent Sample Tabulation]) (Djakarta, 1963).

expected, these percentages declined in the older age groups. Only about 15 per cent of persons aged seventy-five years and older were able to read and write (23.5 per cent of the males and 6.5 per cent of the females). While the percentage of literate persons in each age group was consistently larger for males than for females, the gap was smaller in the younger age groups. This is possibly an indication that the literacy campaign, which has been vigorously conducted for a number of years, had greater success among females.

With respect to the level of education the census gives the following information: 32.1 per cent of persons ten years and over had completed primary school (three to seven years) and 3.1 per cent had successfully completed some school at a higher level. Thus, in 1961 the number of persons aged ten years and

Table 64. Percentage of population (aged ten years and over) by level of education and sex, Indonesia, 1961

Sex	No school	Primary school (3–7 yrs.)	Higher school
Male	53.5	42.1	4.4
Female	75.8	22.4	1.8
Average, both sexes	64.8	32.1	3.1

Source: Biro Pusat Statistik, Sensus Penduduk, 1961—Seluruh Indonesia (Angka2 Sementara Hasil Pengolahan 1 % Sample) (Population Census, 1961—All Indonesia [Preliminary Figures, 1 Per Cent Sample Tabulation]) (Djakarta, 1963).

over who had finished either primary school or some higher school was around 22.5 million, or 35.2 per cent. Of this number more than one-third were females. In terms of percentages Table 64 shows that about 24 per cent of the females aged ten years and over had successfully completed their studies in some type of school, while the percentage for males was almost twice that figure (46.5).

It has been pointed out that according to the census, 46.7 per cent of persons aged ten years and over were able to read and write. Since only 35.2 per cent of that same group had reportedly completed either primary or some higher school, it can be inferred that the remaining 11.5 per cent either had not finished primary school but were still able to read and write, or had attended religious schools or adult classes, where they acquired their ability to read and write. Adult classes had formed part of the literacy campaign and probably account in large measure for the fact that about 25 per cent of literate persons had either never been to school or never completed primary school. The fact that almost 30 per cent of the females aged ten years and over who were able to read and write had either never been to school or had not completed primary school (as compared to 22 per cent for males) can be considered as another indication of the greater success of the literacy campaign among females.

Table 65. Percentage of population (aged ten years and over) by level of education in urban and rural areas, Indonesia, 1961

Area	No school	Primary school (3–7 yrs.)	Higher school
Urban	42.0	45.8	12.2
Rural	69.1	29.5	1.4
Average, urban and rural	64.8	32.1	3.1

Source: Biro Pusat Statistik, Sensus Penduduk, 1961—Seluruh Indonesia (Angka2 Sementara Hasil Pengolahan 1% Sample) (Population Census, 1961—All Indonesia [Preliminary Figures, 1 Per Cent Sample Tabulation]) (Djakarta, 1963).

According to the census, almost 70 per cent of those ten years and over in the rural areas never went to school or did not finish primary school. In the urban areas the percentage was 42 per cent. About 46 per cent of the urban population ten years and over completed primary school and almost one-eighth finished some higher school. As is shown in Table 65, the corresponding percentages for the rural population were 29.5 and 1.4 respectively.

The distribution of persons ten years and over by level of education and region in 1961 is shown in Table 66. The highest percentage of persons ten years and over who had completed

Table 66. Percentage of population (aged ten years and over) by level of
education and region, Indonesia, 1961

Region	No school	Primary school (3–7 yrs.)	Higher school
Java	66.3	30.5	3.2
Sumatra	56.0	39.8	4.2
Kalimantan	65.6	31.9	2.5
Sulawesi	64.8	32.1	3.1
Other islands	70.3	28.1	1.6
Average, Indonesia	64.8	32.1	3.1

Source: Biro Pusat Statistik, Sensus Penduduk, 1961—Seluruh Indonesia
(Angka2 Sementara Hasil Pengolahan 1% Sample) (Population Census, 1961—
All Indonesia [Preliminary Figures, 1 Per Cent Sample Tabulation])
(Djakarta, 1963).

primary education was almost 40 per cent in Sumatra. The
percentage for Java was 30.5 per cent. Sumatra also accounted
for the highest percentage of persons who finished some higher
school (4.2 per cent versus 3.2 per cent in Java).

Table 67 clearly shows the large divergence between levels of
education in the different age groups. The percentage of persons
who never went to school or never completed primary school

Table 67. Percentage of population (aged ten years and over) by level of
education and age group, Indonesia, 1961

Age group	No school	Primary school (3–7 yrs.)	Higher school
10–14	43.4	55.8	0.8
15–19	42.5	50.5	7.0
20–24	54.3	37.9	7.8
25–34	67.9	29.0	3.1
35–44	73.7	24.6	1.7
45–54	82.6	16.1	1.3
55–64	88.6	10.6	0.8
65–74	91.8	7.6	0.6
75+	93.3	6.3	0.6
Unknown	71.6	25.5	0.4
Average, age 10 and over	64.8	32.1	3.1

Source: Based on Biro Pusat Statistik, Sensus Penduduk, 1961—Seluruh
Indonesia (Angka2 Sementara Hasil Pengolahan 1% Sample) (Population
Census, 1961—All Indonesia [Preliminary Figures, 1 Per Cent Sample
Tabulation]) (Djakarta, 1963).

ranged from 42.5 for the 15–19 years age group to as high as 93.3 for persons 75 years and over. On the other hand, the proportion of persons who completed primary school shows a reverse tendency: from 55.8 per cent for the 10–14 years age group to 6.3 per cent for persons 75 years and over. Actually, the 10–24 years age group accounted for 56.1 per cent of persons of all ages who completed primary school. The same age group accounted for almost two-thirds of all persons who finished some school of a higher level. The large discrepancies in

Table 68. Percentage of age groups attending school, by sex,
Indonesia, 1961

Age group	Male	Female	Both sexes
5–9	34.1	32.5	33.3
10–14	64.7	54.4	59.8
15–19	23.2	11.5	17.4
20–24	6.1	1.6	3.6
25+	0.8	0.2	0.5
Unknown	3.3	0.4	1.9
Average, all groups	17.1	12.8	14.9

Source: Based on Biro Pusat Statistik, *Sensus Penduduk, 1961— Seluruh Indonesia* (*Angka2 Sementara Hasil Pengolahan 1% Sample*) (Population Census, 1961—All Indonesia [Preliminary Figures, 1 Per Cent Sample Tabulation]) (Djakarta, 1963).

the level of education of the different age groups are indicative of the progress achieved in the field of education during the fifties.

The census reported that about 15 per cent of persons aged five years and over were attending school. This figure is somewhat misleading, since obviously very few persons aged twenty years and over were still attending school. As shown in Table 68, the proportion of school attendance was highest among the 10–14 years age group: 59.8 per cent for both sexes, 64.7 per cent for males, and 54.4 per cent for females. The 5–9 years age group showed a lower proportion of school attendance, only one-third of them attending school. This low percentage is due to the fact that most children start school at the age of seven or older, particularly since in many regions the increased demand for schools still exceeds the growth of educational facilities. The census data show that the percentages for school attendance of persons aged five, six, seven, eight, and nine years were respectively 4.6, 19.2, 39.9, 51.5, and 56.7 per cent.

A comparison of school attendances in the urban and rural areas in 1961 is shown in Table 69. Almost 80 per cent of the

Table 69. Percentage of age groups attending school in urban and rural areas, Indonesia, 1961

Age group	Urban	Rural	Urban and rural
5–9	49.0	30.9	33.3
10–14	79.8	55.8	59.8
15–19	39.3	12.3	17.4
20–24	10.9	1.9	3.6
25+	1.1	0.4	0.5
Unknown	5.0	1.2	1.9
Average, all groups	24.0	13.3	14.9

Source: Based on Biro Pusat Statistik, *Sensus Penduduk, 1961— Seluruh Indonesia (Angka2 Sementara Hasil Pengolahan 1% Sample)* (Population Census, 1961—All Indonesia [Preliminary Figures, 1 Per Cent Sample Tabulation]) (Djakarta, 1963).

urban population aged 10–14 years were attending school as compared with 55.8 per cent in the rural areas. Almost one-half of the children aged 5–9 years who lived in urban areas did attend school, while the proportion in the rural areas was less than one-third. Among those aged 15–19 years there was a more substantial gap between school attendance in the urban and rural areas: close to 40 per cent in the former and about 12 per cent in the latter. This difference is understandable, however, since the majority of this age group attends secondary schools, and these schools are primarily located in urban areas.

Since school age starts at around seven years, a separate tabulation has been made for the age group 7–13 years in order to facilitate analysis for purposes of educational planning. In 1961 school attendance in this group was about 55 per cent: in the

Table 70. Percentage of children 7–13 years old attending school
in urban and rural areas, by sex, Indonesia, 1961

Area	Male	Female	Both sexes
Urban	77.4	72.4	74.9
Rural	54.5	48.1	51.4
Combined urban and rural	57.7	51.7	54.8

Source: Biro Pusat Statistik, Sensus Penduduk, 1961—Seluruh
Indonesia (Angka2 Sementara Hasil Pengolahan 1% Sample) (Popu-
lation Census, 1961—All Indonesia [Preliminary Figures, 1 Per
Cent Sample Tabulation]) (Djakarta, 1963).

urban areas about three-fourths and in the rural areas a little
more than half. (See Table 70). Furthermore, opportunities to
attend school did not differ greatly between the sexes, particularly in the urban areas: 77.4 per cent of the males and 72.4 per
cent of the females attended school in urban areas, while in the
rural areas the corresponding percentages were 54.5 and 48.1.
A comparison between the school attendance in the different
regions is shown in Table 71. In 1961 the percentage of school
attendance for persons 7–13 years old ranged from 43.5 to 60.2.
The last figure is for Sumatra. Java was second in school attendance for this age group with 55.3 per cent. For males the
percentages were between 46.8 and 62.9 and for females be-

Table 71. Percentage of children 7–13 years old attending school
by region and sex, Indonesia, 1961

Region	Male	Female	Both sexes
Java	58.3	52.2	55.3
Sumatra	62.9	57.4	60.2
Kalimantan	46.8	41.9	44.5
Sulawesi	55.9	52.5	54.3
Other islands	49.1	37.5	43.5
Average, Indonesia	57.7	51.7	54.8

Source: Biro Pusat Statistik, Sensus Penduduk, 1961—Seluruh
Indonesia (Angka2 Sementara Hasil Pengolahan 1% Sample) (Popu-
lation Census, 1961—All Indonesia [Preliminary Figures, 1 Per
Cent Sample Tabulation]) (Djakarta, 1963).

tween 37.5 and 57.4. Thus, while the percentage of school attendance for males and females did not differ greatly within each of the regions, there was a larger discrepancy in school attendance among females of different regions than among males.

CHAPTER 11

The Future Population of Indonesia, 1961-1991

A number of population projections have been developed for Indonesia for the period 1961–1991, using the outcome of the 1961 census as base population. In order to prevent any misinterpretation, it must be stressed that population projections are not forecasts yielding completely realistic pictures of the probable future developments of a population. Rather, they are purely formal calculations, showing the implications of given assumptions concerning the future course of fertility, mortality, and migration. Projections are thus the results of an "If . . . , then . . ." approach, with the outcome depending purely on the underlying assumptions. Innumerable assumptions or sets of assumptions are feasible. Therefore, assumptions are a matter of choice. And even if this choice takes due regard of past trends and allows as much as possible for the likely changes in economic, social, and other conditions that might affect the future growth and structure of the population, there is still no guarantee as to the accuracy of the resulting projections. Particularly where data on the past and present components of population growth (fertility, mortality, and migration) and on the sex-age and geographical distribution of the population are not yet quite adequate, the emerging picture of past trends is not always very clear. Moreover, the future trends of the multiplicity of factors that are likely to have an impact on the course of the growth components of the population cannot be foreseen with any degree of certainty.

Nevertheless, in spite of all these necessary qualifications, a set of alternative population projections, each based on a set of alternative assumptions, can be of some use in providing a picture of the alternative courses of population growth and alternative shifts in its structure. A set of alternative population projections can give an idea of the order of magnitude of the certain variables that have to be taken into account in preparing the future course of planned development for the country. The important thing to remember is that the size of these variables depends on certain sets of assumptions, and if the course of events departs from these assumptions, then the consequent implications will necessarily not conform with the projected magnitudes. Therefore, it is imperative to review, assess, and revise existing projections periodically on the basis of comparative analysis of the underlying assumptions and the actual performances. Thus, population projection is a continuing activity.

Alternative Population Projections

There are several alternative methods of projection. The simplest of these is to estimate future total populations by assuming a certain annual rate of increase, which may be constant or may vary through time. This type of projection is of limited relevance, not only because it disregards the growth of the components of the population, but also because it completely neglects changes in the factors that determine the course of the different components of the population. It only arrives at a total, while for purposes of planning and policy not only the totals but also the components play an important role. Particularly when vital rates in the past were subject to severe changes, it can be expected that these will be reflected in the different sex-age components of the projected population. This problem is taken into account in the component method of projection, since with it each of the components is projected separately.

Using the 1961 census population as a base, alternative projections have been made for the period 1961–1991 with five-year intervals and on the basis of alternative assumptions concerning the future course of fertility and mortality. Since in the past international migration did not play an important role in the growth and structure of the population, it is assumed that its role in the future will also be negligible. For the sake of simplicity, therefore, the projections assume an absence of migration to and from the country. With respect to the base population, some adjustments have been made on the sex-age structure of the data supplied by the 1961 census, while the choice of initial fertility and mortality levels are based on the inferences drawn from the census data discussed earlier.

Census data are always subject to errors owing to inaccurate reporting of ages and to underenumeration of certain ages. For example, it is known that the age group 0–4 years is often subject to serious underenumeration. Also, successive five-year age groups may be alternately overstated and understated owing to the attraction of certain ages. In order to minimize the effect of such irregularities, some simple methods of adjustment have been applied to the sex-age data of the census, while at the same time preserving the census totals for each of the sexes. Thus, the total number of the adjusted population and the ratio between the totals of the two sexes remain identical to those in the unadjusted census data. Moreover, since it is known that the small propor- tion of persons in the 10–19 years age group is indeed a reflec- tion of exceptional developments in vital rates during the forties rather than the result of misstatements of ages or underenumera- tion, no adjustments have been applied to this group. The differ- ence between the adjusted and unadjusted data for this age group is due to prorating as applied to the data as a whole. The resulting adjusted census population is shown in Table 72.

On the basis of the discussion of vital rates inferred from the census data, the following assumptions have been made regard- ing the initial levels of fertility and mortality in the first five- year interval (1961–1966): a sex-age adjusted birth rate of 45 births per 1,000 among a weighted aggregate of numbers of women aged from 15 to 44 years, and an expectation of life at birth of 40 to 42.5 years. With respect to the course of fertility and mortality in the succeeding five-year intervals a number of alternative sets of assumptions have been employed. The first projection, called projection A, assumes a constant level of fertility throughout the thirty-year period at a sex-age adjusted birth rate of 45 births per 1,000, with an initial life expectancy of 40

Table 72. Adjusted census population by sex and age, Indonesia, 1961

Age group	Male No. (in thous.)	Male % of sex group	Female No. (in thous.)	Female % of sex group
0–4	8,869	18.5	8,904	18.1
5–9	7,642	16.0	7,523	15.3
10–14	4,295	9.0	3,802	7.7
15–19	3,813	8.0	3,815	7.7
20–24	3,884	8.1	4,635	9.4
25–29	3,547	7.4	4,431	9.0
30–34	3,588	7.5	3,778	7.7
35–39	3,169	6.6	2,914	5.9
40–44	2,480	5.2	2,309	4.7
45–49	1,941	4.1	1,869	3.8
50–54	1,502	3.1	1,441	2.9
55–59	1,062	2.2	1,189	2.4
60–64	827	1.7	1,182	2.4
65–69	539	1.1	703	1.4
70–74	308	0.6	285	0.6
75–79	143	0.3	140	0.3
80–84	125	0.3	148	0.3
85+	105	0.2	112	0.2
Total, all ages	47,839	100.0	49,180	100.0

years increasing by 0.5 years annually, to an expectation of life at birth of 52.5 years in 1986–1991. This rate of declining mortality has been observed in many populations and is sometimes referred to as the "normal" rate of decline of deaths. The second projection, called projection B, makes the same assumptions regarding the course and level of fertility as projection A.

Mortality is also assumed to decline at a similar rate as in the first projection, but the initial life expectancy for 1961–1966 is assumed to be 42.5 (as against 40 for the first projection), so that by 1986–1991 expectation of life at birth would be 55 years. Thus, projections A and B are similar, the only difference lying in the initial lower level of mortality in projection B. Projection C assumes a constant fertility level at a sex-adjusted birth rate of 42.5 per 1,000, and a rapid mortality decrease, with life expectancy increasing by one year annually or five years in every five-year period. Such a rapid gain in life expectancy has been achieved in a number of countries, although the extent to which it could be sustained in the face of a constantly high level of fertility remains to be seen. If life expectancy is 42.5 years in 1961–1966, this rapid decline in mortality will lead to a life expectancy of 68.2 years in 1986–1991. In projection D the rapid decline in mortality is identical to that in projection C, but, unlike the other projections, fertility is assumed to decline from an initial level of the sex-age adjusted birth rate of 45 per 1,000 in 1961–1966 to 38 per 1,000 in 1976–1981 and 31.8 per 1,000 in 1986–1991. The likelihood of such a future decline in fertility is at present difficult to assess. As has been pointed out, population projections are formal exercises based on certain assumptions. The inclusion of projection D is merely an illustration of the effect on population growth and its constituent components of a certain pattern of fertility decline.

The different alternative projections can be summed up as follows:

Projection A: Constant fertility (a sex-age adjusted birth rate of 45 births per 1,000) and slowly declining mortality (an increase in life expectancy at birth of 2.5 years in every five-year period, from an initial life expectancy of 40 years).

Projection B: Fertility and mortality similar to projection A, but starting from an initial life expectancy of 42.5 years.

Projection C: Constant fertility (a sex-age adjusted birth rate of 45 births per 1,000) and rapidly declining mortality (an increase in life expectancy at birth of 5 years in every five-year period, starting with an initial expectation of life at birth of 42.5 years).

Projection D: Declining fertility (from an initial level of the sex-age adjusted birth rate of 45 births per 1,000 in 1966–1971 to 31.8 births per 1,000 in 1986–1991) and rapidly declining mortality (similar to projection C).

The method used in component projections is identical to that used to estimate the 1930–1960 population from the 1930 figures: the survival ratios of the model abridged life tables are

Table 73. Assumed annual sex-age adjusted birth rate and expectation of life at birth used in population projections A, B, C, and D, Indonesia, 1961–1991

Period	Annual sex-age adjusted birth rate (per 1,000)				Expectation of life at birth (in yrs.)			
	A	B	C	D	A	B	C	D
1961–1966	45.0	45.0	45.0	45.0	40.0	42.5	42.5	42.5
1966–1971	45.0	45.0	45.0	43.0	42.5	45.0	47.5	47.5
1971–1976	45.0	45.0	45.0	40.7	45.0	47.5	52.5	52.5
1976–1981	45.0	45.0	45.0	38.0	47.5	50.0	57.6	57.6
1981–1986	45.0	45.0	45.0	35.0	50.0	52.5	63.2	63.2
1986–1991	45.0	45.0	45.0	31.8	52.5	55.0	68.2	68.2

applied to the base population, and the number of births are calculated from the sex-age adjusted birth rate. The sex-age adjusted birth rates and the expectations of life at birth assumed in the different projections are shown in Table 73.

The Projected Population of 1961–1991

The resulting projections of the total population with five-year intervals until 1991 are shown in Table 74 and in the semilogarithmic graph in Figure 5. The alternative projections show that if there is a "normal" mortality decline during the thirty-year period accompanied by a constant level of fertility,

Table 74. Projected total population and annual rate of increase, Indonesia, 1961–1991

Year	Projection A		Projection B		Projection C		Projection D	
	Total population (in thous.)	Annual rate of increase (per 1,000)	Total population (in thous.)	Annual rate of increase (per 1,000)	Total population (in thous.)	Annual rate of increase (per 1,000)	Total population (in thous.)	Annual rate of increase (per 1,000)
1961	97,019		97,019		97,019		97,019	
		21.6		23.8		23.8		23.8
1966	108,058		109,166		109,166		109,166	
		19.8		22.0		23.2		21.8
1971	119,346		121,717		122,520		121,663	
		20.1		22.3		25.2		22.3
1976	132,062		136,022		138,787		136,012	
		23.5		25.7		29.8		24.9
1981	149,413		154,486		160,916		153,956	
		27.4		29.1		33.8		26.4
1986	171,393		178,454		190,217		175,702	
		28.6		30.1		35.6		26.0
1991	197,843		207,266		226,978		200,057	

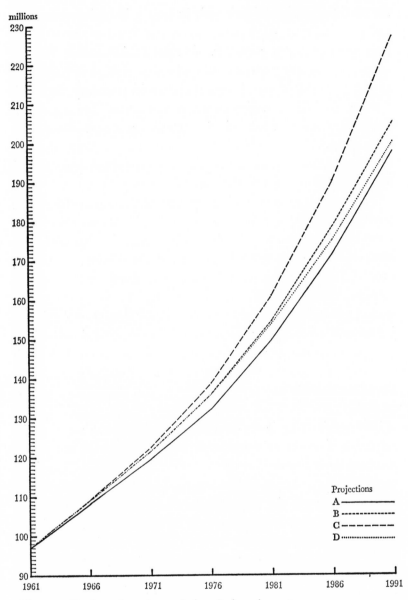

Figure 5. Projected total population, Indonesia, 1961–1991

the total population of Indonesia in 1991 will be between 197.8 and 207.3 million, or between 203.9 and 213.6 per cent of the 1961 population. If mortality declines rapidly while fertility stays constant, the total population in 1991 will be 227.0 million (233.9 per cent of 1961), and if the rapid mortality decline is accompanied by a decline in the fertility level, the 1991 total population will be 200.1 million, or 206.2 per cent of the 1961 population. Thus, the alternative projections indicate that the total population will more than double in the thirty-year period, numbering about two hundred million persons by 1991.

The four alternative projections also indicate that the rate of population increase during the second half of the thirty-year period will be somewhat higher than during the first half. The total population in 1976 will be around 136 million, or 140 per cent of the 1961 population. If there is no change in the level of fertility, the annual growth rate during the first half of the period will be between 20 and 25 per 1,000 persons, and this will increase to 25 to 35 per 1,000 persons in the second half of the period. A fertility decline, commencing in 1966–1971, will result in a rate of population increase of 22 per 1,000 persons in the first half and 26 per 1,000 persons in the second half of the period.

The acceleration in the rate of population growth during the second half of the thirty-year period is mainly due not to the assumed mortality decline but to the recovery in the fifties from the unusual conditions of the forties. The number of births and their survivors in the fifties are much larger than those in the forties. The entry and exit of these birth cohorts into and from the reproductive ages will have an impact on the number of births, and, therefore, on the rate of population increase in the different parts of the thirty-year period. During the first half of the period the majority of women of child-bearing age will have been born in the forties. Since their number is rather small, there will consequently be a small number of births and a decrease in the rate of population increase. After 1976, however, the impact of the survivors of the forties on the number of births will lessen as they start to reach the upper limits of their reproductive ages. At the same time the large cohorts of the fifties will be entering the reproductive ages. The combined effect will be a rapid upsurge in the number of births during the period after 1976, resulting in a higher rate of growth for the total population.

The projected number of births in the five-year periods is shown in Figure 6. Although the level of fertility is assumed to be constant, the number of births according to the first three

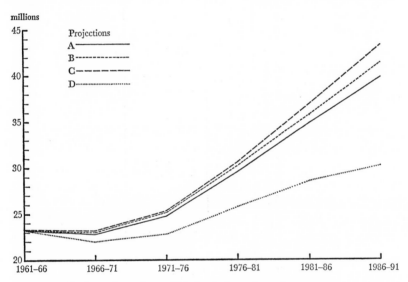

Figure 6. Projected number of births, Indonesia, 1961–1991

projections accelerates rapidly after 1976. Projection B, for example, shows that between 1961–1966 and 1971–1976 the total number of births in the five-year periods will increase from 23.2 million to 25.1 million, while in 1976–1981 the number will reach 30.1 million. This development illustrates the impact of the age structure of the population on the number of births. It also shows the deficiencies of measuring the level of fertility by the crude birth rate, which is dependent on the age distribution of the population. This can be seen from Table 75, which shows

Table 75. Implied annual crude birth rate, crude rate of natural increase, and crude death rate in population projections A, B, C, and D, Indonesia, 1961–1991 (per 1,000 persons)

Period	Annual crude birth rate				Annual crude rate of natural increase				Annual crude death rate			
	A	B	C	D	A	B	C	D	A	B	C	D
1961–1966	45.2	45.1	45.1	45.1	21.6	23.8	23.8	23.8	23.6	21.3	21.3	21.3
1966–1971	40.2	39.9	39.8	38.2	19.8	22.0	23.2	21.8	20.4	17.9	16.6	16.4
1971–1976	39.4	38.9	38.7	35.4	20.1	22.3	25.2	22.3	19.3	16.6	13.5	11.1
1976–1981	42.0	41.4	39.5	35.6	23.5	25.7	29.8	24.9	18.5	15.7	9.7	10.7
1981–1986	43.6	43.1	42.0	34.7	27.4	29.1	33.8	26.4	16.2	14.0	8.2	8.3
1986–1991	43.3	43.1	41.5	32.2	28.6	30.1	35.6	26.0	14.7	13.0	5.9	6.2

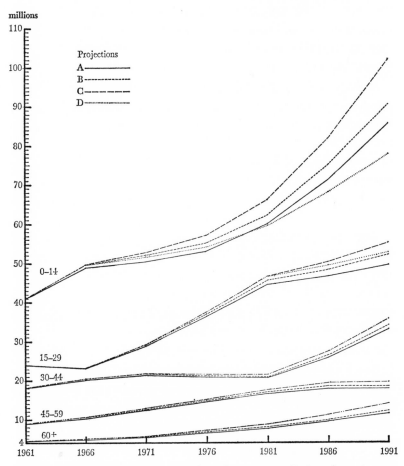

Figure 7. Projected population by broad age group, Indonesia, 1961–1991

the annual crude birth rates implied in the projections. Even though the first three projections assume a constant level of fertility throughout the thirty-year period, the implied crude birth rates in these projections exhibit rather sharp fluctuations. The projections show that the crude birth rate can be expected to slacken between 1966 and 1976. This does not, however, mean that there will be an actual decline in the level of fertility. For even if the actual level of fertility remains constant, the crude birth rate will decline, simply because of the existing age structure of the population, reflecting, as it does, the sudden changes in the vital rates in the past. (The implied crude death rates in the table were found by deducting the implied rate of natural increase from the implied crude birth rate.)

The growth of the different fifteen-year age groups of the population is shown in the semilogarithmic graphs in Figure 7. Between 1961 and 1966 the 0–14 years age group continues the rapid increase started in the fifties. Between 1966 and 1976 its rate of increase declines, but after 1976, and especially after 1981, it resumes its high rate of growth as a result of the entrance of the large cohorts born during the fifties into the reproductive ages.

The 15–29 years age group shows a slight decline from 1961 to 1966, but this is followed by a very rapid rate of increase after 1966. During the period 1961–1966, the 15–29 years age group consists largely of the survivors of the birth cohorts of the forties. After 1966, and particularly after 1971, most of the birth cohorts of the forties leave the 15–29 years age group and enter the 30–44 years age group. The exit of the birth cohorts of the forties from the younger age group is accompanied by the entrance of the birth cohorts of the fifties into that age group. The combined result is the rapid acceleration after 1966 in the growth of the young labor force, aged from 15–29 years.

When in 1971 the survivors of those born during the forties enter the 30–44 years age group, there is a resultant deceleration in the growth of this age group. There will even be a small absolute decrease in the number of persons in this age group. This continues until 1981, when the birth cohorts of the forties begin to enter the older working-age population of 45–59 years. The entry of the large cohorts of the fifties into the 30–44 years age group results again in a rapid acceleration in the growth of this age group in 1981. Similar decreases and increases will be experienced by the older working-age population of 45–59 years in the succeeding years.

Thus, the abrupt changes in vital rates during the forties, and the return to a high level of fertility in the fifties together with a continually decreasing level of mortality, implies unusual fluctuations in the proportions of the different age groups in Indonesia's future population. As the 1940–1950 birth cohort enters a certain age group, there is a resultant decline in the rate of increase of that age group or sometimes even an absolute decline in its numbers. As soon as these cohorts move to the next age group and are followed by the much larger birth cohorts of 1950–1960, the number of persons in that age group will increase sharply. During the thirty-year period under study, only the age group sixty years and over will not be affected by the abrupt changes of the forties and fifties, since none of the cohorts of either period reach the age of sixty before the year 1991.

Changes in the age distribution of the projected population are also shown in Figure 8. The impact of the entry of the 1940–1950 birth cohorts into the different age groups is indicated by the decline in the proportion of persons aged 15–29 years between 1961 and 1966, followed by a decline of the 30–44 years age group from 1971 to 1981, and the beginning of a decrease in the proportion of those aged 45–59 years after 1981, which becomes more pronounced after 1986. In contrast, the entry of the much larger birth cohorts of the fifties into the different age groups is shown by the rapid increase in the proportion of the 15–29 year age group in 1966, followed, after 1981, by an increasing proportion of those aged 30–44 years. Thus, the component projections of the population indicate that *during the next decades the working-age population of Indonesia will undergo a radical rejuvenation.*

The decline in fertility assumed in projection D will primarily affect the 0–14 years age group, and only after 1981 will it have some significance for the 15–29 years age group. Thus only after 1981 will such a decline affect the labor force, and its impact will only be on the younger working-age population, since by 1991 the 1966 birth cohort will only be twenty-five years old. Since women enter the reproductive age at the same time as the work-

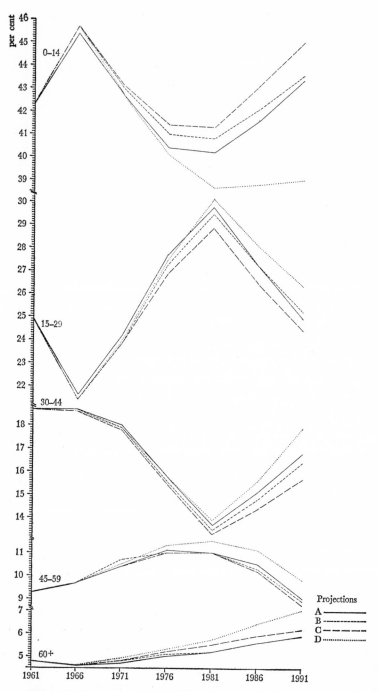

Figure 8. Percentage distribution of projected population by broad age group, Indonesia, 1961–1991

ing age, however, there will also be an impact on the number of births. This is what can be called the secondary effect of fertility decline. The sooner fertility declines, the sooner this effect will be brought about, and the lower will be the resulting rate of population growth. Since ages of high fertility are between twenty and thirty-five years, the secondary effect of a fertility decline may only commence after a minimum of twenty years.

Age Distribution and Labor Force Projections

The growth of the different sex-age categories throughout the thirty-year period for each of the projections is shown in the population pyramids in Figures 9–12. Each of these pyramids shows the sex-age structure of the population at different dates, and by comparing a certain sex-age category at a certain date with the corresponding sex-age group at succeeding dates, some idea can be obtained of the growth of the components of the population.

As previously stated, the sex-age structure of the 1961 population reflects the population history of preceding decades. The abrupt changes in 1940–1950 are clearly exhibited by the very small percentage of the 10–14 and 15–19 years age groups, while the recovery of the fertility level and swift decline in mortality are reflected in the large percentage of persons aged 0–4 and 5–9 years. In addition, it is not unlikely that the relatively small percentage of persons in the 20–24 and 25–29 years age groups indicate the impact of the depression, or they may reflect the fact that during the famines and food shortages of the forties the death toll among those born in the previous decade was enormous.

In comparing the 1961 population with the projected population for 1971—as shown by the population pyramids—one feature stands out very clearly: the great upsurge in the number of persons aged 10–14 years and 15–19 years. Each of the four projections indicates that these age groups will almost double within the ten-year period. It is also noteworthy that there is

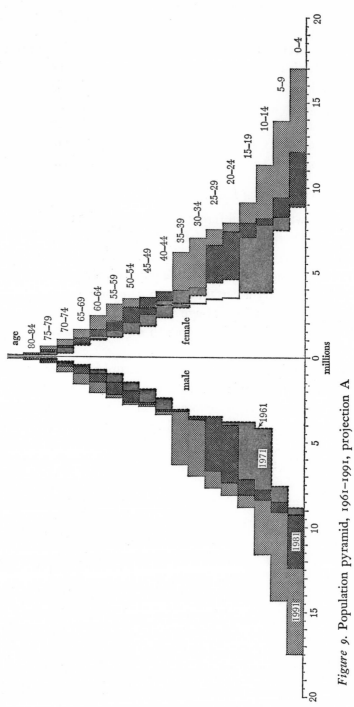

Figure 9. Population pyramid, 1961-1991, projection A

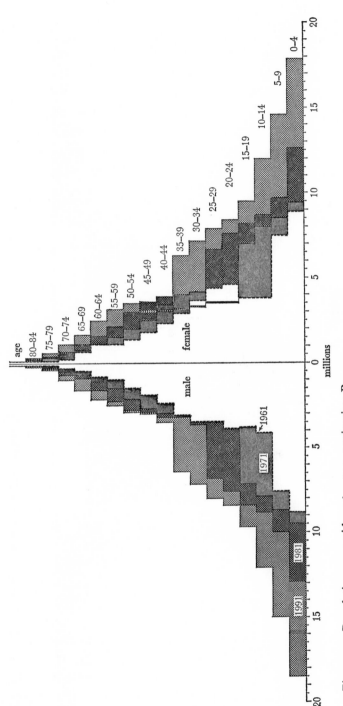

Figure 10. Population pyramid, 1961–1991, projection B

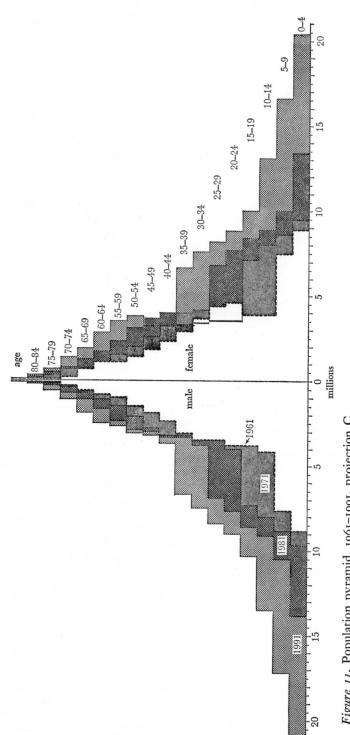

Figure 11. Population pyramid, 1961–1991, projection C

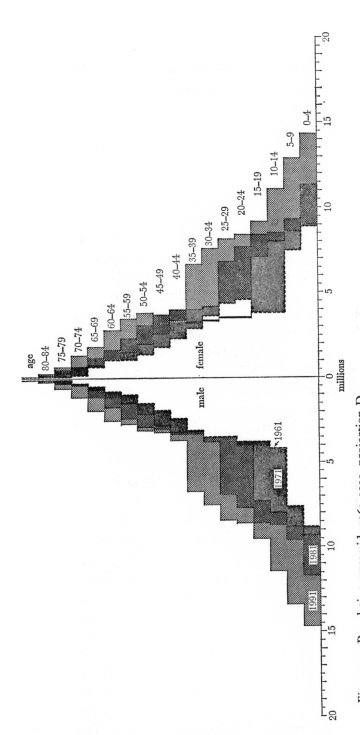

Figure 12. Population pyramid, 1961–1991, projection D

very little difference in the size of the 0–4 years age group between the two populations. This is in conformity with the discussion on the number of births when it was pointed out that the entry of the 1940–1950 birth cohorts into the reproductive ages will probably result in a leveling off in the number of births between 1966 and 1971. Only after 1971, when the birth cohorts of the fifties move up into the reproductive ages, will the number of births—and consequently the age group 0–4 years—increase sharply.

Comparing the 1971 and the 1981 populations, the main increase will be in the 20–24 and 25–29 years age groups, but the 0–4 years age group will also undergo a rapid increase. Between 1981 and 1991 there will apparently be a sharp increase in the number of persons aged 30–34 and 35–39 years, as the 1950–1960 birth cohorts enter these age groups, and the size of the 0–4 years age group will again increase sharply. A new feature in 1991 will be the large increase in the 5–9 and 10–14 years age groups, as a consequence of the upsurge in the number of births after 1971.

Comparisons between the projected populations for the different years—as shown in the population pyramids—indicate the impact of the course of vital events in the forties and fifties on the age structure of the population. They show clearly that during the ensuing decade (1966–1976) the consequence of past events will be a radical rejuvenation of the working-age population in the form of an almost doubling of the number of younger workers aged 15–19 and 20–24 years.

Since the important changes in the immediate future will primarily concern the school-age and younger working-age population, more attention needs to be given to these age groups. One common feature of the alternative projections is the fact that in each of the years there is a point at which a sharp distinction can be drawn between the very small and very large age groups. Thus, in 1961 the 5–9 years age group is far larger than that aged 10–14 years. In 1966 the 10–14 years age group becomes the boundary between the very small (15–19 years) and the very large age groups. In 1971 the big difference will be between the 15–19 years and the 20–24 years age group. In 1976 the age groups below 24 years will be very large, while the older age groups will be small. Table 76 shows the population 0–29 years old by five-year age groups for the years 1961–1981 according to projection B.

Table 76. Projected population aged twenty-nine years and less by age group (projection B), Indonesia, 1961–1981 (in thousands)

Sex and age group	1961	1966	1971	1976	1981
Male					
0–4	8,869	9,467	9,559	10,609	12,938
5–9	7,642	8,158	8,792	8,956	10,020
10–14	4,295	7,456	7,983	8,626	8,807
15–19	3,813	4,191	7,294	7,828	8,477
20–24	3,884	3,679	4,057	7,084	7,623
25–29	3,547	3,718	3,537	3,916	6,863
Female					
0–4	8,904	9,233	9,440	10,340	12,607
5–9	7,523	8,200	8,587	8,858	9,785
10–14	3,802	7,329	8,014	8,416	8,706
15–19	3,815	3,701	7,156	7,847	8,264
20–24	4,635	3,674	3,579	6,948	7,647
25–29	4,431	4,429	3,529	3,454	6,735
Both sexes					
0–4	17,773	18,700	18,999	20,949	25,545
5–9	15,165	16,358	17,379	17,814	19,805
10–14	8,097	14,785	15,997	17,042	17,513
15–19	7,628	7,892	14,450	15,675	16,741
20–24	8,519	7,353	7,636	14,032	15,270
25–29	7,978	8,147	7,066	7,370	13,598

These characteristics can also be viewed from a different angle. Between 1961 and 1966 there is a sharp increase in the age group 10–14 years; in the period 1966–1971 this increase affects the age group 15–19 years; and between 1971 and 1976 it affects the age group 20–24 years. Thus, projection B indicates that in 1961–1966 the number of persons aged 10–14 years increases from 8.1 million to 14.8 million—an increase of 6.7 million, or 82.7 per cent, over the five-year period. Between 1966 and 1971 the younger working-age population of 15–19 years increases from 7.9 million to 14.4 million, an increase of 6.5 million, or 82.3 per cent. From 1971 to 1976 the 20–24 years age group will grow from a total of 7.6 million to 14.0 million, which is an increase of 6.4 million, or 84.2 per cent.

In the years between 1966 and 1971, then, the number of persons aged 15–19 years will increase by 6.5 million, which means an average annual increase for that age group of around 1.3 million persons. The number of males aged 15–19 will increase from 4.2 to 7.3 million, an annual increase of around 0.6 million, and the number of females from 3.7 to 7.1 million, an annual increase of about 0.7 million. In order to arrive at the net increase in the working-age population, of course, the total number of those who died and of those who passed beyond the working ages must be subtracted from these new additions. The total increase between 1966 and 1971 in the 15–29 years age group will be 5.7 million,[1] for those aged 30–44 years 1.4 million, and for the older working-age population of 45–59 years the increase amounts to 2.0 million. Thus the total increase in the working-age population (15–59 years) from 1966 to 1971 will be 9.1 million, out of which 6.5 million belong to the 15–19 years age group. In other words, during that period the number of persons belonging to the working-age population will increase annually by 1.8 million, out of which 1.3 million will be 15–19 years old. The fact that during the same period the annual increase in the total population will be around 2.5 million implies that *more than 50 per cent of the increase in total population will be among persons aged 15–19 years.*

The impact of the sudden increase in the younger working-age population over the next decade has been very well expressed by Nathan Keyfitz:

The most striking feature of the table [see Table 77] is the drop from over 3 million at age 7 to under 1½ million by age 12 or 13. But to call this a drop is only right when the table is read from top

[1] The increase in the 15–29 years age group will be smaller than the increase in the 15–19 years age group, because a decline will occur in the 25–29 years age group.

to bottom. In the book of real History this table is read from the bottom upwards. For the successive ages may be thought of as successive classes or cohorts, and they file past the grandstand of history from the bottom of our list to the top. Those who were age 14 in 1961 are 19 in 1966 and 24 in 1971, etc. It is convenient to take one single age as the point at which we stand in reviewing the march-past of the cohorts, and we choose age 17. This is not the earliest that Indonesians start to work, especially in the villages; on the

Table 77. Population as reported in census and as smoothed by Sprague multipliers, Indonesia, 1961

Age in 1961	Census	Smoothed	Age in 1966	Age in 1971	Year of seventeenth birthday
Less than 1	3,171,000		5	10	1978
1	3,009,000		6	11	1977
2	3,516,000		7	12	1976
3	3,769,000		8	13	1975
4	3,578,000		9	14	1974
5	3,296,000		10	15	1973
6	3,073,000	3,360,000	11	16	1972
7	3,327,000	3,108,000	12	17	1971
8	2,884,000	2,812,000	13	18	1970
9	2,743,000	2,492,000	14	19	1969
10	2,381,000	2,139,000	15	20	1968
11	1,341,000	1,742,000	16	21	1967
12	1,912,000	1,466,000	17	22	1966
13	1,344,000	1,389,000	18	23	1965
14	1,200,000	1,444,000	19	24	1964

Source: Nathan Keyfitz, "Population in Indonesia—The Short and Long Run," in Institute of Economic and Social Research, Faculty of Economics, University of Indonesia, *Workshop Masalah Penduduk*(Workshop on Population Problems) (Djakarta, 1964), p. 8. Based on 1961 census, 1 per cent sample.

other hand one can say that by that age the large majority have left school, and are in the labour market. We see that at the present time, and for many years past, the number that reach 17 year by year is less than 1½ millions; in 1966 it is still less than 1½ million. But then it takes a sudden jump—on the graduated figures, which I am inclined to trust for this purpose, it goes to 1,742,000. By 1968 it has passed the 2,000,000 mark; in 1969 it is close to 2½ million; in 1970 it is approaching 3 million, and in 1971 it has passed that figure. . . .

What ordinarily happens is that the labour force moves up in age each year; people are promoted, retire, or die, and their places are taken by the young entrants who come in at bottom of the hierarchy. This is how the 1 ½ million or those among them who wish to enter the labour force have been absorbed in Indonesia year by year up to now, and will continue to be absorbed up to 1967. But then they will increase so that at the beginning of the new decade the annual entrants are double the number to which the country is now accustomed. Each entrant will literally bring his brother along, and the brother will want a job as well.[2]

In order to relate population projections to the creation of future employment opportunities, labor force projections have to be carried out. These are based on population projections and on the likely percentages of the different sex-age groups in the future population that will belong to the labor force. According to the 1961 population census, as shown in Table 55 Chapter 10, almost 80 per cent of the male population and almost 30 per cent of the female population aged ten years and over belonged to the labor force. The percentages for the different age groups vary widely, between 22.6 and 96.8 per cent for males, and between 15.6 and 39.8 per cent for females. The simplest way to arrive at labor force projections would be to apply these percentages to each of the corresponding sex-age categories in the population projections. The sum of the results will then be the projected labor force for a future date.

This method has two principal disadvantages. It not only assumes a satisfactory degree of accuracy in the census data on the labor force; more importantly, it assumes that the future trend of the labor force will be similar or identical to the past trend. Alternative methods of projecting the labor force do include relating the future trend of the labor force to other variables, such as the likely trends in industrialization and urban-

[2] Nathan Keyfitz, "Population in Indonesia—The Short and Long Run," in Institute of Economic and Social Research, Faculty of Economics, University of Indonesia, *Workshop Masalah Penduduk* (Workshop on Population Problems) (Djakarta, 1964), pp. 8–10.

ization. But in order to illustrate merely the general trend of the working-age population, the simplest method of labor force projection will be used here and no attempt made to relate this trend to other variables. For the purposes of illustrating more clearly the general trends of the projected labor force, only projection B is used and the figures are limited to the years between 1966 and 1976.

The results of applying the simple method of labor force projection are shown in Table 78. For 1961 the "labor force

Table 78. Projected labor force by sex and age (projection B), Indonesia, 1961–1976 (in thousands)

Sex and age group	1961	1966	1971	1976
Male				
10–14	970	1,685	1,804	1,949
15–19	2,543	2,795	4,865	5,221
20–24	3,387	3,208	3,538	6,177
25–34	6,735	6,706	6,705	6,913
35–44	5,468	6,184	6,254	6,297
45–54	3,292	3,878	4,673	5,358
55–64	1,693	1,977	2,463	2,890
65–74	661	798	907	1,143
75+	230	190	216	265
Total, males	24,979	27,421	31,425	36,213
Female				
10–14	593	1,143	1,250	1,313
15–19	1,167	1,133	2,190	2,401
20–24	1,270	1,007	981	1,904
25–34	2,241	2,361	2,121	1,871
35–44	1,739	2,111	2,477	2,650
45–54	1,317	1,547	1,835	2,258
55–64	927	910	1,058	1,266
65–74	311	463	491	501
75+	81	65	93	137
Total, females	9,646	10,740	12,496	14,301

participation rate"—that is, the percentage of the population in the different age groups who belong to the labor force, as found in the census—has been applied to the adjusted census population, resulting in a total labor force population of 34.6 million. In 1966 this figure will be 38.2 million; in 1971, 43.9 million; and in

1976, 50.5 million. Thus, between 1961 and 1966 the labor force increases by around 0.7 million persons each year, while in the period 1966–1971 the annual increase will be 1.15 million persons; in 1971–1976 the labor force will increase by 1.3 million persons each year. One important feature of these increases is the leap from 3.9 million in the labor force population aged 15–19 years in 1966 to 7.1 million persons in this age group in 1971.

It must be remembered that these figures are of an illustrative nature only. For purposes of development planning more complicated and detailed methods will need to be devised that take into account the probable trends of other variables. Furthermore, a breakdown according to region and according to rural and urban areas would be imperative. The future trend in educational level as it affects each of the sexes will also have to be taken into account. Once the probable future number of entrants into the labor force has been estimated, plans can be made to provide them with productive employment. In addition to providing employment for the new entrants into the labor force, plans also need to be formulated for the employment of the overtly unemployed as well as for the fuller employment of the underemployed labor force.

Some Projections of Java's Population

In addition to the projections for Indonesia as a whole, separate population projections have been made for Java. Simple adjustments were applied to the 1961 census population, and the resulting adjusted population was used as the base population for projections. The total number of the census population and the ratio between the totals of the sexes have been retained, as was the case with the adjusted population of Indonesia, and the results are shown in Table 79.

In discussing the vital rates it was found that the fertility level in Java seemed to be somewhat lower than that for the country as a whole. It was therefore assumed that the initial level of fertility could be represented by a sex-age adjusted birth rate of

Table 79. Adjusted census population by sex and age, Java, 1961

Age group	Male No. (in thous.)	Male % of sex group	Female No. (in thous.)	Female % of sex group
0–4	5,636	18.3	5,762	17.9
5–9	4,835	15.8	4,938	15.6
10–14	2,691	8.7	2,416	7.5
15–19	2,394	7.8	2,424	7.5
20–24	2,418	7.8	2,936	9.2
25–29	2,329	7.6	2,819	8.9
30–34	2,377	7.7	2,316	7.1
35–39	2,070	6.7	1,901	5.9
40–44	1,716	5.6	1,625	5.0
45–49	1,355	4.4	1,353	4.2
50–54	1,017	3.3	1,073	3.3
55–59	737	2.4	850	2.6
60–64	509	1.6	845	2.6
65–69	310	1.0	483	1.5
70–74	193	0.6	201	0.6
75–79	82	0.3	97	0.3
80–84	72	0.2	89	0.3
85+	60	0.2	63	0.2
Total, all ages	30,801	100.0	32,191	100.0

44 per 1,000, as compared to 45 per 1,000 for the country as a whole. The initial level of mortality is assumed to resemble that of Indonesia as a whole—a life expectancy at birth of 40 to 42.5 years. In the first three of the four alternative projections the sets of assumptions concerning the course of fertility and mortality are similar to those for projections A, B, and C for Indonesia, the only difference being the somewhat lower level of fertility. For projection D, which shows the results of both a rapidly declining fertility and a rapidly declining mortality, it is assumed that the level of fertility decreases from a sex-age adjusted birth rate of 44 per 1,000 in 1961 to 30.8 per 1,000 in 1986–1991.

The assumed annual sex-age adjusted birth rate and life expectancy for the different projections are shown in Table 80, and the resulting population projections for Java are shown in

Table 80. Assumed annual sex-age adjusted birth rate and expectation of life at birth used in population projections A, B, C, and D, Java, 1961-1991

Period	Annual sex-age adjusted birth rate (per 1,000)				Expectation of life at birth (in yrs.)			
	A	B	C	D	A	B	C	D
1961-1966	44.0	44.0	44.0	44.0	40.0	42.5	42.5	42.5
1966-1971	44.0	44.0	44.0	42.0	42.5	45.0	47.5	47.5
1971-1976	44.0	44.0	44.0	39.7	45.0	47.5	52.5	52.5
1976-1981	44.0	44.0	44.0	37.0	47.5	50.0	57.6	57.6
1981-1986	44.0	44.0	44.0	34.0	50.0	52.5	63.2	63.2
1986-1991	44.0	44.0	44.0	30.8	52.5	55.0	68.2	68.2

Table 81. A "normal" decline in mortality accompanied by a constant level of fertility will result in a total population of between 123.9 and 130.4 million in 1991. A rapidly declining mortality, unaccompanied by changes in fertility, results in a total population of 142.4 million. Should fertility also decrease, the total population in 1991 will be 125.3 million. It thus seems that Java's population will about double in the thirty-year period.

Similar to the projections for the whole country, the rate of population increase in Java during the last part of the thirty-year period will be higher than during the first part, although the resulting rates of increase in each of the projections is smaller than for Indonesia as a whole. The more rapid increase in total population from 1976 to 1991 is also due largely to the recovery in the fifties from the unusual conditions of the forties: a large number of women born during the fifties start to enter the reproductive ages, resulting in a rapid upsurge of the number of births. The implied annual crude birth rates, together with the rates of natural increase and the corresponding crude death rates, are shown in Table 82. Again, this table shows clearly the deficiencies of crude rates in that they are too dependent on the age structure of the population. Thus, the projections imply a decline in crude birth rates between 1961 and 1976, even though fertility is assumed to remain constant.

Table 81. Projected total population and annual rate of increase, Java, 1961–1991

Year	Projection A		Projection B		Projection C		Projection D	
	Total population (in thous.)	Annual rate of increase (per 1,000)	Total population (in thous.)	Annual rate of increase (per 1,000)	Total population (in thous.)	Annual rate of increase (per 1,000)	Total population (in thous.)	Annual rate of increase (per 1,000)
1961	62,992	18.9	62,992	21.9	62,992	21.9	62,992	21.9
1966	69,236	17.6	70,295	20.5	70,295	21.8	70,295	20.3
1971	75,603	20.1	77,756	21.4	78,362	24.1	77,821	21.2
1976	83,635	24.3	86,547	25.1	88,397	28.5	86,549	23.7
1981	94,402	26.9	98,182	27.8	101,921	32.4	97,428	25.3
1986	107,967	27.6	112,851	28.8	119,874	34.4	110,604	25.0
1991	123,889		130,392		142,412		125,293	

Table 82. Implied annual crude birth rate, crude rate of natural increase, and crude death rate in population projections A, B, C, and D, Java, 1961–1991 (per 1,000 persons)

Period	Annual crude birth rate				Annual crude rate of natural increase				Annual crude death rate			
	A	B	C	D	A	B	C	D	A	B	C	D
1961–1966	42.1	43.2	43.2	43.2	18.9	21.9	21.9	21.9	23.2	21.3	21.3	21.3
1966–1971	36.7	38.6	38.4	36.8	17.6	20.5	21.8	20.3	19.1	18.1	16.6	16.5
1971–1976	38.7	38.3	37.8	34.6	20.1	21.4	24.1	21.2	18.6	16.9	13.7	13.4
1976–1981	41.9	41.0	39.8	34.6	24.3	25.1	28.5	23.7	17.6	15.9	11.3	10.9
1981–1986	43.2	42.6	41.1	33.8	26.9	27.8	32.4	25.3	16.3	14.8	8.7	8.5
1986–1991	42.2	42.1	40.1	31.5	27.6	28.8	34.4	25.0	14.6	13.3	5.7	5.5

Table 83. Projected population by sex and broad age group (projection B), Java, 1961–1991 (in thousands)

Sex and age group	1961	1966	1971	1976	1981	1986	1991
Male							
0–14	13,162	15,764	16,446	17,543	19,905	23,804	28,541
15–29	7,141	7,251	9,379	11,911	14,437	15,221	16,381
30–44	6,163	6,427	6,482	6,295	6,480	8,504	10,918
45–59	3,109	3,711	4,364	4,993	5,302	5,442	5,382
60+	1,226	1,417	1,735	2,159	2,680	3,276	3,906
Total, males	30,801	34,570	38,406	42,901	48,804	56,247	65,128
Female							
0–14	13,116	15,828	16,271	17,095	19,428	23,217	27,816
15–29	8,179	7,492	9,215	11,834	14,480	15,056	15,974
30–44	5,842	6,678	7,340	7,193	6,691	8,371	10,883
45–59	3,276	3,738	4,247	4,875	5,688	6,355	6,306
60+	1,778	1,989	2,277	2,649	3,091	3,605	4,285
Total, fe-males	32,191	35,725	39,350	43,646	49,378	56,604	65,264
Both sexes							
0–14	26,278	31,592	32,717	34,638	39,333	47,021	56,357
15–29	15,320	14,743	18,594	23,745	28,917	30,277	32,355
30–44	12,005	13,105	13,822	13,488	13,171	16,875	21,801
45–59	6,385	7,449	8,611	9,868	10,990	11,797	11,688
60+	3,004	3,406	4,012	4,808	5,771	6,881	8,191
Total, both sexes	62,992	70,295	77,756	86,547	98,182	112,851	130,392

Table 83 shows the growth of the different age groups of projection B throughout the thirty-year period. The growth of these age groups is quite similar to the course of the corresponding age groups in the projections for Indonesia as a whole. The growth of the different broad age groups as well as the changes in the proportions of the age groups clearly reflects the abrupt changes in vital rates in the forties and the recovery of the fifties. The future population of Java will also undergo a rejuvenation of the working-age population as the survivors of the large number of births of the fifties follow the very small number of survivors of the births of the forties into the working ages.

The Impact of Out-Migration on the Future Population of Java

A further study has been conducted to assess the impact on the future growth of Java's population of alternative patterns of out-migration to the other Indonesian islands. These projections use different sets of assumptions from the earlier ones and are based on the estimated population of 1960 rather than the census population of 1961.

Given a base population of 62.5 million in 1960, and assuming a constant fertility level (a sex-age adjusted birth rate of 46.4 births per 1,000 persons) and a rapidly declining mortality level (from a life expectancy of 42.5 years in 1960–1965 to 68.2 years in 1985–1990), the population of Java in 1990 will be 146.2 million. This projection assumes that there will be neither any out-migration from Java nor any in-migration into Java.

This projection is then compared with another projection which assumes identical courses of fertility and mortality but which in addition also assumes that 200,000 young persons will migrate annually from Java, or one million young persons over each five-year period. It is assumed that the out-migration starts in 1960–1965 and continues throughout the whole thirty-year period. The assumption concerning the youth of the migrants refers to their sex-age distribution at the actual time of their departure, which is assumed to be at the last moment of the five-year period.[3] Assuming further that no vital change occurs between the last moment of any five-year period and the first moment of the following five-year period, the different sex-age groups of the migrant population can then be subtracted from the corresponding sex-age group of the population as it would exist at the beginning of the following five-year period if there had been no out-migration.[4]

[3] More precisely, it refers to the sex-age distribution of the migrant population that would have occurred at the last moment (or on the last day) of each five-year period if no migration took place. This is equal to the sex-age distribution of the migrant population at the moment of departure only if their departure is assumed to occur at the last moment of the five-year period.

[4] If it were assumed that the departures were spread out over the whole five-year period, then the calculation of the sex-age distribution of the migrant population and their descendants at the beginning of the

By assuming that one million migrants leave Java at the last moment of each five-year period, it is possible to estimate the 1965 population as one million less than in the original projection. The 1970 population will be equal to the original number minus the one million migrants who left between 1965 and 1970, and also minus the survivors and descendants of the one million migrants who had departed during the earlier period, 1960–1965.

The result of a net migration of one million young persons in each five-year period, assuming constant fertility and rapidly declining mortality, would then yield a total population of 86 million in 1975 and 136 million in 1990. These figures are respectively 4.2 and 6.8 per cent less than the projected population numbers in the absence of out-migration. Thus by the end of the thirty-year period this rate of out-migration would result in a total population of 10.2 million less than the original projected population figure.

Although the annual rate of population growth will be somewhat lower than in the absence of out-migration, all the effects on the projected population of the sudden changes in vital rates between 1940 and 1950 are reproduced in the population resulting from the net migration: an acceleration of the growth rate of the total population after 1975 and a slackening of the rate of increase of the 0–14 years age group in 1965–1975 and of the working-age population before 1965. Constant or even slightly negative rates of increase are noticeable for the 15–29 years age group in 1960–1965, for the 30–44 years age group in 1970–1980, and for the 45–59 years age group after 1985. The entry of the relatively small birth cohorts of 1965–1970, generated by the birth cohorts of the forties, results in a deceleration of the growth rate of the younger working-age population in the eighties, but this will have little effect on the growth rate of the working-age population as a whole, since during the same period

following five-year period would have to take into account the aging and the survivorship of the migrants during the intervening period as well as the births during that period.

the large birth cohorts of the fifties enter the middle-aged work-ing population.

It is instructive to compare the effect of out-migration with that of a fertility decline. In doing this, one projection assumes that Java's projected population has a constant fertility level and a rapidly declining level of mortality and that there is an out-mi-gration of 200,000 young persons annually. For purposes of comparison, another projection assumes a declining level of fer-tility, a rapidly declining mortality level, and no out-migration. The sex-age adjusted birth rate is assumed to decline from 46.4 births per 1,000 persons in 1960–1965 to 35.0 in 1985–1990, while life expectancy increases from 42.5 years in 1960–1965 to 68.2 years in 1985–1990. This latter projection gives an esti-mated population of Java of 88 million in 1975 and of 132 million in 1990. A comparison between the two projections (see Table 84) shows that a "normal" decline in fertility will have a

Table 84. Projected population of Java based on alternative assump-tions of fertility, mortality, and out-migration, 1960–1990 (in millions)

Alternative sets of assumptions	1960	1975	1990
Constant fertility, rapidly declining mortality, no out-migration	62.5	89.8	146.2
Constant fertility, rapidly declining mortality, out-migration of 200,000 young persons annually	62.5	86.1	136.0
Declining fertility, rapidly declin-ing mortality, no out-migration	62.5	88.4	132.1

comparable, if not a stronger, impact on the future growth of Java's population than an out-migration of 200,000 young per-sons annually.

Additional projections have also been made assuming a net out-migration of one million young persons annually or five million young persons in each five-year period. Although such a rate of out-migration is unlikely to occur, the projection has been carried out for purposes of comparison. It has been found that in this case Java's population will be 70.8 million in 1975 and 94.9 million in 1990. Thus, a net out-migration of one million young persons annually from Java will still result in an increase in the remaining population of around 50 per cent in a thirty-year period.

Conclusions

Indonesia possesses the usual traits of the populations of developing countries: a high rate of increase in the total population, a large dependency ratio, and a rapid rate of growth among the urban population. There are also other features, however, of which one is the well-known discrepancy in the geographical distribution of the population.

The existing population differential between Java and the rest of the Indonesian islands has in the past led to widespread speculation concerning a "population explosion" in Java during the nineteenth century. On the basis of existing population data, very high growth rates have been computed for the nineteenth-century population of Java. Such computations, however, have in most cases been carried out without actually appraising the original sources of the data, and many, in fact, defy the warnings contained in most of the original data concerning the limitations of the information. On the basis of a detailed study of the original data references and official colonial reports, the present study shows that the existing data on Java's nineteenth-century population are actually gross underestimates and that there was a high degree of underreporting.

The allegedly rapid population increase was supposedly due to widespread improvements in health conditions and rapid increases in the standard of living of Java's population during the past century. However, there is no evidence to support these contentions. Health improvements were carried out on a much more limited scale than is generally believed, and official reports abound with accounts on famines. The notion of a "population explosion" in Java during the nineteenth century is thus based on questionable evidence, evdience that endeavors to show the blessings of a colonial regime by exaggerating those factors favorable to population growth. Most probably the population of the island of Java was already large long before the nineteenth century.

In addition to the wide discrepancy in the geographical distribution of the population of Indonesia, there is another, lesser-known feature related to its present age composition. This reflects the changes in fertility and mortality levels in the past and, in turn, will affect the growth and composition of Indonesia's future population.

The last census during the colonial era was conducted in 1930. Employing demographic tools of analysis the present study arrives at estimates of the growth and age composition of the population during the period 1930–1960, together with estimates of the levels and courses of fertility and mortality for that period.

During the 1930's fertility as well as mortality levels were high. Abrupt changes in vital rates took place during the following decade as a consequence of the occupation and the war of independence. During that decade the level of fertility declined rapidly while the mortality level increased sharply, resulting in a very low population growth—probably even a population decrease.

In the decade of the fifties fertility resumed its prewar level, and might be even higher, owing to family reunions after the war and an increase in marriages. On the other hand, the level of mortality, and in particular infant mortality, has decreased steadily since the early fifties as a result of the spread of improved public health measures. The result was a tremendous upsurge in the number of infants and young children during the fifties.

The developments in the forties as well as in the fifties had an immediate impact on the age composition of the present population and will continue to have an effect on the growth and age composition of the future population. The abrupt changes in vital rates result in unusual fluctuations in the proportions of the different age groups of the population. As the small birth cohort of the forties enter a certain age group, a small increase occurs in the number of persons in that age group. When that cohort moves up to the next age group, the much larger birth cohort of the fifties enters the original age group, and a sharp increase takes place in the number of persons in that group.

In this respect the population census of 1961, the first held in independent Indonesia, provides relevant material. Age data from censuses are never to be taken at face value. Nevertheless, after taking due account of inaccuracies in age reporting, the age composition of the 1961 population shows certain features which can be traced to past changes in vital rates. Thus, the number of persons aged 10–19 years in 1961 was relatively small. These were survivors of the births between 1942 and 1951. On the other hand, the 0–9-year age group was very large in 1961. It consisted of the survivors of the births of 1952–1961. This large burden of child dependency continues after 1961.

During the period 1962–1966 a sharp increase occurred in the number of persons aged 10–14 years, since the large number of persons aged 5–9 years in 1961 became the 10–14-year age group in 1966. It is estimated that during 1962–1966 the 10–14-year age group almost doubled. As a consequence, the pressure on educational facilities, in particular at elementary and secondary levels, has been increasing.

The period 1967–1971 is undergoing a rapid increase in the 15–19-year age group, while the period 1972–1976 will experience an upsurge of persons aged 20–24 years. These developments take place as the small birth cohort of the forties moves out of these age groups and is replaced by the large birth cohort of the fifties. Thus, during the period 1967–1976 the population of Indonesia will undergo a radical rejuvenation of its working-age population because the number of young workers aged 15–19 and 20–24 years will almost double. In the years 1967–1971 more than 50 per cent of the increase in total population, which amounts to 2.5 million persons annually, consists of those aged 15–19 years. The creation of employment opportunities for these new entrants into the labor force is clearly essential.

Past changes in fertility and mortality levels also have their impact on present and future rates of population increase. As soon as the large number of females born in the fifties enters the marriage age group a more rapid increase in the number of children born takes place. In 1971 the women aged 20–29 years are survivors of the small number of births of 1942–1951, while in 1981 the same age group will consist of the survivors of the large number of births of 1952–1961. Therefore, given certain fertility and mortality levels, the number of births will increase more rapidly after 1971.

As to the future population, the present study arrives at a number of alternative population projections based on alternative sets of assumptions concerning the future courses of fertility and mortality. A rapid decline in mortality, unaccompanied by changes in fertility, gives a total population for Java in 1991 of more than 140 million, whereas if fertility also declines Java's population will be about 125 million. Furthermore, the impact of out-migration on the future population of Java has also been investigated. A net out-migration from Java of 200,000 young persons annually will decrease by only about 7 per cent the 1991 population as computed on the basis of no out-migration.

Thus, the high rate of population increase, the large burden of child dependency, the rapid process of urban growth, the heavy concentration of the population on a relatively small island, and the radical rejuvenation of the working-age population, all point sharply to the need for a massive development effort to create expanding employment opportunities, accompanied by a rapid spread of fertility control.

Population by Sex and
Region, Indonesia, 1961

Region	Male	Female	Both sexes	No. of females per 1,000 males
I. DJAKARTA RAYA	1,480,771	1,425,762	2,906,533	953
1. North Djakarta	486,698	467,635	954,333	961
2. Central Djakarta	425,157	412,203	837,360	970
3. South Djakarta	610,450	570,909	1,181,359	935
II. WEST JAVA	8,657,815	8,956,740	17,614,555	1,035
Municipality:	682,676	682,719	1,365,395	1,000
1. Bogor	77,012	77,080	154,092	1,001
2. Bandung	488,911	483,655	972,566	989
3. Sukabumi	39,323	41,115	80,438	1,046
4. Tjirebon	77,430	80,869	158,299	1,044
Regency:	7,975,139	8,274,021	16,249,160	1,037
1. Pandeglang	219,394	220,819	440,213	1,006
2. Serang	354,783	365,386	720,169	1,030
3. Lebak	212,678	215,124	427,802	1,012
4. Bekasi	342,479	350,338	692,817	1,023
5. Krawang	414,049	419,691	833,740	1,014
6. Purwakarta	537,137	549,285	1,086,422	1,023
7. Tangerang	421,311	429,079	850,390	1,018
8. Bogor	658,379	655,777	1,314,156	996
9. Sukabumi	477,171	487,424	964,595	1,021
10. Tjiandjur	446,106	453,397	899,503	1,016
11. Bandung	786,387	810,022	1,596,409	1,030
12. Sumedang	257,491	269,948	527,439	1,048
13. Garut	444,349	480,194	924,543	1,080

Region	Male	Female	Both sexes	No. of females per 1,000 males
14. Tasikmalaja	488,790	528,886	1,017,676	1,082
15. Tjiamis	495,417	519,209	1,014,626	1,048
16. Tjirebon	434,269	469,845	904,114	1,082
17. Kuningan	255,144	271,857	527,001	1,066
18. Indramaju	419,696	442,552	862,248	1,054
19. Madjalengka	310,109	335,188	645,297	1,081
III. CENTRAL JAVA	8,967,714	9,439,757	18,407,471	1,053
Municipality:	591,412	625,352	1,216,764	1,057
1. Magelang	47,534	48,920	96,454	1,029
2. Pekalongan	49,821	52,559	102,380	1,055
3. Tegal	42,555	46,461	89,016	1,091
4. Semarang	247,434	255,719	503,153	1,033
5. Salatiga	27,689	30,446	58,135	1,100
6. Surakarta	176,379	191,247	367,626	1,084
Regency:	8,376,302	8,814,405	17,190,707	1,052
1. Banjumas	444,654	462,588	907,242	1,040
2. Purbolinggo	250,662	265,057	515,719	1,057
3. Tjilatjap	447,767	461,000	908,767	1,030
4. Bandjarnegara	254,459	265,294	519,753	1,043
5. Magelang	351,473	368,430	719,903	1,048
6. Temanggung	188,423	193,793	382,216	1,028
7. Wonosobo	210,137	215,680	425,817	1,026
8. Purworedjo	266,122	285,577	551,699	1,073
9. Kebumen	404,653	428,213	832,866	1,058
10. Pekalongan	415,665	435,559	851,224	1,048
11. Pemalang	333,787	365,852	699,639	1,096
12. Tegal	360,648	403,637	764,285	1,119
13. Brebes	424,749	469,922	894,671	1,106
14. Semarang	280,387	292,815	573,202	1,044
15. Kendal	259,962	269,023	528,985	1,035
16. Demak	231,219	237,550	468,769	1,027
17. Grobogan	341,584	348,107	689,691	1,019
18. Pati	342,656	356,187	698,843	1,039
19. Djepara	239,625	249,745	489,370	1,042
20. Rembang	146,234	150,580	296,814	1,030
21. Blora	248,353	259,022	507,375	1,043
22. Kedu	180,146	193,452	373,598	1,074
23. Klaten	394,900	427,923	822,823	1,084
24. Bojolali	294,196	309,307	603,503	1,051
25. Sragen	262,252	268,081	530,333	1,022
26. Sukohardjo	196,827	206,830	403,657	1,051

Region	Male	Female	Both sexes	No. of females per 1,000 males
27. Karanganjar	205,956	211,940	417,896	1,029
28. Wonogiri	398,806	413,241	812,047	1,036
IV. JOGJAKARTA	1,092,403	1,149,074	2,241,477	1,052
Municipality:	156,191	156,507	312,698	1,002
1. Jogjakarta	156,191	156,507	312,698	1,002
Regency:	936,212	992,567	1,928,779	1,060
1. Bantul	240,780	258,814	499,594	1,075
2. Sleman	250,435	269,070	519,505	1,074
3. Gunung Kidul	281,761	290,519	572,280	1,032
4. Kulon Progo	163,236	174,164	337,400	1,067
V. EAST JAVA	10,602,448	11,220,572	21,823,020	1,058
Municipality:	917,096	961,532	1,878,628	1,048
1. Surabaja	498,569	509,376	1,007,945	1,022
2. Modjokerto	24,427	27,305	51,732	1,118
3. Madiun	59,089	64,284	123,373	1,088
4. Kediri	76,999	81,919	158,918	1,064
5. Blitar	30,003	32,969	62,972	1,099
6. Malang	164,524	176,928	341,452	1,075
7. Pasuruan	30,641	32,767	63,408	1,069
8. Probolinggo	32,844	35,984	68,828	1,096
Regency:	9,685,352	10,259,040	19,944,392	1,059
1. Surabaja	322,117	343,885	666,002	1,068
2. Sidoardjo	260,438	280,613	541,051	1,077
3. Modjokerto	240,800	253,692	494,492	1,054
4. Djombang	335,485	350,877	686,362	1,046
5. Bodjonegoro	348,310	360,261	708,571	1,034
6. Tuban	310,403	327,781	638,184	1,056
7. Lamongan	375,377	397,222	772,599	1,058
8. Madiun	249,328	260,100	509,428	1,043
9. Ngawi	283,733	298,584	582,317	1,052
10. Magetan	238,959	259,476	498,435	1,086
11. Ponorogo	340,140	359,725	699,865	1,058
12. Patjitan	205,504	225,518	431,022	1,097
13. Kediri	451,760	466,276	918,036	1,032
14. Ngandjuk	332,042	343,864	675,906	1,036
15. Blitar	413,178	426,774	839,952	1,033
16. Tulungagung	327,553	347,796	675,349	1,062

Region	Male	Female	Both sexes	No. of females per 1,000 males
17. Trenggalek	213,528	225,329	438,857	1,055
18. Malang	715,208	758,898	1,474,106	1,061
19. Pasuruan	346,505	382,862	729,367	1,105
20. Probolinggo	318,496	337,511	656,007	1,060
21. Lumadjang	319,979	337,508	657,487	1,055
22. Bondowoso	245,026	258,434	503,460	1,055
23. Panarukan	210,767	221,280	432,047	1,050
24. Djember	740,000	761,763	1,501,763	1,029
25. Banjuwangi	530,458	533,075	1,063,533	1,005
26. Pamekasan	188,064	208,349	396,413	1,108
27. Sampang	226,720	258,166	484,886	1,139
28. Sumenep	329,106	365,441	694,547	1,110
29. Bangkalan	266,368	307,980	574,348	1,156
VI. SOUTH SUMATRA	2,465,562	2,381,662	4,847,224	966
Municipality:	357,921	336,564	694,485	940
1. Palembang	244,245	230,726	474,971	945
2. Bengkulu	12,963	12,367	25,330	954
3. Tandjung Karang and Teluk Betung	69,982	63,919	133,901	913
4. Pangkal Pinang	30,731	29,552	60,283	962
Regency:	2,107,641	2,045,098	4,152,739	970
1. Musi Banjuasin	148,838	147,388	296,226	990
2. Ogan Komering Ilir	184,388	193,874	378,262	1,051
3. Ogan Komering Ulu	192,207	189,317	381,524	985
4. Muara Enim	165,576	166,880	332,456	1,008
5. Lahat	155,001	155,034	310,035	1,000
6. North Bengkulu	43,346	43,777	87,123	1,010
7. Musi Rawas	95,577	90,116	185,693	943
8. South Bengkulu	69,454	69,729	139,183	1,004
9. Redjang Lebong	78,826	75,787	154,613	961
10. South Lampung	353,492	331,900	685,392	939
11. Central Lampung	267,617	246,467	514,084	921
12. North Lampung	171,551	162,583	334,134	948
13. Bangka	128,793	122,846	251,639	954
14. Belitung	52,975	49,400	102,375	933
VII. DJAMBI	386,109	358,272	744,381	928
Municipality:	61,599	51,481	113,080	936
1. Djambi	61,599	51,481	113,080	936

Region	Male	Female	Both sexes	No. of females per 1,000 males
Regency:	324,510	306,791	631,301	945
1. Batanghari	133,287	116,977	250,264	878
2. Merangin	115,373	109,627	225,000	950
3. Kerintji	75,850	80,187	156,037	1,057
VIII. RIAU	637,064	597,920	1,234,984	939
Municipality:	38,983	31,838	70,821	817
1. Pakanbaru	38,983	31,838	70,821	817
Regency:	598,081	566,082	1,164,163	946
1. Kampar	103,982	105,322	209,304	1,013
2. Indragiri	186,869	190,342	377,211	1,019
3. Bengkalis	155,854	142,828	298,682	916
4. Riau Islands	151,376	127,590	278,966	843
IX. WEST SUMATRA	1,117,669	1,201,388	2,319,057	1,075
Municipality:	118,436	114,516	232,952	967
1. Bukittinggi	25,942	25,514	51,456	984
2. Padang	73,730	69,969	143,699	949
3. Sawah Lunto	6,312	5,964	12,276	945
4. Padang Pandjang	12,452	13,069	25,521	1,050
Regency:	999,233	1,086,872	2,086,105	1,088
1. Agam	137,937	166,516	304,453	1,207
2. Pasaman	108,063	109,248	217,311	1,011
3. Limapuluh Kota	121,719	128,968	250,687	1,060
4. Solok	129,351	141,883	271,234	1,097
5. Padang Pariaman	213,443	229,206	442,649	1,074
6. South Pasisir	109,055	112,394	221,449	1,031
7. Tanah Datar	115,244	131,219	246,463	1,139
8. Sawah Lunto/ Sidjundjung	64,421	67,438	131,859	1,047
X. NORTH SUMATRA	2,514,328	2,450,406	4,964,734	975
Municipality:	377,375	355,863	733,238	943
1. Medan	246,061	233,037	479,098	947
2. Pematang Siantar	59,202	55,668	114,870	940
3. Tandjung Balai	14,932	14,220	29,152	952
4. Bindjai	23,456	21,779	45,235	929
5. Tebing Tinggi	13,488	12,740	26,228	945
6. Sibolga	20,236	18,419	38,655	910

Region	Male	Female	Both sexes	No. of females per 1,000 males
Regency:	2,136,953	2,094,543	4,231,496	980
1. Deli Serdang	495,993	475,628	971,621	959
2. Langkat	176,217	165,398	341,615	939
3. Karo	72,126	75,547	147,673	1,047
4. Simalungun	249,826	246,412	496,238	986
5. Asahan	208,451	200,555	409,006	962
6. Labuhan Batu	131,771	124,226	255,997	943
7. Central Tapanuli	50,968	49,827	100,795	978
8. South Tapanuli	248,692	246,368	495,060	991
9. North Tapanuli	272,261	288,123	560,384	1,058
10. Nias	161,253	153,576	314,829	952
11. Dairi	69,395	68,883	138,278	993
XI. ATJEH	822,102	806,881	1,628,983	981
Municipality:	22,494	17,573	40,067	781
1. Banda Atjeh	22,494	17,573	40,067	781
Regency:	799,608	789,308	1,588,916	987
1. Greater Atjeh	79,357	76,610	155,967	965
2. Pidie	124,734	134,839	259,573	1,081
3. North Atjeh	191,477	192,178	383,655	1,004
4. East Atjeh	125,296	114,019	239,315	910
5. Central Atjeh	84,793	86,432	171,225	1,019
6. West Atjeh	96,720	88,607	185,327	916
7. South Atjeh	97,231	96,623	193,854	994
XII. WEST KALIMANTAN	802,010	779,024	1,581,034	971
Municipality:	77,240	72,980	150,220	945
1. Pontianak	77,240	72,980	150,220	945
Regency:	724,770	706,044	1,430,814	974
1. Pontianak	192,367	186,140	378,507	968
2. Sambas	208,747	204,574	413,321	980
3. Ketapang	79,355	77,150	156,505	972
4. Sanggau	111,647	107,895	219,542	966
5. Sintang	89,569	86,011	175,580	960
6. Kapuas Hulu	43,085	44,274	87,359	1,028
XII. CENTRAL KALIMANTAN	251,316	245,206	496,522	976
Municipality:	4,074	2,786	6,860	684
1. Palangka Raya	4,074	2,786	6,860	684
Regency:	247,242	242,420	489,662	980
1. Kapuas	78,027	77,021	155,048	987

Region	Male	Female	Both sexes	No. of females per 1,000 males
2. North Barito	36,444	35,404	71,848	971
3. South Barito	36,788	36,578	73,366	994
4. West Kotawaringin	25,975	25,174	51,149	969
5. East Kotawaringin	70,008	68,243	138,251	975
XIV. SOUTH KALIMANTAN	725,959	747,196	1,473,155	1,029
Municipality:	107,530	106,566	214,096	991
1. Bandjarmasin	107,530	106,566	214,096	991
Regency:	618,429	640,630	1,259,059	1,036
1. Barito Kuala	44,003	44,834	88,837	1,019
2. Bandjar	155,249	155,313	310,562	1,000
3. Central Hulusungai	87,893	95,630	183,523	1,088
4. South Hulusungai	115,109	121,768	236,877	1,058
5. North Hulusungai	156,775	165,664	322,439	1,057
6. Kota Baru	59,400	57,421	116,821	967
XV. EAST KALIMANTAN	286,963	263,801	550,764	919
Municipality:	84,896	76,525	161,421	901
1. Balikpapan	48,707	42,999	91,706	883
2. Samarinda	36,189	33,526	69,715	926
Regency:	202,067	187,276	389,343	927
1. Kutai	114,784	105,472	220,256	919
2. Berau	14,845	13,590	28,435	915
3. Bulongan	48,812	46,873	95,685	960
4. Pasir	23,626	21,341	44,967	903
XVI. NORTH AND CENTRAL SULAWESI	1,015,050	988,161	2,003,211	974
Municipality:	99,988	101,302	201,290	1,013
1. Menado	66,052	63,860	129,912	967
2. Gorontalo	33,936	37,442	71,378	1,103
Regency:	915,062	886,859	1,801,921	969
1. Sangir Talaud	97,734	96,519	194,253	988
2. Minahasa	228,815	223,109	451,924	975
3. Bolaang Mongondow	76,391	73,826	150,217	966
4. Gorontalo	156,110	156,260	312,370	1,001

Region	Male	Female	Both sexes	No. of females per 1,000 males
5. Bual-Toli2	42,665	39,955	82,620	936
6. Donggala	147,960	142,495	290,455	963
7. Poso	89,985	85,350	175,335	948
8. Banggai	75,402	69,345	144,747	920
XVII. SOUTH AND SOUTH-EAST SULAWESI	2,474,747	2,601,391	5,076,138	1,051
Municipality:	228,898	223,253	452,151	975
1. Makasar	194,851	189,308	384,159	972
2. Pare-Pare	34,047	33,945	67,992	997
Regency:	2,245,849	2,378,138	4,623,987	1,059
1. Mamudju	32,247	28,115	60,362	872
2. Luwu	144,410	156,089	300,499	1,081
3. Madjene	21,584	22,412	43,996	1,038
4. Polewali/Mamasa	112,815	115,016	227,831	1,020
5. Tana Toradja	140,488	138,725	279,213	987
6. Pinrang	104,668	109,208	213,876	1,043
7. Enrekang	73,286	81,024	154,310	1,106
8. Sidenreng/Rappang	70,798	77,930	148,728	1,101
9. Wadjo	167,145	178,851	345,996	1,070
10. Soppeng	95,016	97,994	193,010	1,031
11. Barru	62,702	65,286	127,988	1,041
12. Pangkadjene	83,264	84,332	167,596	1,013
13. Bone	246,147	269,635	515,782	1,095
14. Maros	77,055	77,740	154,795	1,009
15. Gowa	147,180	151,227	298,407	1,027
16. Sindjai	48,810	54,455	103,265	1,116
17. Bulukumba	101,376	108,259	209,635	1,068
18. Bonthain	35,304	36,242	71,546	1,027
19. Djeneponto	111,055	116,558	227,613	1,050
20. Takalar	64,894	67,773	132,667	1,044
21. Selajar	42,182	45,096	87,278	1,069
22. Kolaka	17,685	17,403	35,088	984
23. Kendari	79,889	79,589	159,478	996
24. Muna	52,079	59,687	111,766	1,146
25. Buton	113,770	139,492	253,262	1,226
XVIII. BALI	883,512	899,017	1,782,529	1,018
Regency:	883,512	899,017	1,782,529	1,018
1. Buleleng	158,449	164,633	323,082	1,039

Region	Male	Female	Both sexes	No. of females per 1,000 males
2. Djembrana	64,934	64,600	129,534	995
3. Tabanan	135,545	138,015	273,560	1,018
4. Badung	156,100	154,470	310,570	990
5. Gianjar	115,323	117,244	232,567	1,017
6. Klungkung	62,078	65,815	127,893	1,060
7. Bangli	62,106	61,899	124,005	997
8. Karangasem	128,977	132,341	261,318	1,026
XIX. WEST NUSA TENGGARA	893,469	914,361	1,807,830	1,023
Regency:	893,469	914,361	1,807,830	1,023
1. West Lombok	202,104	208,854	410,958	1,033
2. Central Lombok	194,113	200,965	395,078	1,035
3. East Lombok	242,105	252,093	494,198	1,041
4. Sumbawa	98,389	97,165	195,554	988
5. Dompu	28,765	27,553	56,318	958
6. Bima	127,993	127,731	255,724	997
XX. EAST NUSA TENGGARA	984,415	982,882	1,967,297	998
Regency:	984,415	982,882	1,967,297	998
1. East Sumba	48,912	45,990	94,902	940
2. West Sumba	79,240	76,984	156,224	972
3. Manggarai	125,927	127,757	253,684	1,015
4. Ngada	59,781	62,280	122,061	1,042
5. Endeh	81,123	81,818	162,941	1,009
6. Sikka	83,096	85,787	168,883	1,032
7. Flores	91,116	103,087	194,203	1,131
8. Kupang	137,777	129,839	267,616	942
9. South-central Timor	103,732	99,232	202,964	957
10. North-central Timor	52,238	49,470	101,708	947
11. Belu	66,434	63,916	130,350	962
12. Alor	55,039	56,722	111,761	1,031
XXI. MALUKU	402,500	387,034	789,534	962
Municipality:	29,947	26,090	56,037	871
1. Ambon	29,947	26,090	56,037	871
Regency:	372,553	360,944	733,497	969
1. North Maluku	123,607	115,359	238,966	933
2. Central Maluku	150,819	145,214	296,033	963
3. Southeast Maluku	98,127	100,371	198,498	1,023

Region	Male	Female	Both sexes	No. of females per 1,000 males
XXII. WEST IRIAN	375,154	383,242	758,396	1,022
1. Tidore	29,928	28,468	58,396	951
2. West Irian	345,226	354,774	700,000	1,028 *
INDONESIA	47,839,080	49,179,749	97,018,825	1,028

* Applying the sex ratio of the population of Indonesia excluding this area.
Source: Biro Pusat Statistik, Sensus Penduduk 1961 (Population Census, 1961) (Djakarta, 1962). Figures for Djakarta Raya, Java, and Indonesia have been revised.

Population by Sex and Age Group, Indonesia, 1961–1991, According to Projection A

(in thousands)

Sex and age group	1961	1966	1971	1976	1981	1986	1991
Male							
0–4	8,869	9,247	9,298	9,807	12,495	15,038	17,503
5–9	7,642	8,069	8,505	8,635	9,188	11,801	14,313
10–14	4,295	7,432	7,873	8,322	8,472	9,035	11,631
15–19	3,813	4,179	7,252	7,702	8,160	8,325	8,898
20–24	3,884	3,665	4,032	7,021	7,480	7,949	8,135
25–29	3,547	3,701	3,509	3,877	6,777	7,247	7,730
30–34	3,588	3,367	3,533	3,366	3,735	6,555	7,038
35–39	3,169	3,386	3,197	3,374	3,231	3,602	6,349
40–44	2,480	2,959	3,185	3,028	3,215	3,095	3,468
45–49	1,941	2,277	2,741	2,975	2,849	3,044	2,947
50–54	1,502	1,740	2,063	2,508	2,745	2,648	2,849
55–59	1,062	1,301	1,527	1,831	2,248	2,483	2,415
60–64	827	876	1,089	1,296	1,572	1,951	2,177
65–69	539	633	683	863	1,041	1,280	1,608
70–74	308	368	442	486	625	767	958
75–79	143	176	217	267	301	396	496
80–84	125	63	81	103	131	152	206
85+	105	57	32	31	39	50	63
Total, males	47,839	53,496	59,259	65,492	74,304	85,418	98,784
Female							
0–4	8,904	9,018	9,069	10,034	12,180	14,654	17,038
5–9	7,523	8,107	8,305	8,434	9,416	11,526	13,975

Sex and age group	1961	1966	1971	1976	1981	1986	1991
Female (continued)							
10–14	3,802	7,303	7,898	8,116	8,266	9,254	11,355
15–19	3,815	3,688	7,108	7,711	7,947	8,116	9,109
20–24	4,635	3,657	3,552	6,874	7,487	7,744	7,936
25–29	4,431	4,403	3,494	3,412	6,634	7,258	7,539
30–34	3,778	4,190	4,192	3,346	3,285	6,418	7,053
35–39	2,914	3,558	3,976	4,003	3,213	3,171	6,225
40–44	2,309	2,731	3,361	3,782	3,831	3,091	3,066
45–49	1,869	2,145	2,559	3,172	3,593	3,661	2,969
50–54	1,441	1,708	1,980	2,381	2,973	3,391	3,475
55–59	1,189	1,284	1,539	1,801	2,185	2,751	3,160
60–64	1,182	1,015	1,111	1,348	1,595	1,955	2,484
65–69	703	942	822	914	1,125	1,349	1,673
70–74	285	502	687	612	693	867	1,056
75–79	140	172	311	437	399	461	590
80–84	148	66	84	157	227	214	255
85+	112	70	39	36	60	92	101
Total, females	49,180	54,559	60,087	66,570	75,109	85,973	99,059
Both sexes							
0–4	17,773	18,265	18,367	19,841	24,675	29,692	34,541
5–9	15,165	16,176	16,810	17,069	18,604	23,327	28,288
10–14	8,097	14,735	15,771	16,438	16,738	18,289	22,986
15–19	7,628	7,867	14,360	15,413	16,107	16,441	18,007
20–24	8,519	7,322	7,584	13,895	14,967	15,693	16,071
25–29	7,978	8,104	7,003	7,289	13,411	14,505	15,269
30–34	7,366	7,557	7,725	6,712	7,020	12,973	14,091
35–39	6,083	6,944	7,173	7,377	6,444	6,773	12,574
40–44	4,789	5,690	6,546	6,810	7,046	6,186	6,534
45–49	3,810	4,422	5,300	6,147	6,442	6,705	5,916
50–54	2,943	3,448	4,043	4,889	5,718	6,039	6,324
55–59	2,251	2,585	3,066	3,632	4,433	5,234	5,575
60–64	2,009	1,891	2,200	2,644	3,167	3,906	4,661
65–69	1,242	1,575	1,505	1,777	2,166	2,629	3,281
70–74	593	870	1,129	1,098	1,318	1,634	2,014
75–79	283	348	528	704	700	857	1,086
80–84	273	129	165	260	358	366	461
85+	217	127	71	67	99	142	164
Total, both sexes	97,019	108,055	119,346	132,062	149,413	171,391	197,843

Population by Sex and Age Group, Indonesia, 1961–1991, According to Projection B

(in thousands)

Sex and age group	1961	1966	1971	1976	1981	1986	1991
Male							
0–4	8,869	9,467	9,559	10,609	12,938	15,706	18,470
5–9	7,642	8,158	8,792	8,956	10,020	12,314	15,053
10–14	4,295	7,456	7,983	8,626	8,807	9,876	12,161
15–19	3,813	4,191	7,294	7,828	8,477	8,673	9,745
20–24	3,884	3,679	4,057	7,084	7,623	8,284	8,498
25–29	3,547	3,718	3,537	3,916	6,863	7,413	8,083
30–34	3,588	3,386	3,566	3,407	3,788	6,653	7,226
35–39	3,169	3,407	3,234	3,423	3,286	3,669	6,470
40–44	2,480	2,981	3,227	3,082	3,279	3,164	3,548
45–49	1,941	2,298	2,785	3,036	2,918	3,122	3,029
50–54	1,502	1,759	2,103	2,569	2,822	2,731	2,941
55–59	1,062	1,318	1,561	1,885	2,324	2,574	2,509
60–64	827	889	1,188	1,340	1,636	2,037	2,277
65–69	539	645	704	955	909	1,349	1,698
70–74	308	378	459	510	703	680	1,025
75–79	143	181	229	284	323	455	448
80–84	125	66	86	112	143	168	242
85+	105	61	35	34	44	58	72
Total, males	47,839	54,038	60,399	67,656	76,903	88,926	103,495
Female							
0–4	8,904	9,233	9,440	10,340	12,607	15,228	17,966
5–9	7,523	8,200	8,587	8,858	9,785	12,223	14,687
10–14	3,802	7,329	8,014	8,416	8,706	9,640	12,079

Sex and age group	1961	1966	1971	1976	1981	1986	1991
Female (continued)							
15–19	3,815	3,701	7,156	7,847	8,264	8,569	9,510
20–24	4,635	3,674	3,579	6,948	7,647	8,080	8,405
25–29	4,431	4,429	3,529	3,454	6,735	7,444	7,895
30–34	3,778	4,218	4,242	3,398	3,341	6,545	7,262
35–39	2,914	3,585	4,028	4,074	3,280	3,240	6,374
40–44	2,309	2,753	3,410	3,853	3,920	3,171	3,146
45–49	1,869	2,163	2,598	3,239	3,684	3,765	3,060
50–54	1,441	1,725	2,012	2,435	3,057	3,497	3,593
55–59	1,189	1,299	1,569	1,847	2,253	2,848	3,279
60–64	1,182	1,029	1,138	1,390	1,653	2,034	2,593
65–69	703	958	846	950	1,176	1,415	1,760
70–74	285	513	713	641	732	921	1,125
75–79	140	177	326	464	427	498	639
80–84	148	68	89	170	249	236	282
85+	112	74	42	40	67	104	116
Total, females	49,180	55,128	61,318	68,364	77,583	89,458	103,771
Both sexes							
0–4	17,773	18,700	18,999	20,949	25,545	30,934	36,436
5–9	15,165	16,358	17,379	17,814	19,805	24,537	29,740
10–14	8,097	14,785	15,997	17,042	17,513	19,516	24,240
15–19	7,628	7,892	14,450	15,675	16,741	17,242	19,255
20–24	8,519	7,353	7,636	14,032	15,270	16,364	16,903
25–29	7,978	8,147	7,066	7,370	13,598	14,857	15,978
30–34	7,366	7,604	7,808	6,805	7,129	13,198	14,488
35–39	6,083	6,992	7,262	7,497	6,566	6,909	12,844
40–44	4,789	5,734	6,637	6,935	7,199	6,335	6,694
45–49	3,810	4,461	5,383	6,275	6,602	6,887	6,089
50–54	2,943	3,484	4,115	5,004	5,879	6,228	6,534
55–59	2,251	2,617	3,130	3,732	4,577	5,422	5,788
60–64	2,009	1,918	2,326	2,730	3,289	4,071	4,870
65–69	1,242	1,603	1,550	1,905	2,085	2,764	3,458
70–74	593	891	1,172	1,151	1,435	1,601	2,150
75–79	283	358	555	748	750	953	1,087
80–84	273	134	175	282	392	404	524
85+	217	135	77	74	111	162	188
Total, both sexes	97,019	109,166	121,717	136,020	154,486	178,384	207,266

Population by Sex and Age Group, Indonesia, 1961–1991, According to Projection C

(in thousands)

Sex and age group	1961	1966	1971	1976	1981	1986	1991
Male							
0–4	8,869	9,467	9,758	10,907	13,897	17,485	21,225
5–9	7,642	8,158	8,870	9,288	10,523	13,570	17,252
10–14	4,295	7,456	8,004	8,742	9,189	10,443	13,501
15–19	3,813	4,191	7,311	7,882	8,640	9,110	10,381
20–24	3,884	3,679	4,070	7,114	7,743	8,528	9,031
25–29	3,547	3,718	3,551	3,958	6,993	7,624	8,441
30–34	3,588	3,386	3,582	3,449	3,871	6,881	7,541
35–39	3,169	3,407	3,250	3,469	3,366	3,802	6,794
40–44	2,480	2,981	3,246	3,129	3,369	3,292	3,739
45–49	1,941	2,298	2,804	3,091	3,009	3,266	3,213
50–54	1,502	1,759	2,120	2,624	2,927	2,876	3,146
55–59	1,062	1,318	1,577	1,934	2,427	2,738	2,715
60–64	827	889	1,132	1,382	1,725	2,195	2,505
65–69	539	645	714	933	1,164	1,479	1,910
70–74	308	378	467	534	718	917	1,189
75–79	143	181	234	302	358	497	651
80–84	125	66	89	121	164	203	292
85+	105	61	37	39	52	74	98
Total, males	47,839	54,038	60,816	68,898	80,135	94,980	113,624
Female							
0–4	8,904	9,233	9,511	10,796	13,483	16,876	20,400
5–9	7,523	8,200	8,664	9,071	10,439	13,201	16,694
10–14	3,802	7,329	8,037	8,536	8,976	10,368	13,151

Sex and age group	1961	1966	1971	1976	1981	1986	1991
Female (continued)							
15–19	3,815	3,701	7,176	7,911	8,439	8,909	10,322
20–24	4,635	3,674	3,593	7,017	7,783	8,347	8,851
25–29	4,431	4,429	3,546	3,498	6,881	7,681	8,280
30–34	3,778	4,218	4,264	3,446	3,425	6,783	7,611
35–39	2,914	3,585	4,051	4,136	3,369	3,371	6,710
40–44	2,309	2,753	3,431	3,917	4,032	3,306	3,326
45–49	1,869	2,163	2,615	3,296	3,796	3,935	3,244
50–54	1,441	1,725	2,027	2,482	3,160	3,670	3,829
55–59	1,189	1,299	1,583	1,889	2,341	3,011	3,526
60–64	1,182	1,029	1,151	1,429	1,733	2,177	2,831
65–69	703	958	859	985	1,249	1,543	1,967
70–74	285	513	726	728	794	1,031	1,300
75–79	140	177	334	494	515	581	776
80–84	148	68	92	184	287	313	367
85+	112	74	44	45	80	134	169
Total, females	49,180	55,128	61,704	69,860	80,782	95,237	113,354
Both sexes							
0–4	17,773	18,700	19,269	21,703	27,380	34,361	41,625
5–9	15,165	16,358	17,534	18,359	20,962	26,771	33,946
10–14	8,097	14,785	16,041	17,278	18,165	20,811	26,652
15–19	7,628	7,892	14,487	15,793	17,079	18,019	20,703
20–24	8,519	7,353	7,663	14,131	15,526	16,875	17,882
25–29	7,978	8,147	7,097	7,456	13,874	15,305	16,721
30–34	7,366	7,604	7,846	6,895	7,296	13,664	15,152
35–39	6,083	6,992	7,301	7,605	6,735	7,173	13,504
40–44	4,789	5,734	6,677	7,046	7,401	6,598	7,065
45–49	3,810	4,461	5,419	6,387	6,805	7,201	6,457
50–54	2,943	3,484	4,147	5,106	6,087	6,546	6,975
55–59	2,251	2,617	3,160	3,823	4,768	5,749	6,241
60–64	2,009	1,918	2,283	2,811	3,458	4,372	5,336
65–69	1,242	1,603	1,573	1,918	2,413	3,022	3,877
70–74	593	891	1,193	1,262	1,512	1,948	2,489
75–79	283	358	568	796	873	1,078	1,427
80–84	273	134	181	305	451	516	659
85+	217	135	81	84	132	208	267
Total, both sexes	97,019	109,166	122,520	138,758	160,917	190,217	226,978

Population by Sex and Age Group, Indonesia, 1961–1991, According to Projection D

(in thousands)

Sex and age group	1961	1966	1971	1976	1981	1986	1991
Male							
0–4	8,869	9,467	9,326	10,031	11,738	13,583	14,761
5–9	7,642	8,158	8,870	8,876	9,678	11,462	13,402
10–14	4,295	7,456	8,004	8,742	8,781	9,604	11,403
15–19	3,813	4,191	7,311	7,882	8,640	8,705	9,547
20–24	3,884	3,679	4,070	7,144	7,743	8,528	8,629
25–29	3,547	3,718	3,551	3,958	6,993	7,624	8,441
30–34	3,588	3,386	3,582	3,449	3,871	6,881	7,541
35–39	3,169	3,407	3,250	3,469	3,366	3,802	6,794
40–44	2,480	2,981	3,246	3,129	3,369	3,292	3,739
45–49	1,941	2,298	2,804	3,091	3,009	3,266	3,213
50–54	1,502	1,759	2,120	2,624	2,927	2,876	3,146
55–59	1,062	1,318	1,577	1,934	2,427	2,738	2,715
60–64	827	889	1,132	1,382	1,725	2,195	2,505
65–69	539	645	714	933	1,164	1,479	1,910
70–74	308	378	467	534	718	917	1,189
75–79	143	181	234	302	358	497	651
80–84	125	66	89	121	164	203	292
85+	105	61	37	39	52	74	98
Total, males	47,839	54,038	60,384	67,640	76,723	87,726	101,976
Female							
0–4	8,904	9,233	9,086	9,714	11,383	13,110	14,332
5–9	7,523	8,200	8,664	8,665	9,392	11,145	12,968

Sex and age group	1961	1966	1971	1976	1981	1986	1991
Female (*continued*)							
10–14	3,802	7,329	8,037	8,536	8,574	9,328	11,103
15–19	3,815	3,701	7,176	7,911	8,439	8,510	9,287
20–24	4,635	3,674	3,593	7,017	7,783	8,347	8,455
25–29	4,431	4,429	3,546	3,498	6,881	7,681	8,280
30–34	3,778	4,218	4,264	3,446	3,425	6,783	7,611
35–39	2,914	3,585	4,051	4,136	3,369	3,371	6,710
40–44	2,309	2,753	3,431	3,917	4,032	3,306	3,326
45–49	1,869	2,163	2,615	3,296	3,796	3,935	3,244
50–54	1,441	1,725	2,027	2,482	3,160	3,670	3,829
55–59	1,189	1,299	1,583	1,889	2,341	3,011	3,526
60–64	1,182	1,029	1,151	1,429	1,733	2,177	2,831
65–69	703	958	859	985	1,249	1,543	1,967
70–74	285	513	726	728	794	1,031	1,300
75–79	140	177	334	494	515	581	776
80–84	148	68	92	184	287	313	367
85+	112	74	44	45	80	134	169
Total, females	49,180	55,128	61,279	68,372	77,233	87,976	100,081
Both sexes							
0–4	17,773	18,700	18,412	19,745	23,121	26,693	29,093
5–9	15,165	16,358	17,534	17,541	19,070	22,607	26,370
10–14	8,097	14,785	16,041	17,278	17,355	18,932	22,506
15–19	7,628	7,892	14,487	15,793	17,079	17,215	18,834
20–24	8,519	7,353	7,663	14,161	15,526	16,875	17,084
25–29	7,978	8,147	7,097	7,456	13,874	15,305	16,721
30–34	7,366	7,604	7,846	6,895	7,296	13,664	15,152
35–39	6,083	6,992	7,301	7,605	6,735	7,173	13,504
40–44	4,789	5,734	6,677	7,046	7,401	6,598	9,065
45–49	3,810	4,461	5,419	6,387	6,805	7,201	6,457
50–54	2,943	3,484	4,147	5,106	6,087	6,546	6,975
55–59	2,251	2,617	3,160	3,823	4,768	5,749	6,241
60–64	2,009	1,918	2,283	2,811	3,458	4,372	5,336
65–69	1,242	1,603	1,573	1,918	2,413	3,022	3,877
70–74	593	891	1,193	1,262	1,512	1,948	2,489
75–79	283	358	568	796	873	1,078	1,427
80–84	273	134	181	305	451	516	659
85+	217	135	81	84	132	208	267
Total, both sexes	97,019	109,166	121,663	136,012	153,956	175,702	202,057

Index